EUROPE WITHOUT ILLUSIONS

The Paul-Henri Spaak Lectures, 1994-1999

Edited by

Andrew Moravcsik

**Weatherhead Center for International Affairs,
Harvard University**

**University Press of America,® Inc.
Lanham · Boulder · New York · Toronto · Oxford**

University Press of America,® Inc.
4501 Forbes Boulevard
Suite 200
Lanham, Maryland 20706
UPA Acquisitions Department (301) 459-3366

PO Box 317
Oxford
OX2 9RU, UK

Printed in the United States of America
British Library Cataloging in Publication Information Available

Copublished by arrangement with
Weatherhead Center for International Affairs,
Harvard University

Library of Congress Control Number: 2004117820
ISBN 978-0-7618-3128-0

The paper used in this publication meets the minimum requirements of American National Standard for Information Sciences—Permanence of Paper for Printed Library Materials, ANSI Z39.48—1984

In memory of

Maurits and Sophie Boas

CONTENTS

WEATHERHEAD CENTER FOR INTERNATIONAL AFFAIRS
Executive Committee, 2003-2004 vii

THE PAUL-HENRI SPAAK LECTURES—1994 -1999 x

FOREWORD
Jorge I. Domínguez xi

PREFACE
Frank Boas xiv

PART I
EDITOR'S INTRODUCTION

Europe without Illusions
Andrew Moravcsik 3

PART II
THE PAUL-HENRI SPAAK LECTURES, 1994-1999

1. The Disappointing Partnership between British Governments and Europe: Why the Paul-Henri Spaak Tradition Rarely Embraces London
Right Honorable Lord Roy Jenkins 47

2. The Global Challenge: Opportunities and Choices in the Multilateral Trading System
Ambassador Renato Ruggiero 61

3. From Europe to *EU*rope: A Story of Hope, Trial and Error
Ralf Dahrendorf 77

4. The New Europe: How to Overcome Forty Years of Division 91
Uffe Ellemann-Jensen

5. Europe and the Balkans: The Role of Greece
George Papandreou 103

PART III
CONFERENCE PROCEEDINGS

6. Transatlantic Relations One Year after September 11 121

CONFERENCE PARTICIPANTS 191

ABOUT THE AUTHOR 195

WEATHERHEAD CENTER FOR INTERNATIONAL AFFAIRS

Executive Committee, 2003-2004

Peter Hall, Director, Minda de Gunzburg Center for European Studies; Krupp Foundation Professor of European Studies; Harvard College Professor

J. Bryan Hehir, President, Catholic Charities, Archdiocese of Boston

Stanley H. Hoffmann, Paul and Catherine Buttenwieser University Professor

Samuel P. Huntington, Chairman, Harvard Academy for International and Area Studies; Albert J. Weatherhead III University Professor

A. Iain Johnston, The Governor James Albert Noe and Linda Noe Laine Professorship of China in World Affairs, Department of Government

Herbert C. Kelman, Cabot Research Professor of Social Ethics

William C. Kirby, Edith and Benjamin Geisinger Professor of History; Dean of the Faculty of Arts and Sciences

Steven Levitsky, Associate Professor of Government

Charles S. Maier, Leverett Saltsonstall Professor of History

Lisa L. Martin, Professor of Government; editor-in-chief, International Organization

David Maybury-Lewis, Edward C. Henderson Professor of Anthropology; Director, Program on Nonviolent Sanctions and Cultural Survival

Kathleen Molony, Director, Fellows Program

Joseph S. Nye, Jr., Don K. Price Professor of Public Policy; Dean, John F. Kennedy School of Government

Susan J. Pharr, Director, Program on U.S.-Japan Relations; Edwin O. Reischauer Professor of Japanese Politics

Robert D. Putnam, The Peter and Isabel Malkin Professor of Public Policy; Director, Saguaro Seminar, John F. Kennedy School of Government

The Center is a multidisciplinary research institution within Harvard University's Faculty of Arts and Sciences. The Center for International Affairs was founded in 1958 and was renamed the Weatherhead Center for International Affairs in 1998 in gratitude for the magnificent endowment established by Albert and Celia Weatherhead and the Weatherhead Foundation. The Center seeks to foster a vibrant research community for a diverse group of scholars and practitioners studying various aspects of international affairs. The work produced by the Center seeks to deepen the understanding of the forces, both domestic and international, that are transforming many countries as well as the international system.

The Paul-Henri Spaak Lectures

1994 - 1999

Right Honorable Lord Roy Jenkins: "The Disappointing Partnership between British Governments and Europe: Why the Paul-Henri Spaak Tradition Rarely Embraces London," Chancellor of Oxford University, and leader of the Liberal Democrats in the House of Lords, November 1994

Ambassador Renato Ruggiero: "The Global Challenge: Opportunities and Choices in the Multilateral Trading System," Director General of the World Trade Organization, October 1995

Ralf Dahrendorf: "From Europe to *EU*rope: A Story of Hope, Trial and Error," Warden, St. Antony's College, Oxford, October 1996

Uffe Ellemann-Jensen: "The New Europe: How to Overcome Forty Years of Division," former Minister of Foreign Affairs of Denmark, October 1997

George Papandreou: "Europe and the Balkans: The Role of Greece," Minister of Foreign Affairs of the Hellenic Republic, November 1999

FOREWORD

Jorge I. Domínguez

The Atlantic Alliance was one of the great political and military achievements of the second half of the twentieth century. It codified and institutionalized a permanent relationship between the United States, Canada, and Western Europe to ensure their collective security and to deter the Soviet Union from military actions in Western Europe. The very existence of the Atlantic Alliance provided a security framework for the consolidation of European democracies and, in due course, the expansion of democracy throughout Southern Europe. Such security and democracy were the foundation for the creation of a zone of peace in Western Europe, and contributors to the birth and development of what we have come to know as the European Union and the long wave of prosperity that marked the continent for the past half-century.

And yet this first paragraph highlights a problem. Nearly all of the most impressive accomplishments of the Atlantic Alliance were already history by 1960. True, the continued existence of the alliance remained very important for the endurance of these salutary trends, but the thrill of political creativity and the satisfaction of bold and evident accomplishment belong to the statesmen of the late 1940s and the 1950s. The more distant the time from the founding of the Atlantic Alliance, the more dismissive the assessment tends to become.

Will the Atlantic Alliance's triumphs be the cause of its demise? Although the Alliance's central practical task was military deterrence, at its very heart there was a commitment to the defense of democracy and the liberties that characterize its polities, economies, and societies. At its founding, it might have been difficult to envisage a day when these core values would triumph as they have and that Western Europe would no longer fear the Soviet Union or the spread of communism. Today, with its enemies defeated, some can and do argue that the Alliance should declare victory and disband.

The fate of the Atlantic Alliance during the first decade of the twenty-first century remains unclear, therefore. U.S. political ambitions and military-technological developments have also made it possible for the United States to think that it no longer needs the alliance. Most allies are no longer capable of accompanying U.S. forces as equal partners into war. As the United States prepared for a second Gulf War with Iraq in 2002–03, key U.S. government officials—especially the U.S. Secretary of Defense—displayed condescending irritability in their public and private commentary about leading European governments, while the German chancellor ran for and won re-election on a platform deliberately opposed to U.S. war policy. The United States seems to have become more comfortable with the concept of a coalition of the willing while much of the European Union's public and some of Europe's key politicians seem to prefer a coalition of abstention.

In that context, the European Union, too, enters the twenty-first century layered with complexities. Its governments and its citizens have become accustomed to considering the opportunities and problems posed by expansion and deepening. New members from Central and Eastern Europe are about to join the European Union just as it deepens its integrative policies across many spheres of action. Less clear is whether the European Union is ready for a world without the Atlantic Alliance. Would it matter if the Eastern European countries looked exclusively to Washington and London for their security, not to Berlin and Paris? Would it matter if U.S. forces were to depart permanently from Germany to move to new bases in Poland? Would it matter if a Franco-German *entente* were to become the core of a larger version of a permanently neutral Switzerland—prosperous, democratic, polyglot, collectively governed, but militarily and politically uninfluential *by its own choice* in the world beyond its boundaries?

Many European citizens everywhere would probably welcome this vision of a Suissified "core" continental Western Europe. However, no government of France has ever seemed interested in such a role, and the trends in German politics in the aftermath of unification seemed to portend a more active albeit peaceful global role for Germany. The European Union, moreover, has been discussing the development of common security and foreign policies and even the formation of a military force that could be deployed for specific purposes, mainly perhaps in the Balkans. There seems to be, therefore, a disjunction between trends pertinent for the European Union—between its publics and its leaders and between European leaders and U.S. leaders.

This is the third book in the series of Spaak Lectures. In the foreword to the first, Center Director Robert D. Putnam wrote that "the founders of this [U.S.-European] alliance would probably be pleasantly surprised to discover how durable it has been." In the foreword to the second, Center Director Joseph S. Nye, Jr. wrote that the "question for the current volume is whether and how long that situation will continue." The question has not changed between the second and this third volume but its urgency has.

Nye also wrote in his foreword to that second volume that "predicting the future is beyond the scope of this foreword or this volume." Instead, then and today, "we present these lectures and conference proceedings with the hope that they will inform our understanding of the policy choices before us in this period of major change."

The Spaak Lectures Series, founded in 1981, is half as old as the Weatherhead Center for International Affairs, which was founded under a slightly different name in 1958. The series and the Center remain committed to improving and deepening our understanding of the central issues for the Atlantic Alliance and the European Union.

On behalf of the Executive Committee of the Weatherhead Center for International Affairs, I express our thanks to those who have made this book possible, above all to Frank Boas and the Boas Foundation. Our gratitude goes also to the Spaak Lecturers, Andrew Moravcsik for providing the key paper to stimulate the discussion at the conference that concluded the cycle toward this book, Etienne Davignon for chairing and hosting the conference in Brussels, and Amanda Pearson for the book's copy editing and production.

PREFACE

Frank Boas

In April 1981, Fernand Spaak, Chief of Cabinet of the President of the European Commission, inaugurated a series of lectures that would bring to Harvard, under the auspices of what would become the Weatherhead Center for International Affairs, distinguished European leaders to address issues in U.S.-European relations. These presentations, known as the Paul-Henri Spaak Lectures, honor Fernand Spaak's father, who was one of the founding fathers of postwar Europe. Paul-Henri Spaak, three times Prime Minister of Belgium and the first President of the United Nations General Assembly, was not only a signatory of the Rome Treaty establishing the European Common Market, but also served as the first President of the Organization for Economic Cooperation and Development (the forerunner of the OECD) and as Secretary General of NATO.

Fernand Spaak's inaugural lecture in 1981 was followed by four lectures delivered respectively by Senator Jean Francois-Poncet, former French Minister of Foreign Affairs; Viscount Etienne Davignon, Vice President of the European Commission; Pieter Dankert, President of the European Parliament; and Lamberto Dini, Director General of the Bank of Italy.

In October 1985, a conference was held in Brussels, co-sponsored by the Weatherhead Center, the Paul-Henri Spaak Foundation, and the Frank Boas Foundation, to review the major themes of the first five Spaak Lectures and to discuss U.S.-European relations with reference to a conference paper prepared by Dr. Richard C. Eichenberg of Tufts University. Several Spaak Lecturers, a delegation of senior Harvard faculty from the Weatherhead Center, as well as a large number of European Union officials and diplomats, attended the conference. The result was the 1986 publication of the book, *Drifting Together or Apart?*

A second volume, *Allies or Adversaries?*, was published in 1993, following the Second Harvard University–Spaak Foundation Conference held in Brussels in October 1991. In addition to the conference proceedings, this volume contains a paper presented by Professor Eichenberg and the texts of the six lectures delivered respectively from 1985 to 1990 by Sir Michael Palliser, Chairman of the Board of Montagu and Company and former Head of the British Foreign Office; Karl Otto Pohl, Member of the Monetary Committee of the European Community and Chairman of the "Group of Ten" Central Bank Governors; Felipe Gonzalez, Prime Minister of Spain; Raymond Barre, Member of the National Assembly of France and former Prime Minister; Frans Andriessen, Vice President of the European Communities; Jiri Dienstbier, Minister of Foreign Affairs of Czechoslovakia. It also contains an appendix, the 1992 lecture by Manfred Woerner, Secretary General of NATO.

The present volume, *Europe without Illusions*, contains the texts of the next five Spaak Lectures, a paper prepared by Professor Andrew Moravcsik, as well as the conference proceedings of the Third Harvard University–Spaak Lecture Conference, which was held in Brussels in September 2002.

The Spaak Lectures and Conferences have spanned a period of more than two decades, during which time the world has witnessed the collapse of the Soviet Union and the end of the cold war, the reunification of Germany, the first Gulf War, the Balkan wars, the attacks on September 11, a second war against Iraq, and now a possible nuclear crisis on the Korean Peninsula.

While anti-Americanism is now very much on the rise in Europe and the rest of the world, according to a recent survey of people in forty-two countries by the Pew Research Center, and published by the *Economist*, it remains a minority opinion, albeit a vocal one. During a recent debate in the United Nations Security Council concerning Iraq, the French Foreign Minister declared that if the U.S. were to attack Iraq on its own, it would be "a victory for the law of the strongest." This led U.S. Defense Secretary Donald Rumsfeld to respond that France and Germany "were history."

The relationship between Europe and the U.S. is beyond doubt changing. The European Union is rapidly expanding to the East and is grappling with pressing issues of governance, which greatly influence its relationship with the U.S. The expansion of NATO by the inclusion of former Warsaw Pact members (of which Poland and the Czech Republic are at present more pro-American than France or Germany) also drastically changes the U.S.-European relationship.

During the cold war, a shared threat of the spread of communism strengthened the transatlantic alliance, and this bond was briefly revived at the time of September 11. Fortunately, the cooperation between Europe and the U.S. with respect to the war on terrorism continues. As Jean Francois-Poncet pointed out at the September 2002 Spaak Conference in Brussels, however, it is a new phenomenon when a German chancellor uses anti-Americanism for electoral purposes.

In the course of the tumultuous and often acrimonious debates about Iraq, the leaders of Spain, Britain, Italy, Poland, Hungary, the Czech Republic, Denmark, and Portugal published an open letter in the *Wall Street Journal* on January 30, 2003. This letter contains two passages that I believe describe the basic fundamentals underpinning the relationship between Europe and the U.S.:

> The real bond between the U.S. and Europe is the values we share: democracy, individual freedom, human rights and the rule of law. These values crossed the Atlantic with those who sailed from Europe to help create the United States of America. Today, they are under greater threat than ever. We in Europe have a relationship with the U.S. that has stood the test of time. Thanks in large part to American bravery, generosity and far-sightedness, Europe was set free from the two forms of tyranny that devastated our continent in the twentieth century: Nazism and communism.

It is significant that France and Germany were not invited to sign this letter, which also expresses solidarity with the U.S. in dealing with Iraq. Once again, this not only demonstrates that Europe does not speak with one voice on foreign policy, but that the attempt to revive the old Gaullist idea of a French-German *Directoire* to formulate European foreign policy has failed. What this letter also reveals is that there are still European leaders today who will stand up for the transatlantic alliance, even if this is not politically correct in their own countries.

This calls to mind the vote in the Belgian Parliament on June 17, 1966, when Paul-Henri Spaak and his friend Antoine Spinoy cast the only two socialist votes in support of the government's decision to allow SHAPE, the Supreme Headquarters Allied Powers Europe, to relocate from France to Belgium after France withdrew from the NATO military alliance. On the previous day, Spaak had made his last speech before Parliament, in which he marshaled his great eloquence to defend the Atlantic Alliance he had always championed, arguing that there was no viable alternative to it. This was the conclusion of his remarkable political career, which ended, as he wrote in his memoirs, on an issue of important principle.

It is my hope that European statesmen will continue to journey to Harvard to lecture on U.S.-European relations and that these lectures, conferences, and books will continue to enlighten and promote good relations between our two continents.

Finally, I want to express my appreciation to the Spaak Lecturers, and to the Weatherhead Center for International Affairs at Harvard, its Director, Professor Jorge Dominguez, and its Executive Director, Dr. James Cooney, for organizing these lectures. My thanks also go to the Paul-Henri Spaak Foundation, its President, Viscount Davignon, and its Secretary General, Mr. Francois Danis, for hosting the Brussels Spaak Conferences. Last but not least I want to thank Ms. Amanda Pearson, Director of Publications of the Weatherhead Center, for her work in making this book possible.

PART I

EDITOR'S INTRODUCTION

Introduction

Europe Without Illusions

Andrew Moravcsik

Future historians may someday look back on the 1990s as the decade when Europeans began to view the European Union without illusions.[1] For almost fifty years after World War II, geopolitical imperatives—the democratization of Germany and Italy, the communist menace at home and abroad, and the omnipresence of United States military power—masked the foundation on which postwar European integration was built; namely, the management of commercial and financial interdependence. Instead, integration was justified on ideological and geopolitical grounds. Support for the European Union (EU) in this period rested on a "permissive consensus" of favorable public opinion, which permitted centrist political parties to satisfy the economic demands of powerful producer groups, while justifying their actions with arguments about the role of the EU in promoting democracy and peace.

---

1. The first draft of this paper was delivered as the opening lecture at the Third Harvard University—Spaak Foundation Conference, "Les relations tranatlantiques un an après le 11 septembre 2001" (Brussels, September 6–8, 2002). I am grateful to Renato Ruggiero and other participants at that conference for their comments and criticisms.

With the exception of a few salient episodes—the French debate over the European Defense Community and the British referendum of 1975 come to mind—fundamental assumptions about the proper form and substance of European economic integration were almost never put to public debate. The future of Europe was instead placed in the hands of prominent statesmen (and sometimes officials and judges) who believed in the European project, Paul-Henri Spaak being a noble example. They charted the way forward and constructed the major pillars of the EU: the customs union, the Common Agricultural Policy, the supremacy of European law as proclaimed by the European Court of Justice, the directly elected European Parliament, the single market, and monetary integration.

This quiet, elite-driven style of EU politics came to an end a decade ago. In the wake of the Single European Act of 1986, the Maastricht Treaty of 1991 and enlargement to include three new members, the old basis of European integration began to be questioned. Referenda on the 1991 Maastricht Treaty in Denmark, France, and Ireland sparked widespread, if somewhat demagogic, public deliberation, and national constitutional courts, notably in Germany, squarely placed the issue at the heart of national legal debates. Discussion was later energized by new challenges—regional stabilization, democratization, and enlargement—emerging out of the post–cold war world.

In the decade that followed, a wide-ranging debate has emerged over the deeper purposes, technical efficiency, institutional appropriateness, and democratic legitimacy of the EU. While Oxford don Larry Siedentop recently asked in a widely read book "Where are the Madisons for Europe?",[2] a more appropriate question for those who follow continental debates, is: "Why are there so many Madisons?" For the debate over the future of the EU has engaged an extraordinary number of Europe's leading public intellectuals, journalists, and politicians. Jürgen Habermas, Alain Minc, Anthony Giddens, and Timothy Garton Ash head the list of hundreds of scholars debating its democratic legitimacy, while elite European newspapers devote entire sections to proposed provisions for a European constitution. In fact, one is hard-pressed to find a leading European prime minister, president, or foreign minister who has not advanced a detailed scheme for reform of the European constitutional order. In the past two years alone, Prime Ministers Tony Blair of the United Kingdom and Jose-

---

2. Larry Siedentop, *Democracy in Europe* (New York: Columbia University Press, 2001).

Maria Aznar of Spain, French President Jacques Chirac, German Foreign Minister Joschka Fischer, former Italian Premier Giuliano Amato, European Commission President Romano Prodi, and many others have done so. And now a constitutional convention is charged with crafting something enduring from all these ideas.

This criticism and debate does not mean that European integration is faltering. The decade from 1993 to 2003 may indeed be the most successful in EU history, marked by deepening of the internal market program; realization of a single currency; enlargement to include Austria, Sweden and Finland; increased activities on social, defense, and immigration policy; the conclusion of negotiations for enlargement to include five to eight new members to the East and South, and, we expect, a new constitutional document for Europe. The EU has been and remains, by any reasonable standard, the most successful voluntary international organization in world history, and understanding its distinctive dynamics has become essential for any serious analyst of world politics.

The shift in European discourse from uncritical public acceptance of integration to a more critical yet still constructive tone is reflected in the five statesmen—Roy Jenkins, Renato Ruggiero, Ralf Dahrendorf, Uffe Ellemann-Jensen, and George Papandreou—who delivered Spaak Lectures at Harvard University in the period from 1994 through 2000. Their reflections command our attention not just because in each case they were written by practitioners of considerable intelligence, insight and, in two cases, scholarly credentials, but because they differ so strikingly in both tone and topic from the Spaak Lectures of the preceding decade and a half:[3] Three differences in particular illustrate the depth and direction of recent changes of the political mood in Europe.

First, there is a shift from military to civilian topics. Whereas earlier speakers focused primarily on NATO and transatlantic relations, these five speakers hardly mention such matters; indeed, they hardly discuss pure geopolitical or security affairs at all.[4] Instead, four of the five focus on

---

3. For previous lectures, see Richard C. Eichenberg, *Drifting Together or Apart? U.S.-European Relations in the Paul-Henri Spaak Lectures, Harvard University, 1981-1984* (Lanham, MD: University Press of America, 1986); Center for International Affairs, *Allies or Adversaries? U.S.-European Relations in the Paul-Henri Spaak Lectures, Harvard University, 1985-1992* (Lanham, MD: University Press of America, 1993).
4. Papandreou's discussion of the Balkans is the only major exception.

policies directly related to the EU, while Ruggiero dwells on the relationship between the General Agreement on Tariff and Trade/World Trade Organization (GATT/WTO) system and regional institutions like the EU. This indicates not just a shift in public attention from transatlantic relations to European events, but signals an even deeper shift from the unquestioned primacy of security matters in the cold war to a more balanced attention to social and economic interactions among countries in the post–cold war period.

Second, greater attention is paid to historical change. As befits commentators in any period of fundamental transformation, each speaker seeks to situate the current state of the EU in historical perspective. This is particularly striking in the cases of Lord Jenkins and Lord Dahrendorf, who devote the greater part of their essays to the history of the EU. Ellemann-Jensen, Ruggiero, and Papandreou also advance intriguing historical claims. This implies that the fundamental concerns regarding European integration have shifted in recent years.

Third, while each of the five speakers sincerely professes to be a "European," most are deeply critical of past and current EU policy. This reflects one of the most intriguing developments in contemporary Europe—the emergence among national political elites of a range of more skeptical positions with regard to the EU. Before 1991, with the exception of the French Gaullists of the early 1960s and the British Tories of the 1980s, it would have been difficult to find a governing party in Europe that was fundamentally critical of the course of European integration. To be sure, there was much criticism in opposition, and there were endless squabbles, some quite heated, over the distribution of funds, not least in the agricultural sector. And, of course, many European leaders were far more skeptical in private—Helmut Schmidt and Valéry Giscard d'Estaing are examples. Yet fundamental criticism of the legitimacy or desirability of the current EU structure remained essentially outside the scope of acceptable public debate for all except the representatives of the extreme left and right. Instead, politicians invoked a set of symbols and myths, of varying degrees of appropriateness and accuracy, about the beneficial consequences of integration and the continuing need for "ever closer union." After 1991, however, major European politicians began to stake out a series of subtly differentiated critiques and proposals for EU reform, some quite unorthodox—of which the essays by Lord Dahrendorf, Ellemann-Jensen, and Ruggiero provide particularly thoughtful examples.

Taken together, these critiques cast doubt on nearly all the underlying core beliefs used to legitimate European integration during Spaak's generation: the central role of integration in preventing war in Europe; the use of European ideals as an antidote to nationalism; the need for Europeanism as a bulwark against domestic and foreign communism; the inevitability of spillover into ever expanding activities; the destiny of the EU to become a centralized federal state; the conception of EU officials as impartial administrators of the common interest; and the higher purpose justifying the EU's lack of traditional democratic institutions. All these things, and more, are questioned by these writers, just as they have been in recent European debates.

For each speaker, as for many Europeans, the central question for the future is: How can we justify and legitimate European integration in an era when it is increasingly viewed without the help of ideological and geopolitical illusions? Consideration of what public justification is required for European integration raises a number of significant issues, which I have used to organize my commentary on the Lectures. Each of these issues is central to the future constitutional evolution of a united Europe.

First, there is matter of the historical role of the founding European myths and beliefs on the continent. Which specific myths were most important? What precise role did they play? This issue is raised by Lord Dahrendorf, as well as Ullemann-Jensen and Ruggiero, and is addressed in the first section of this essay.

Second, there is the curious history of the United Kingdom and a few other more pragmatic and sometimes outright "Euroskeptical" countries that resisted the lure of such ideologies. Britain has long harbored lukewarm attitudes toward the EU. What makes Britain distinctive in this regard, and what does British "exceptionalism" tell us about the European project? This issue is addressed in the lecture by Lord Jenkins, and in the second section of this essay.

Third, there is the question whether the founding myths of the EU are in fact true. Is it in fact the case that economic integration prevents war, or that it necessarily leads to political union? This issue is raised with particular force by Lord Dahrendorf, while interesting contributions to the analysis are made by Ellemann-Jensen and Papandreou as well. This is the topic of the third section of this essay.

Fourth, and most important for current policy, is the issue of whether the recent deepening of European integration has pushed the EU too far; that is, beyond the constraints imposed by sensible policy analysis and the need for democratic legitimacy. This is, in one form or another, the concern of every one of the Spaak Lecturers.

This essay takes the opposite position. My central contention is that the EU, the most successful example of peaceful, voluntary international cooperation in world history, remains stable and strong. It is easy—too easy, recent public debates suggest—to criticize the EU by holding it up against a philosophical ideal of a unified national state governed by a sovereign parliament. This idealistic starting point naturally gives rise to criticisms such as those we have just considered—that is, that the current institutional structure of the EU, with its complex compromises of nationally and regionally specific elements, breeds insularity and protectionism, generates division and conflict, and exacerbates the perception that the EU is democratically illegitimate.

I reject each of these criticisms. The EU is democratically legitimate as it stands, and widespread efforts to reform it in a more participatory or majoritarian direction, not least in the current constitutional convention, are therefore unwarranted. It is no surprise that the new constitution seems destined to be a conservative, consolidating document, rather than revolutionary one; when governments are taking a good close look at EU institutions, they seem to reflect the complex trade-offs of this extraordinary multilevel polity. In particular, I argue in the fourth section below, the past ten years have not, in fact, confirmed most of the concerns voiced by the Spaak lecturers, and by critics of the EU's democratic legitimacy more general. Instead, the EU has deepened the single market, established a single currency, and agreed to expand to the East—all without a noticeable diminution in either efficiency or legitimacy. The EU is here to stay, and while not all aspects of European regional governance are laudable, the institution is, on balance, stronger and larger than ever. Rather than asking, as many have in the recent constitutional deliberation, when the EU will become more like the U.S., we should be asking when the U.S. will become more willing to accept the sort of effective multilateral institutions Europe has pioneered.[5]

The Power of European Myths

The conventional wisdom about the origins of the European Union, repeated in endless Commission pamphlets, Sunday speeches, and

---

5. This is one way to respond to the challenge set forth by Robert Kagan in *Of Paradise and Power: America and Europe in the New World Order* (New York: Knopf, 2003).

journalistic commentaries—and not a few historical monographs—is that the EU was not simply an economic project, but was above all a response to overarching geopolitical concerns. In his 1996 Spaak Lecture, "From Europe to *EU*rope: A Story of Hope, Trial and Error," Lord Ralf Dahrendorf states this view with great clarity, stressing the role of political ideology in motivating European integration on the continent since 1957.

Lord Dahrendorf recognizes that European integration, despite being an essentially economic project, was consistently justified in idealistic and geopolitical terms. For Lord Dahrendorf, as for most Germans, the key source of such ideological support for the EU was never simply "European federalist" idealism or cold war anticommunism. What held together the project, in his view, was above all the desire to restrain Germany.

> [European integration] since 1945...was always about Germany...At least three German chancellors—Adenauer, Schmidt, and Kohl—showed a strong sense of the need for German *Selbsteinbindung*...All the way to monetary union, one motive force of European integration has remained the desire to keep Germany within the fold...of the liberal democracies of the world...[D]emocracy at home is also as solid a guarantee against aggression abroad as one can hope for.[6]

This view is echoed by former Danish Foreign Minister Uffe Ellemann-Jensen, whose 1997 Spaak Lecture, "The New Europe: How to Overcome Forty Years of Division," restates the political interpretation of European integration in its strongest possible form.

> [Y]ou must know what really lies behind European integration ...Out of the despair [of World War II] grew the idea that a united Europe would make war impossible...Although the agreement evolved from an arrangement initially dominated by economic issues to one increasingly dominated by political concerns, the fundamental objective remained the same: integration should lead to peace and liberty. *That* was always the goal. Economic integration—pooling the resources—was always the means, not the end...It is very important to keep this in mind: *European integration is first and foremost a political endeavor.*[7]

6. Dahrendorf, pp. 82-83.
7. Ellemann-Jensen, pp. 96-97.

European integration, in Ellemann-Jensen's account, was meant to render war between European governments impossible, to support the West in a continent "divided between two ideological systems" and, more recently, to strengthen new democracies in Southern and Eastern Europe. Ambassador Renato Ruggiero, in his 1995 Lecture, "The Global Challenge: Opportunities and Choices in the Multilateral Trading System," takes the same view not just of the EU but also of the global trading regime. It was designed, above all else, not to promote economic welfare per se, but to promote peace and security within the cold war context.[8]

There is some truth to this account. From the launching of the Schuman Plan to the Maastricht Treaty, major decisions in the history of the EU were often pursued by those who had the threats of Soviet expansionism and German nationalism in mind. This was particularly true of the German conservative leaders Konrad Adenauer and Helmut Kohl. As a matter of international relations theory, there is reason to believe, in Europe as in the global system, that such concerns added to the incentives of particularly powerful and competitive states to promote multilateral trade liberalization.[9]

Yet it is important not to exaggerate this point. The newest generation of historiography on the EU, based on the recent release of confidential documents, reveals that elite decision-makers among the Six were generally more obsessed with economic policy goals than with geopolitical aims.[10] European integration has in fact always been more about commercial gain and less about peace and liberty than politicians have admitted publicly. Non-economic arguments for integration were more often used as a public justification for policies that reflected rather narrow economic self-interest.

Consider first the Schuman Plan, later the European Coal and Steel Community (ECSC) of the early 1950s—perhaps the clearest case of a

---

8. Ruggiero, p. 63.
9. For analyses along these lines, see Joanne Gowa, *Allies, Adversaries and International Trade* (Princeton: Princeton University Press, 1994); Marc Trachtenberg, *A Constructed Peace? The United States, the NATO Allies, and the Making of the European Settlement, 1949–1963* (Philadelphia: University of Pennsylvania Press, 1998).
10. By this I mean economic interest as defined by powerful domestic interest groups and electoral pressures, not aggregate welfare, although the two sometimes overlap. Many economists take the view that if the EU cannot be economically motivated, a strict economic assessment would favor a multilateral trading system instead, but this overlooks the domestic political imperatives of trade policy.

European proposal undoubtedly motivated by the desire to stabilize peace, democracy, and centrist domestic coalitions in Western European countries. The rhetoric of the Schuman Plan, with its vision of ridding the continent of war, has influenced perceptions of European integration ever since. Yet even in this case, recent historical research reveals the considerable extent to which the ECSC was also motivated by narrow economic self-interest. We forget that Jean Monnet was at the time not just an activist for Europe but also the chief of French planning, and his domestic goals required him to obtain the natural resources, notably steel, necessary to fulfill his industrial schemes abroad, not least in Germany.[11]

Even if we were to concede the dominance of geopolitical concerns in this case, things had changed fundamentally just five years later. It is often forgotten that the customs union plan of 1955–57 that gave rise to the European Economic Community (EEC) was perceived by the "founding fathers" of the EU as a decisive break with the initial conception of the European economic integration as a means to prevent war. When discussions began in 1955, Spaak, Monnet, and Pierre Uri had proposed to carry on in the spirit of the ECSC by regulating "strategic" sectors that could support warfare, notably transport and atomic energy, and doing so through a centralized regulatory agency. Within a matter of days, however, German business leaders, who had resented meddling by the ECSC High Authority between 1950 and 1955, and who had grown internationally competitive enough to favor trade liberalization, vetoed any such proposal outright. European leaders therefore sought another proposal.

The proposal for a customs union was the brainchild of the Dutch Foreign Minister Willem Beyen, not particularly known for his pro-European views, and was only reluctantly accepted by Spaak and Monnet as a quid pro quo to keep the transport and atomic energy plans alive. Over the next eighteen months, Monnet visited Adenauer several times to beg him to kill the EEC, arguing not just that it was unrealistic, but that trade

11. Alan S. Milward, *The Reconstruction of Western Europe, 1945–1951* (Berkeley: University of California Press, 1994); Francis M. B. Lynch, *France and the International Economy: From Vichy to the Treaty of Rome* (London: Routledge, 1997). Some have challenged details of this analysis, but not its core.

liberalization, by its very nature, was apolitical.[12] Yet the EEC, as the only acceptable proposal for most of the major economic interests involved, remained at the core of the discussions and became the major substantive basis for the "relaunching" of Europe in the mid-1950s. Transport cooperation and EURATOM, the residue of the old Monnetist conception of integration as a means to prevent war embodied in the ECSC, persisted only in a moribund, essentially symbolic form. Thereafter, if not before, European integration was an essentially commercial project.

During much of the subsequent history of the EEC, European governments continued to be motivated more by butter than by guns—quite literally so, in the case of the Common Agricultural Policy. Consider the episode widely considered to be the most salient geopolitically motivated act of European policy in the 1960s: de Gaulle's veto of the first British EU membership bid in 1963. De Gaulle's celebrated action is almost universally interpreted as having resulted from his geopolitical aim of establishing France and Europe as a political-military entity independent of the U.S. and, therefore, of Britain. Yet the documents now demonstrate—unambiguously, in my view—that de Gaulle was motivated primarily not by geopolitical rivalry with Atlanticist Britain, but by the desire to protect French commercial prerogatives, most importantly in agriculture. Certainly commercial concerns were more salient in the internal deliberations, to an extent that appears sufficient to have triggered a veto.[13]

The motivations behind other major decisions through the years were similarly commercial. There is general agreement among scholars today that the desire to overcome economic "Eurosclerosis" was the primary motivation behind the Single European Act of 1986.[14] It can quite plausibly be argued that the support for monetary integration between 1970 and 1992

12. This interpretation is not controversial. See the finest biography of Monnet, by his former close associate, François Duchêne: *Jean Monnet: The First Statesman of Interdependence* (New York: Norton, 1995). Also Moravcsik, *Choice for Europe*, pp. 145; also 140, 151-152.
13. Andrew Moravcsik, "De Gaulle between Grain and *Grandeur*: The Economic Origins of French EC Policy, 1958–1970 (Parts I and II)" *Journal of Cold War Studies* (Spring 2000 and Fall 2000). See also Moravcsik, "Le grain et la grandeur: les origines économiques de la politique européenne du général de Gaulle (Partie I et II)" *Revue française de science politique* (August 1999 and February 2000).
14. For example, Wayne Sandholtz and John Zysman, "1992: Recasting the European Bargain," *World Politics* 42 (December 1989), pp. 95-128.

by leaders like Schmidt, Giscard d'Estaing, and François Mitterrand owed as much to the economic interest of their respective nations as to geopolitics. Monetary integration did not simply reduce the transaction costs of investment in Europe, it freed European monetary policies from constraints imposed by an unstable U.S. dollar and an unaccountable German Bundesbank—or it was at least widely perceived as doing so.[15]

Overall, it is hard to deny that European politicians have always been pragmatists quite attentive to commercial considerations, no matter what additional geopolitical and ideological considerations were adduced to support their positions. Though economists rarely see it this way, producer groups believed that the EU had considerable advantages over the multilateral trading system under GATT and the WTO, since it permitted trade liberalization that has been at once more intense and more closely tailored to European interests. To be sure, as Dahrendorf notes, geopolitical concerns rendered Germany somewhat more forthcoming than pure economic interest would have dictated. In a series of crises with the Soviet Union and its client state on German soil, Adenauer, Brandt, and Kohl employed European integration effectively to muster support among the Western allies.[16] German willingness to fund the Common Agricultural Policy in the 1950s is difficult (though perhaps not impossible) to explain any other way.[17] Most of the time, however, European integration has been powered by the pragmatic search for commercial benefits in the world's most economically interdependent continent.

---

15. Thomas H. Oatley, *Monetary Politics: Exchange Rate Cooperation in the European Union* (Ann Arbor: University of Michigan Press, 1997); Jeffry Frieden, "The Impact of Goods and Capital Market Integration on European Monetary Politics," *Comparative Political Studies* 29 (1996), pp. 193-222; Kathleen McNamara, *The Currency of Ideas: Monetary Politics in the European Union* (Ithaca, NY: Cornell University Press, 1997); Moravcsik, *Choice for Europe,* Chapters 4, 6, and, for a balanced assessment of economic and geopolitical concerns, Chapter 7.
16. Dahrendorf, p 83.
17. Though, of course, the German government demanded and received high support prices as a quid pro quo, with the result that a country that had exported almost no agricultural goods in the 1950s became the world's sixth largest agricultural exporter.

Life Without Illusions: The Exceptional Role of Britain

Some countries have consistently resisted both commercial and geopolitical justifications for European integration. It is in Britain that we find generally lukewarm support for the EU, and a vociferous, deeply entrenched "Euroskeptical" minority.[18] European integration has been more controversial there than in almost any other member state. In his 1994 Spaak Lecture, "The Disappointing Partnership Between British Governments and Europe: Why the Paul-Henri Spaak Tradition Rarely Embraces London," the late Lord Jenkins, leader of pro-European forces, former president of the Commission and then a leading member of the House of Lords, addresses the central puzzle of British EU policy over the past half century: How can we account for Britain's "persistent self-defeating semi-detachment" with respect to the European project?[19]

British "exceptionalism" on Europe poses a double puzzle. First, why have the British tended to hang back from new European initiatives, whether the ECSC in the early 1950s or Economic and Monetary Union (EMU) in the 1990s? Second, why have the British also tended to (in Lord Jenkins's apt metaphor) "running along the track of the departing train and hoping that we can clamber aboard" at the next convenient point? The latter is a habit, he rightly notes, "conducive neither to comfort nor to national dignity," one that in practical terms, "guarantees that we never play an effective role in shaping the institutions which we subsequently join."[20] Such demands, needless to say, elicit little sympathy from other European governments. Indeed, until very recently, the result has been a policy at the "extreme of illogicality," in which, on the one hand, the British government generally supports à la carte or multiple-speed policies, yet violently opposes any effort by others to move ahead without the UK, on the other.[21]

---

18. For an overview of Euroskeptical opinion with somewhat greater attention to France, see Ronald Tiersky, *Euroskepticism: A Reader* (Lanham: Rowman and Littlefield, 2001). Jenkins cites Thatcher as rarely saying anything positive about the EU, and he cites her amusing judgment of her continental counterparts as "a rotten lot, except maybe for Schmidt." Jenkins, p. 57.
19. Jenkins, p. 60.
20. Jenkins, p. 55.
21. Jenkins, p. 59.

Lord Jenkins sets out in search of a "general theory" to explain this phenomenon. He begins, in fine social scientific form, by succinctly and convincingly dismissing some spurious explanations.[22] British exceptionalism, he concludes, is too consistent to be attributed only to particular individuals, too enduring to be the result of nostalgia for empire, and too much in conflict with U.S. policy to stem from a hankering after an Atlanticist "special relationship." Nor can it be attributed to poor British linguistic skills (for the French are worse) or to Lockean skepticism of continental Cartesianism *à la française* (for the Irish have managed, at least until recently, rather well in Europe).

What, then, is the explanation? To be sure, it is with some disappointment that one turns to the last page of Lord Jenkins's essay to find a brief concluding paragraph that begins, "I am sorry not to give you a more definitive answer ...,"[23] yet his search uncovers two very promising leads.

The first has to do with what Lord Jenkins terms the "peculiar rigidities of the British political system."[24] British parliamentary support for Europe rests on a cross-party coalition between center-right and center-left. Over the years, this is how it has been in most European political systems: support for the EU comes from the center, while opposition arises on the far left (e.g., French and Italian communists, the left wing of the British Labour Party, and even the social democratic parties of Scandinavia) and the nationalist far right (e.g., Poujadists, Thatcherite British Tories, current anti-immigrant parties, and sometimes the French Gaullists). What is distinct in Britain, Lord Jenkins rightly observes, is a singular inability to manage this delicate political situation so as to permit the government to act.

This persistent failure to manage domestic conflict productively invites us to reflect on deeper characteristics of the British political system. While many factors might contribute to this pathology,[25] perhaps the most

---

22. Jenkins, pp. 59-60.
23. Jenkins, p. 61.
24. Jenkins, p. 59.
25. One is the lack of presidential government, an institutional characteristic that appears to have contributed much to French support for the EU under both the right (de Gaulle and Chirac) and the left (Mitterrand). Another is the "first past the post" electoral system, which undermines the power of smaller centrist parties—one thinks of the German Free Democrats, the French UDF, and many others on the continent—that often contribute to pro-European centrist parliamentary coalitions. The positive role of the Liberal Democrats in Britain, weakened though they are, is striking in this regard. Also, the

important for our purposes here is the lack of a large, organized communist opposition, a characteristic that strikingly differentiates Britain from Italy, France, and (albeit indirectly, via national division) even Germany. In these countries the threat from a highly organized radical left, powered in part by internationalist views, led postwar centrists to embrace European integration as an alternative conception of cosmopolitan idealism.[26] The lack of such a threat is a characteristic that Britain shares with other less federalist countries, notably Denmark, Sweden, Norway, Switzerland, and Ireland, and it lends European integration less ideological force.

The second intriguing lead uncovered by Lord Jenkins is the British tendency to view European integration primarily as a matter of trade. Jenkins maintains that trade is an inherently uninspiring matter. As the ambitious young Gladstone bitterly complained a century and a half ago after he was relegated early in his career to head the Board of Trade, it is the management of "packages." Trade still fails to inspire widespread public support, while "Europe is and must be about men and women, and peace and politics and security, and art and life and buildings and ecology, and wider purpose than packages."[27] The argument appears to be that Britain failed to generate widespread belief in the 'European myths' discussed earlier.

Lord Jenkins is quite correct that economic incentives have dominated British policymaking over the past half century. Indeed, recently released confidential documents reveal that commercial concerns were far more important than most, even Jenkins, believed at the time or have believed ever since. In 1955, the British government's choice to favor the maintenance of Commonwealth trade over trade with the Six made perfect sense in commercial terms: the Commonwealth took 52 percent of British exports, the Six only 12 percent. France and Germany, by contrast, exported two to three times as much to each other and members of the proposed EEC. As

---

selection of candidates for parliamentary elections by decentralized party activists, notably in the Conservative Party, tends to encourage the selection of more or less centrist candidates.

26. The trajectory of the French Christian Democratic Party, the Movement Républicain Populaire (MRP) of Jean Monnet and Robert Schuman, is a good example. The MRP began the postwar period a Euroskeptical party, but switched in large part in order to contest the communists for the rural electorate. See Serge Berstein, S. J. M. Mayeur, and Pierre Milza. *Le MRP et la construction européenne* (Bruxelles: Éditions Complexe, 1993).
27. Jenkins, p. 58.

the relative weights of British trade with Commonwealth and continent reversed between 1955 and 1965, so did British policy. We now know that Harold Macmillan's primary motivation for launching the first British application to the EEC in 1961 was his understanding that trade was shifting rapidly from the Commonwealth to the continent. Avoiding commercial exclusion from Europe became the single most important priority of British policy, for if Britain were unable to export, neither guns nor butter would be affordable.[28]

Commercial concerns continued to dominate British policy over the decades that followed. The positive outcome of the referendum of 1975, for example, was decisively shaped by the intervention of British big business, which permitted the "Yes" campaign—in which Jenkins played a leading role—to outspend their opponents ten to one.[29] In the years that followed, the major issue around which British opposition formed was the Common Agricultural Policy, which burdened British taxpayers while creating relatively few allies in Britain's tiny agricultural sector. Jenkins notes also the particular irony of Margaret Thatcher, the most Euroskeptical leader of Britain in the postwar period, who presided over the advance to the Single Market—"the one major step towards integration taken in Europe in the past half century in which Britain was not left tagging along behind"—in large part due to her commitment to free trade.[30]

The non-ideological nature of the British approach to Europe may well account for the characteristic passivity of British policy toward Europe. At most turning points, as Jenkins suggests, economic interest rather than geopolitical calculation or federal idealism dictated British participation in Europe. Yet the absence of a domestic political rationale for action—in particular, the absence of organized communist opposition at home—meant

---

28. For the argument in detail, see Andrew Moravcsik, *The Choice for Europe: Social Purpose and State Power from Messina to Maastricht* (Ithaca: Cornell University Press, 1998), pp. 122-135, 164-176, 274-285. Also Jacqueline Tratt, *The Macmillan Government and Europe: A Study in the Process of Policy Development* (New York: St. Martin's Press, 1996.) More recently, see Alan S. Milward, *The Rise and Fall of a National Strategy: The UK and the European Community* (London: Oxford University Press, 2002).
29. David Butler and Uwe Kitzinger, *The 1975 Referendum* (London: Macmillan, 1976); Anthony King, *Britain says Yes—The 1975 Referendum* (Washington: American Enterprise Institute, 1977.
30. Jenkins, p. 57. This was true when Lord Jenkins spoke. Now we must add Tony Blair's recent proposals in foreign and security policy.

that partisan and public support was weak. Accordingly, British participation was less enthusiastic (and often slower to emerge) than that of its continental counterparts.[31] Rather than responding swiftly or strongly, Britain became "an awkward partner."[32]

While this explains British policy through the mid-1990s, one cannot help but perceive that in today's post–cold war period Britain is less exceptional in Europe than ever before. This is so in part because creative diplomacy has moved Britain closer to the heart of Europe. Though Britain remains a persistent objector on EMU, Prime Minister Tony Blair has moved Britain to the middle of efforts to construct a common foreign and security policy. He has brilliantly usurped the traditional position of the French by advancing proposals for foreign policy cooperation that contain a tinge of idealism and not a little self-interest, and doing so in a way that makes it impossible for either France or Germany to oppose them.

The United Kingdom is also less exceptional because Europe has become more British. Public debate within other EU member states, even the original Six, has moved in a more skeptical direction. On the continent, the end of the cold war and the disappearance of a domestic communist opposition (with former communist voters disseminated among other parties) appear to have legitimated more pragmatic views. The addition of new members with very different political traditions, most notably in Scandinavia, adds to the momentum. In the former Eastern Europe, many governments take a more pragmatic view of the EU. Britain's traditional concerns about the "democratic deficit" are shared by others, and its view that the Council should be strengthened commands widespread support, while traditional federalists like Germany and Belgium are on the defensive. At the current moment, Britain's more pro-American position on the Middle East and the Iraq War appears to commend as much support across European governments (though not necessarily European publics) as does Franco-German skepticism of U.S. policy—as attested by a letter signed by

31. One might also argue that Britain benefited less broadly from membership in economic terms, thereby undermining domestic support. For a consistent economic interpretation of cross-national public opinion support for the EU, see Matthew Gabel, *Interests and Integration: Market Liberalization, Public Opinion, and European Union* (Ann Arbor: University of Michigan Press, 1998).
32. Stephen George, *An Awkward Partner: Britain in the European Community* (Oxford: Oxford University Press, 1990).

nine governments in support of U.S. policy. All this seems to suggest that however important the 'European myths' may or may not have been in the past, EU politics is now justified in a more concrete and pragmatic way—and not just in Britain.

Are the European Myths Accurate?

Some may find the preceding discussion a somewhat arcane historical diversion into national motivations. After all, from *Sonntagsreden* in Germany to the abstract analyses of American academics, nearly every commentator on European politics over the past fifty years has viewed the EU, after the fact, as a decisive force preventing a European war. The practical-minded reader might thus conclude that whatever the motivations—that is, whether politicians really believed what they said or simply used geopolitical concerns as justification for the pursuit of commercial gain—European integration has had stabilizing impact on European politics. Is this not the EU's real contribution to postwar regional order?

Here Lord Dahrendorf finds convincing reasons for skepticism. Politicians may have sincerely believed over the years that economic liberalization promotes democracy and peace, but Lord Dahrendorf believes they were mistaken and that the linkage was spurious all along. Worse, the notion that economic integration can spill over into geopolitics, as founding fathers like Robert Schuman, Spaak, and Monnet believed, is not just fallacious, it is the "fatal flaw" of the EU. This public ideology, Lord Dahrendorf asserts, is based on two questionable connections between economic integration and geopolitical stabilization, one direct and indirect. In his view, it encourages the acceptance of schemes that lack a sound economic or public rationale, and thus undermines the European integration process. Let us examine this argument in detail.

First, does European economic integration inevitably spill over into political and security cooperation? Some believe that success in economic areas, say trade, necessarily creates political or institutional support for cooperation elsewhere. This was the view of Monnet, Spaak, Walter Hallstein, and others of that generation—though most of them tended to believe that areas of strategic significance and high government regulation, such as atomic energy, would work best.

Lord Dahrendorf is dismissive. "If we want political union," he states flatly, "no economic subterfuge will get us there."[33] And again he has a valid point.[34] Economic integration seems to have done relatively little over the years to advance European cooperation in non-economic matters. There have been notable successes in deploying international institutions to stabilize postwar Europe—the Marshall Plan, NATO, the Organization of Security and Cooperation in Europe, and the European Convention on Human Rights come to mind—but these lie outside the EU, and all but one predate it.[35] Those areas of EU success in foreign policy coordination appear to have proceeded parallel to economic integration, rather than as a result of it.

Second, does European economic integration actually promote peace by removing incentives for war? This view, first developed by Schuman and Monnet, remains widespread. It is advanced in classic form by Ellemann-Jensen, who argues that the EU has succeeded in rendering war between its members "not only unlikely and unbelievable, but also impossible for practical reasons."[36] Ruggiero voices concern about the possibility of excessive regionalism, "with all the consequences this would imply for political stability and security." He concludes: "If we decrease our imports from the developing countries, we decrease their growth and our growth alike...[and] will just increase instability, violence, war and terrorism." [37]

---

33. Dahrendorf, p. 89.
34. This conclusion is surely a bit overstated, since spillover does appear to exist within the economic area, from trade to money, for instance, and has had important political consequences. For example, the creation of the Single Market contributed to investment and capital flows that encouraged monetary union—though even here the most recent research suggests that high trade and capital flows in Europe are, for the most part, not induced by European integration but are largely a function of underlying resource endowments and global economic trends. For state-of-the-art econometrics on the question, see Jeffrey A. Frankel, Ernesto Stein, and Shang-Jinwei, *Regional Trading Blocs in the World Economic System* (Washington DC: Institute for International Economics, 1997.)
35. Even EU institutions for foreign policy coordination lie outside the supranational "first pillar."
36. Ellemann-Jensen, this page will have to be changed, argues that "today war between member states of the European Union is not only unlikely and unbelievable, but also impossible for practical reasons"—an outcome he attributes to the EU.
37. Ruggiero, pp. 77-78.

Lord Dahrendorf will have none of it. "One must be allowed to wonder," he writes, "whether it was actually European integration which has prevented wars at least among the members of Europe's communities after 1945."[38] And he is no longer alone in voicing skepticism about this linkage. The issue was publicly debated, with considerable sophistication, during the French referendum on the Maastricht Treaty, and is increasingly challenged in European circles.

Both the historical record and social scientific analysis seem to confirm Lord Dahrendorf's skepticism—at least in the postwar European case. Nearly everything we know about international security affairs suggests that democratic governance alone is sufficient to prevent war; trade has a secondary impact, and membership in international organizations almost none.[39] And in the particular case of postwar Europe, the evidence is scant that the EU either prevented war or promoted democracy among the Six. From the beginning of this period to the end, no two Western European governments (members of the EU or not) even considered threatening one another with military attack. The resolution of territorial disputes in the Saarland and the integration of Germany into the Western alliances, the last outstanding issues that might plausibly have eventually led to war, took place before the founding of the European Community in 1957. By that time, democracy in the *Bundesrepublik* had been consolidated, and it is far-fetched to assert that the ECSC, launched in 1952, contributed much to a process of German democratization that was also propelled forward by the Nazi debacle, Allied occupation, the Soviet threat, and Adenauer's strong leadership. Lord Dahrendorf, who is as qualified as any living scholar to make such a judgment, is correct to "doubt whether the role of European institutions in creating a firm social basis for Germany's democratic political institutions was more than marginal."[40]

---

38. Dahrendorf, p. 82.
39. For a detailed discussion, see John R. O'Neal and Bruce Russett, *Triangulating Peace: Democracy, Interdependence, and International Organizations* (W.W. Norton & Company, 2001).
40. Dahrendorf goes even further and disputes the link between economic growth and democracy. He writes, "It is tempting to interpret the history of postwar Europe as one of political stabilization by economic growth and prosperity. Yet here as elsewhere one must beware of the elementary confusion between correlation and causality. The economic and the political miracle happened at much the same time, but it does not follow that one caused the other." Dahrendorf, p. 83.

The strongest evidence for a linkage between economic integration and regional peace and security is not, in fact, to be found in the early days of European integration, but today. It is difficult to account entirely for the recent decision to enlarge the EU to include Eastern Europe without invoking the belief that economic integration will stabilize Eastern European democracies and ameliorate the resulting social and political dislocation. As Ellemann-Jensen states:

> If popular support of the political and economic reforms weaken, it...may not bring us back to the old days of East-West confrontations, with its threat of mutual destruction, but it may unleash the nationalistic forces buried in the soil of Europe...If we should face a situation of turmoil...with new massive movements of refugees and immigrants, the costs will be greater than those needed to prevent it.[41]

Here George Papandreou, in his 1999 Spaak Lecture, "Europe and the Balkans: The Role of Greece," adds a strong voice for viewing the EU as an effective means to stabilize fledgling democracies. He sketches a vision of a united Europe based on democratic governance:

> [T]he practice of democracy, the strengthening of institutions, the reduction of economic inequalities, and the rule of law...lies in being members of the European Union and NATO...Every country in Southeastern Europe...[should join the] European Union...We see one sole and unifying path: from totalitarianism to democracy, from violence to peace, from poverty to prosperity. Each country in Southeastern Europe might stand today on a different ground but, they should all be heading in the same direction. There is only one path to becoming part of Europe.[42]

Enlargement, Papandreou argues, is the surest way to eliminate nationalist conflict and other causes of war.

There is an irony here. Belief in the myth that the EU stabilized postwar Europe is greatly exaggerated, yet it has encouraged efforts to pursue the same policy today, with much more convincing results. Access to the vast European market, with far fewer exceptions and limitations than under the WTO, appears to have created a nearly irresistible impetus to political and economic reform. In Romania (1996), Bulgaria (1997), Slovakia (1998),

---

41. Ellemann-Jensen, pp. 112-113.
42. Papandreou, pp. 103-104.

and in both Croatia and Serbia (2000), authoritarian, ethnically intolerant, and corrupt governments lost elections to democratic, market-oriented coalitions held together above all by the promise of eventual EU membership. Serbia and Montenegro tottered on the brink of civil war and separation until EU foreign policy czar Javier Solana recently threatened that they would not be considered for membership unless they applied together. Without the military-political impetus, one wonders whether enlargement would have proceeded nearly as fast; and without enlargement, one wonders whether recent democratic transitions would have been as successful.[43]

The promise of membership in the EU is perhaps the most powerful and unique instrument of European foreign policy. Indeed, it may well be the most powerful instrument for global peace and security pursued by any countries in the world today—at least equal to U.S. military might.[44] With this observation we move from the assessment of Europe's past to the topic of the final section, the prognosis for Europe's future.

Has European Integration Gone Too Far?

We have seen that the 'European myths' played an important, though secondary, role in motivating European integration over the years, and we have observed disagreements about the accuracy of those myths.[45] Yet Lord Dahrendorf goes further. Economic integration, he argues, not only fails to promote democracy, liberty, and political union, but the fallacious belief that it can do so—the myth of spillover—is harmful. This belief is no less than a "fatal flaw" that has led the EU "seriously astray." The illusory quest for political union via economic integration, he states categorically, has become an "obstacle rather than a motive force for real political cooperation."[46] This, Lord Dahrendorf believes, is the primary reason why

---

43. Andrew Moravcsik and Milada Vachudova, "National Interest, State Power, and EU Enlargement," *East European Politics and Society* (forthcoming)
44. Andrew Moravcsik, "The Quiet Superpower," *Newsweek* (June 17, 2002, Atlantic Edition).
45. For a precise balancing of the relative contribution, see Andrew Moravcsik, *The Choice for Europe: Social Purpose and State Power from Messina to Maastricht* (Ithaca: Cornell University Press, 1998).
46. Lord Dahrendorf, pp. 10-11.

integration proceeded beyond initial plans for a customs union, and the source of the current difficulties facing the EU.

Lord Dahrendorf is not alone. Two other Spaak Lecturers—Ellemann-Jensen and, at least implicitly, Ruggiero—highlight the dangers of excessive deepening, another central concern of the ongoing European debate. All tend to be skeptical of monetary union, the Common Agricultural Policy, and many aspects of the general trend toward deeper economic cooperation among existing member states. (The two remaining speakers, Jenkins and Papandreou, are more supportive of a broad European agenda.) One suspects that Lord Dahrendorf's complaint is not so much with ideological justifications for pragmatic policies per se, but with the particular policies that the EU has charted over the last decade. Lord Dahrendorf, here joined by Ellemann-Jensen, is deeply dissatisfied with both the procedural and substantive nature of recent EU reforms—most notably EMU. Not by chance are both Lord Dahrendorf and Ellemann-Jensen leading spokesmen for liberal political parties that are suspicious of government regulation and centralized bureaucracy.

Still, the concerns they raise deserve close examination. They revolve around the status of three core European values: free markets, European unity, and democratic legitimacy. Is the deepening of European integration undermining free trade? Is it fragmenting the EU internally and cutting it off from the outside world? Is it eroding democratic legitimacy? Let us consider each concern in turn.

Free Markets and the Threat of Protectionism

The first danger posed by deepening of the EU is greater European protectionism. Yet is European integration really beginning to turn protectionist?

Lord Dahrendorf, Ellemann-Jensen, and Ruggiero hint that new reforms threaten to close Europe off from the rest of the world. Economic liberals, among them most professional economics, have long viewed the EU's carefully crafted compromise between free trade and domestic political stability with suspicion. Self-interest has led the British, Danish, and Dutch governments, not to mention that of the U.S., to take a similar view. The greatest conflict is found in agriculture and other sensitive sectors.

Current developments threaten new protection. In EMU and other recent projects, Lord Dahrendorf detects an "inward-looking bias" and warns, "protectionism and parochialism would be the end of a Europe that matters in the world."[47] Ruggiero documents the striking extent to which the cosmopolitan aspirations of the global trading system are in conflict with the dictates of regional agreements:

> Since the creation of the GATT nearly fifty years ago, one hundred and eight regional agreements have been notified. Eighty existing agreements have so far been examined, and only six have been found consistent with the rules I mentioned above (the EU is not one of them)....Clearly there is a need to improve the rules and the procedures under which the WTO's members can assess this crucial relationship...Regional agreements are becoming more and more important...These are elements that could break up the parallelism between regional and multilateral progress.[48]

Viewed from Geneva, the choice is stark. Ruggiero writes: "[T]here is the basic question of the kind of international system we want: a global system based on the principle of non-discrimination embodied in agreed and enforced rules, or a world divided into regional blocs with all the consequences this would imply for political stability and security."[49] For his part, Ellemann-Jensen calls for the EU to offer Central and Eastern European governments "access to our markets—even in sensitive areas like agricultural products, textiles, and steel."[50] He doubts that reform of the EU's Common Agricultural Policy will be easy, and thus he considers WTO pressure a fortunate development in this regard.

With the passage of a decade, however, concerns about the tension between regionalism and globalism apparent in the mid-1990s seem overdrawn. EU protectionism, while certainly a constant concern, is not worsening. The Single European Act (SEA) and, to a surprising extent, the EMU have been implemented with minimal disturbance to the global trading and financial systems. European agricultural policy remains, to be sure, a major barrier to developing country prosperity. Though the recent agreement to perpetuate the Common Agricultural Policy is sobering, it essentially continues the status quo and may be bargained away, at least in part, in the upcoming Doha Round of WTO negotiations. The internal politics of the EU, however, are moving slowly toward renationalization of

47. Lord Dahrendorf, pp. 88, 91.
48. Ruggiero, pp. 76-77.
49. Ruggiero, p. 77.
50. Ellemann-Jensen, p. 103.

the Common Agricultural Policy, a process likely to continue unless pressure from new applicants prevents it.

Perhaps more fundamental is the increasing acceptance (in large part thanks to appreciation of the EU experience) of the notion that trade policy must acknowledge the legitimacy of domestic regulatory protection. The Europeans have learned that this effort cannot be carried by mutual recognition alone, but requires a measure of minimal regulatory harmonization. Whether in environmental, consumer, competition, monetary or social policy, deregulation without "re-regulation" has often proved neither feasible nor desirable. Deepening is therefore required. Jenkins and Papandreou, whose instincts are more favorable to regulation than their three more liberal counterparts, stress the need for balance in which they pay more attention to issues like art, ecology, education, and development—in Jenkins's words, about "wider purposes than packages."[51] The proof lies in the experience of the EU, which over the past twenty years appears to have pursued deepening successfully without succumbing to the protectionist temptation.

European Unity and the Threat of Fragmentation

The second danger posed by EU deepening is internal fragmentation. Yet, is the EU really disintegrating?

One common concern in this regard, voiced by Lord Dahrendorf and Ellemann-Jensen, is that deepening will slow or block efforts to enlarge the EU. According to this argument, by differentiating among states within the EU and raising the barriers to entry for those outside the EU, excessive deepening increases divisions and conflict within Europe. Lord Dahrendorf charges: "Western Europe has betrayed its principles and promises when, instead of stretching out its hands to Central Europe, it has turned inward to its own so-called *approfondissement* á la Maastricht."[52] Lord Dahrendorf warns of divisive splits between "ins" and "outs;"[53] Ellemann-Jensen warns that critical questions such as the relative voting weights of respective

51. Jenkins, p 58; Papandreou, p 115.
52. Dahrendorf, p. 84.
53. Dahrendorf, p. 88.

member states, the number of commissioners and the reform of the Common Agricultural Policy, have yet to be resolved.[54]

Whereas a decade ago many believed that schemes for deepening monetary, social, and foreign policy might slow or derail enlargement, this fear too has receded. The EU has moved with surprising speed. Surely this critique is unsustainable on the eve of a "big bang" enlargement now slated to include ten new members, with at least two more on the doorstep. To be sure, negotiations with the applicant countries have been difficult, and they have been conducted on terms extraordinarily advantageous to the interests of existing EU member states.

We should not forget that Eastern European states are taking part in this laborious accession process primarily because EU membership brings tremendous economic and geopolitical benefits, particularly as compared to the uncertain and potentially catastrophic costs of being left behind as others move forward. Though the very real danger of a backlash in some applicant countries cannot be ignored, most have already moved substantially toward more open trade with Europe on a bilateral basis and seek an even closer relationship. While the candidates have had to comply with the EU's requirements and acquiesce to certain unfavorable terms, EU membership remains for each a matter of net national interest. (This is precisely why their bargaining power is so weak.) On balance, moreover, the sacrifices demanded of them seem entirely in keeping with the immense adjustment, and the immense benefits, involved. Consistent with Papandreou's analysis, which stresses the fundamental political and economic transformations required for stable democracy, development, and EU membership, most requirements motivate Eastern European governments to implement reforms undeniably required to improve the structure of the state and increase aggregate economic welfare.[55] To oppose this process would seem churlish, even if, in a utopian world, one might hope that the self-interest of existing member states would be less pronounced.

Another cost of deepening may be greater fragmentation within the EU itself. Over the past decade, new forms of EU cooperation have been all but impossible without "multi-track" or "flexible" arrangements—meaning,

---

54. Ellemann-Jensen, p. 104.
55. For a more detailed analysis along these lines, see Andrew Moravcsik and Milada Anna Vachudova, "National Interests, State Power, and EU Enlargement," *East European Politics and Society* 17, Issue 1 (February 2003).

effectively, that countries can opt in or out. We see such provisions in many policy areas. Initial decisions were taken at Maastricht to move ahead in social policy with fourteen of the fifteen member states and in monetary policy with eleven of the fifteen members. Foreign and defense policy coordination assembles "coalitions of the willing," in which those governments that wish to pursue a particular policy may move ahead without fully committing the others. Similar ad hoc arrangements have long existed in transport, R&D and structural fund policies. The Schengen Agreement, which established a zone free of customs checks, has increasingly been integrated into the EU, though it does not include all EU members and not all participants belong to the EU. Similarly, there will very likely be long transition periods in extending the Common Agricultural Policy to Eastern Europe. General provisions for flexibility have been written into the amended Treaty of Rome, with the intention of resisting both obstructions by Euroskeptical governments and (one suspects) demands for redistribution by newly admitted governments. Such provisions have been uncomfortable for some countries, not least those, like Britain, that are subject to threats of exclusion.

Yet it is unclear why we—and, in particular, why pragmatist liberals like Lord Dahrendorf and Ellemann-Jensen—should be critical of such flexible arrangements. As with enlargement, the record of the past decade is quite positive. A subset of countries moving ahead toward a single currency, a tendency that might have appeared divisive six years ago, now appears rather benign and conflict-free—and the number of members has increased since.[56] The pessimistic prognoses envisaged by Lord Dahrendorf—"political non-viability," shocks derailing the transition, massive domestic unrest—simply have not come to pass. Similarly, can common policies on immigration, social protection, or foreign policy really be viewed, on balance, as divisive?

---

56. Lord Dahrendorf also believes that monetary union was simply the wrong policy, which may well be true. But this is not the basis of a general critique of the EU. For skeptical views, see Peter Hall and Robert Franzese, "Central Bank Independence, Coordinated Wage-Bargaining, and European Monetary Union." *International Organization* 52 (Summer 1998), pp. 505-35; and in the same issue, Torben Iversen, "Wage Bargaining, Central Bank Independence and the Real Effects of Money," *International Organization* 52 (Summer 1998), pp. 469-504.

Such a critical position toward flexibility is particularly odd for a sociologist of Lord Dahrendorf's pluralist persuasion about modern society in general. One associates Lord Dahrendorf's brand of liberal sociology with the fundamental premise that a certain amount of political disagreement and conflict is an inevitable and desirable feature of modern politics. Lord Dahrendorf's professed ideal of a "Europe of trial and error" seems well served by flexible arrangements; governments ought to be free to experiment not simply with new unilateral policies but with new multilateral arrangements. The result would be something like the "laboratories of democracy" of the U.S., but with the added option of experimenting with international cooperation. Lord Dahrendorf's own position seems contradictory here. His emphasis on policy experimentation seems to argue for policies that encourage flexibility and diversity with regard to international commitments, like those currently in place in Europe, rather than for the centralized uniformity of a unit veto system that Lord Dahrendorf advocates.[57] Again Lord Jenkins is a useful counterpoint. He notes that tolerance of an open-ended, multispeed EU is surely more consistent with pragmatic British objections to European centralization than is the dogmatic insistence on a right to veto the collective actions of other governments.[58]

European Democracy and the Threat of Popular Discontent

Given the lack of evidence for either protection or fragmentation, the liberal case against deepening comes down to the essential belief that it exacerbates the "democratic deficit" in Europe. Democratic legitimacy is, of course, the major issue in the EU today and the primary topic of the ongoing constitutional convention. Thus it is fitting that our discussion culminates here.

Today, the EU is almost universally viewed as democratically illegitimate. Ellemann-Jensen takes the liberal (and conventionally Danish) view that this lack of popularity is a function of the EU's ambition to encompass new policy areas and to expand its bureaucracy.

> It seems as though some of [what Robert Schuman called the] "sense of common purpose" was lost when integration was speeded up in order to

57. Dahrendorf, p. 91.
58. See footnote 21 above.

> respond to the changes in Europe and has promoted significantly, I believe, the widespread notion of the European Community as a haven for bureaucrats and a centralized organization with too little democratic control. This is why *decentralization, participation, openness, information, and democracy* have become key concepts in the debate on how to reform...the European Union.[59]

Like many European observers, the primary evidence is the behavior of voters in referenda, not least in Denmark.

> Developments in my own country can be taken as an example. The Danes voted "No" to the Maastricht Treaty in 1992, causing much delay in the process, but other countries have also witnessed a growing popular discontent with the European Union...The Danish and French referendums on Maastricht clearly showed that the people wanted information and influence on EC decisions, *not* that they were against a unified Europe...It was widely believed that the Community had become too centralized, too bureaucratic, and too removed from the lives of ordinary citizens.[60]

Lord Dahrendorf is similarly critical of the EU's "serious lack of democratic accountability."[61] His assessment of the 1970s ("A democrat must be ashamed to see grown-up parliamentarians enact the farce they have to play ten times a year in Strasbourg and Luxembourg.") appears to have changed little over the past quarter century.[62]

It is not hard to see why this perception is so widespread in Europe today. Arbitrary rule by national and supranational technocrats—"bureaucratic despotism" by a "superstate" in Brussels, as Siedentop puts it—is a widespread concern in regard to contemporary EU politics.[63] This is the stuff of British tabloid articles, often fueled by ignorance of what the EU actually does, but it also underlies much legitimate concern, particular by those at the libertarian end of the political spectrum. This concern, shared by Lord Dahrendorf and Ellemann-Jensen, appears to gain plausibility from the overtly technocratic nature of much EU regulation, the open role played by non-elected officials in Brussels, and the geographical and cultural distance between these regulators and the average European

59. Ellemann-Jensen, p. 102.
60. Ellemann-Jensen, p. 101.
61. Dahrendorf, p. 88.
62. Dahrendorf, p. 87.
63. Siedentop, *Democracy in Europe*.

"person in the street." All this raises suspicions based on the classic liberal justification for democracy; namely, to check and channel the arbitrary and potentially corrupt power of the state.

Nonetheless, it is odd—and, I believe, deeply misleading—to view the EU as democratically illegitimate, much less as a centralized, arbitrary "despotism."[64] It is neither. The threat of arbitrary rule by a European superstate is an illusion. Narrow substantive, fiscal, administrative, legal, and procedural constraints on EU policymaking are embedded in the Treaty of Rome. These exceed the most extreme limitations imposed by national systems, whether consociational or consensus democracies (beyond, say, the Netherlands or Austria of years past), federal systems (e.g., Switzerland, Canada), separation of powers systems (e.g., the United States), and systems with weak fiscal competences (e.g., the United States, Switzerland). To see precisely how and why this is so, let us now consider the most relevant characteristics of EU policymaking.

(1) Narrow Substantive Scope: The EU's current activities are restricted to a modest number of the myriad substantive activities pursued by the modern state—primarily those linked to the regulation of policy externalities directly resulting from cross-border economic activity. The core of EU activity and its strongest institutional prerogatives still lie almost exclusively in the area of trade in goods and services, the movement of factors of production, the production of and trade in agricultural commodities, exchange rates and monetary policy, foreign aid, and trade-related environmental, consumer, and competition policies.[65] Excluded from the EU policy agenda are taxation and the setting of fiscal priorities, social

---

64. This section follows Moravcsik, "In Defense of the Democratic Deficit: Reassessing Legitimacy in the European Union," *Journal of Common Market Studies* 40:4 (November 2002); and Moravcsik, "Federalism in the European Union: Rhetoric and Reality," in Robert Howse and Kalypso Nicolaïdis, eds. *The Federal Vision: Legitimacy and Levels of Governance in the US and the EU* (Oxford: Oxford University Press, 2002).
65. To be sure, there are exceptions. These include a modest level of regional and structural funding of infrastructure (primarily as a side payment for the creation of core policies) and some regulatory controls exceeding narrow market-making functions in a few areas. There is also emerging legislation in immigration and foreign policies, but these often tend to be treated in more intergovernmental procedures, whereas the strongest constitutional prerogatives of the EU remain primarily concerned with market regulation.

welfare provision, defense and police powers, education policy, cultural policy, non-economic civil litigation, direct cultural promotion and regulation, the funding of civilian infrastructure, and most other regulatory policies unrelated to cross-border economic activity.

To be sure, the EU has made modest inroads into some of these areas, but only where it is directly related to cross-border flows.[66] Even within the core functions of the EU, governments are allowed to exempt themselves to maintain high regulatory protection (e.g., environmental and social policy) or to act unilaterally where the EU has not effectively legislated (e.g., air transport). These limitations are not just happenstance; they are the direct result of enduring characteristics of the EU's treaty-based constitutional structure.

(2) Modest Fiscal Resources: The EU's institutional capacity to act in new areas is further constrained by its lack of fiscal resources. The ability to tax and spend is what most strikingly distinguishes the modern European state from its predecessors, yet the EU's ability to tax is miniscule. It is capped at about 2-3 percent of national and local government spending (1.3 percent of GDP) and is unlikely to change soon. The spending of these funds, moreover, is explicitly dedicated to a small range of essential policies—the Common Agricultural Policy, structural funding, and development aid—that must periodically be renewed by unanimous consent of the member states.

Consequently, there is little room for discretionary funding by Brussels technocrats, who are generally constrained by the need for unanimous intergovernmental agreement. It is not coincidental that the policies absent from the EU's policy portfolio—notably social welfare provision, defense, education, culture, and infrastructure—require high government expenditure. The EU is thereby rendered what Giandomenico Majone terms a "regulatory polity"—a polity with legal instruments but little fiscal

66. The scholarly literature on European integration seems to pay disproportionate attention to exceptional cases of spillover in cases such as gender discrimination, the initial experience with environmental policy and structural funding, the jurisprudence of supremacy and direct effect, the Commission's use of Article 90, and the possible, but as yet undocumented effects of the Open Method of Coordination. These are intriguing trends, to be sure, but atypical of the EU as a whole.

capacity.[67] If we define tyranny, as James Otis did over two hundred years ago, as "taxation without representation," the EU surely does not qualify.

(3) Limited Manpower: Analysts often observe that the essential politics of regulation lie in implementation—particularly, one would expect, in a "regulatory polity"—yet the EU implements very few of its own regulations. With the exception of monetary policy, competition policy, and the conduct of, though not the ultimate control over, external trade negotiations (I will address the exceptions to these below), the powers of the EU to administer and implement are in fact exceptionally weak. How could it be otherwise, given the extraordinarily small size of the Brussels bureaucracy? The EU employs fewer officials than a modest European city. They total about one-fortieth the number of comparable civilian federal employees even in the United States, a slightly smaller jurisdiction noted in cross-national perspective for the small size of its national government workforce. In all but a few areas, the task of legally or administratively implementing EU regulations falls to national parliaments and administrations. Furthermore, the EU has no police, military force, or significant investigatory capacity—and no realistic prospect of obtaining any of these. Even if, for example, the most ambitious plans currently on the table in European defense were fully realized, the EU would control only two percent of European NATO forces—and these could be only employed for a narrow range of regional peacekeeping and peacemaking tasks.

(4) Institutional Checks and Balances: The EU's ability to act, even in those areas where it enjoys clear competence, is constrained by institutional checks and balances, a multilevel structure of decision-making, separation of powers, and a plural executive. This makes arbitrary action—indeed, any action—difficult, and tends to empower veto groups that can capture a subset of national governments. Such institutional procedures are the conventional tool for protecting the interests of vital minorities—a design feature generally thought to be most appropriate to polities like the EU, that are designed to accommodate heterogeneous cultural and substantive interests.[68] The most fundamental constraint is the requirement of unanimity for amendment of the Treaty of Rome, followed by electoral, parliamentary,

---

67. Giandomenico Majone, *Regulating Europe* (London: Routledge, 1996).
68. Arend Lijphart, *Patterns of Democracy* (New Haven: Yale University Press, 1990).

or administrative ratification—a high standard for any fundamental act of substantive redirection or institutional delegation.

The EU has accordingly developed over the past two decades only by focusing on core areas of exceptionally broad consensus, backed by large financial side payments to persuade recalcitrant member states. Whereas judicial decisions like the celebrated *Cassis de Dijon* case may have helped set the agenda for initiatives like the Single Market, monetary union and enlargement, there is now agreement in the scholarly literature that they could not do so without nearly consensual support from the member states. Even "everyday" EU directives must be promulgated under rules that require the concurrent support of between 74–100 percent of the weighted votes of territorial representatives in the Council of Ministers—a level of support higher than required for legislation in any existing national polity or, indeed, to amend nearly any national constitution in the world today. Any piece of EU legislation must therefore command an exceptional level of transnational consensus across Europe.

The EU is not a system of parliamentary sovereignty but one of separation of powers. Power is divided horizontally among the Commission, Council, Parliament, and Court, and vertically among local, national, and transnational levels. Concurrent majorities, generally greater than 50 percent, are required for action. For effective legislation, the Commission must propose, the Council must approve and amend, the Parliament must consent, European and national courts must confirm, national parliaments or officials must transpose into national law, and national bureaucracies must implement.

Even *within* each branch and level of EU governance, we encounter extraordinary pluralism. The Commission itself is a plural executive—so much so that experts disagree whether it is an executive at all. The Council works by deference to consensus opinion; the European Parliament requires unusually high majorities to act; the Court is effective only where supported by national judiciaries. The result is that an exceptionally broad range of interests, represented in an exceptionally broad range of procedures, have a say in EU policymaking.

(5) Direct and Indirect Accountability: In nearly all the most important matters of market regulation, the EU is directly accountable to the EP and indirectly accountable to elected national officials. The European Parliament (EP) must approve most EU economic legislation, and it is directly elected, generally by proportional representation within nation-states, and often acts independently of ruling national parties. Whereas one might

criticize the absence of clear programmatic elections, the EP nonetheless has an effective system of party cooperation, with votes most often splitting along party lines and in which recognizable ideological cleavages shape voting patterns. Among the most relevant differences between the EP and national parliaments appears to be the former's tendency to reach decisions by large majorities. Yet this simply further underscores the tendency of the EU to reach decisions by consensus—which is unsurprising, given the high level of support required in the Council of Ministers.

For over a decade, the EU legislative process has evolved to permit the EP to progressively usurp the role of the Commission as the primary interlocutor vis-à-vis the national governments in the Council. It is now the EP that, late in the legislative process, accepts, rejects or amends legislation in a manner that is easier for the Council to accept than reject—an "agenda-setting" prerogative traditionally accorded the Commission. This should give us considerable confidence that it is legislating in the "European" interest. [69]

Still, there might be reason for concern if the relatively weak EP were the only democratic check, or even the most important one. Yet a still more important channel of accountability lies in the democratically elected governments of the member states, which dominate the still largely territorial and intergovernmental structure of the EU. In the European Council, which is consolidating its position as the EU's dominant institution, elected heads of state and government wield power directly.[70] In the Council of Ministers, which imposes the most important binding constraint on everyday EU legislation, permanent representatives, ministerial officials, and the ministers from each country act under constant instruction from national executives, much as they would at home.

The bonds of accountability are tight: these representatives can be recalled or reinstructed at will, often more easily than parliamentarians in national systems. In addition, national parliaments can consider and comment on many EU policies, though their de facto ability to influence policy fluctuates greatly by country. In some countries, such as Denmark, they provide real-time input into national positions—a procedure open to,

69. Simon Hix, Abdul Noury, and Gerard Roland. 'Normal' Parliament? Party Cohesion and Competition in the European Parliament, 1979-2001" (paper presented at the Public Choice Society conference, San Diego March 21–23, 2002).
70. Peter Ludlow, *The Laeken Council* (Brussels: Intercommunity, 2002).

but not chosen by, other governments. If there is a democratic deficit, then it is at home, not in the European system.[71]

(6) Transparency: In contrast to the widespread impression of a cadre of secretive gnomes in Brussels, supranational officials in fact work under intense public scrutiny. In part this is a function of the broad and diffuse forms of representation we have just analyzed. With twenty commissioners and their staffs, fifteen national delegations, over six hundred parliamentarians, hundreds of national ministers and thousands of national officials, *ex ante* parliamentary scrutiny in some countries and *ex post* parliamentary scrutiny in nearly all, combined with the subsequent need for domestic administrative implementation, there can be no such thing as a monopoly of information in the EU. The legislative process works slowly, without any equivalent to ruling by executive decree or pushing legislation swiftly through a friendly parliament, and information appears as plentiful about the EU political and regulatory process, at least at the Brussels level, than about similar processes in nearly all of its member states.

Whereas it is true that certain aspects of the system, such as early discussions in the lower levels of the Committee of Permanent Representatives (COREPER), tend to take place in relative secret, the same might be said of the de facto preparation of legislation in national systems. As for regulatory procedures, recent research seems to reveal that the EU processes are as open to input from civil society, and as constrained by norms of "reason-giving," as the (relatively open) systems of Switzerland and the U.S. Recent research reveals that even discussions within the secretive *comitologie* appear to take due account of public interest considerations.[72]

The conclusion should by now be obvious. No matter what institutional measure we use—substantive scope, fiscal resources, administrative manpower, institutional checks and balances, direct and indirect accountability, and an exceptional amount of transparency—the EU operates under tight legal and democratic constraints. Furthermore, these constraints mandate a level of consultation and openness unheard of in most national polities, dominated as they are by strong prime ministers and often-secretive political party structures.

---

71. As suggested by the massive literature over the past generation, not least in Britain, on the "decline of Parliament."

72. Christian Joerges and E. Vos, eds., *EU Committees: Social Regulation, Law and Politics* (Oxford: Hart Publishing, 1999).

The Roots of Popular Discontent with the EU

If all this is so, then one might well inquire, why is the EU so widely perceived as undemocratic? Many factors contribute to this perception. Most governmental institutions are viewed negatively these days, and the EU is tarred with the same brush.[73] Member states exacerbate the consequences for the EU by blaming it for unpopular but necessary policies—budgetary consolidation, liberalization of service industries, and rejection of demands for protection or subsidies, to name three—which has given it the reputation of being an all-powerful, neo-liberal technocracy. The EU has also manifestly failed to provide the sort of face-to-face political interaction that prevails in small countries such as Denmark. Furthermore, the decentralized EU form of government, with its complex horizontal and vertical separation of powers, appears foreign to most Europeans, who are used to an ideal model of governance that functions, at least in theory, according to parliamentary sovereignty. Yet two other points are particularly relevant to our understanding public dissatisfaction with the EU.

The first is that there is little distinctively "European" or "supranational" about the pattern of delegation to supranational officials we observe in the EU, (except, as we have seen, that these officials are far less numerous and their roles far more circumscribed than their national counterparts.)The late twentieth century saw the "decline of parliaments" and the rise of courts, public administrations, and the "core executive" in almost all advanced industrialized democracies. Accountability is being increasingly imposed not simply through direct participation in majoritarian decision-making, though these remain important (as in the EU), but through complex systems of indirect representation, selection of representatives, professional socialization, *ex post* review, and balances between branches of government.[74]

The critical point for understanding the EU is this: Within the multilevel governance system prevailing in Europe, EU officials (or insulated national representatives) enjoy autonomy in precisely those areas—central banking, constitutional adjudication, criminal and civil prosecution, technical

---

73. Joseph S. Nye, Philip D. Zelikow, and David C. King, eds., *Why People Don't Trust Government* (Cambridge: Harvard University Press, 1997).
74. Giandomenico Majone, *Regulating Europe* (New York: Routledge, 1998).

administration, and economic diplomacy—that many advanced industrial democracies, including most EU member states, insulate from being directly politically contested. The apparently "undemocratic" nature of the EU as a whole is therefore largely a function of the curious selection of tasks delegated to it.

This pattern of delegation to insulated authorities gives the impression of an undemocratic technocracy (hence the public criticism), but is in fact often fully justified, as it is in many nation-states, by reference to legitimating normative and pragmatic considerations. The most important of these include the need for greater attention, efficiency, and expertise in areas where most citizens remain "rationally ignorant" or choose not to participate; the desire to promote justice, equality, and rights for individuals and minority groups; and the need to provide majorities with unbiased representation.

Consider, for example, one case of the latter: the use of "fast-track" provisions in the U.S. Congress to pass trade legislation. This institutional maneuver is designed to serve the interests of consumers and future producers, both of which are weak, unorganized constituencies, over the opposition of smaller but exceptionally self-conscious and powerful minorities comprised of sectorally organized protectionists. Europeans tend to strongly favor the use of such techniques in the U.S., where trade liberalization would otherwise probably be impossible. Yet these same analysts often tend to overlook that the EU, by virtue of its insulation, performs much the same function in Europe. Similar arguments can be made in favor of courts, central banks, environmental ministries, and many other such insulated institutions. The existence of this justification may help explain why, in those advanced industrial democracies where they play an important role, non-elected branches of government, most notably the judiciary, are often among the most popular. To the extent policies work this way, the EU is more "representative" precisely because it is, in a narrow sense, less "democratic."

The second point critical to understanding public discontent in Europe—and why holding European elections and calling constitutional conventions does not reduce it—is that the issues handled by the EU are relatively unimportant to European voters (and this is even more so for the second-order institutional choices about how to manage those issues). Of the five most salient issues in most Western European democracies—health care, education, law and order, pension and social security policy, and taxation—none is primarily an EU competence. Among the next ten, only a few (managing the economy and the environment, along with the anomalous issue of "Europe" itself) could be considered major EU concerns, but none exclusively so.[75] By contrast, the issues in which the EU specializes—trade liberalization, monetary policy, the removal of nontariff barriers, technical regulation in the environmental and other areas, foreign aid, and general foreign policy coordination—tend not to inspire electorates. It is reasonable to believe, therefore, that lack of interest, not lack of opportunity, imposes the binding constraint on European political participation. This explains why European citizens fail to exploit even the limited opportunities they have to influence EU politics—even when polls show that they recognize that the EU is powerful and their own influence is considerable.[76]

Referenda, parliamentary elections, or constitutional conventions based on issues of secondary concern simply encourage informationally impoverished and institutionally unstructured deliberation, which in turn generates unstable plebiscitary politics in which individuals have no incentive to reconcile their concrete interests with their immediate choices. Under such circumstances, public opinion and mass political behavior are notoriously unstable. A typical result is the debacle of the recent Irish referenda on the Nice Treaty, in which public opinion swerved in response to a misleading minor incident involving the Commission, leading to a negative vote—followed by a positive vote some time later. Not only does this demonstrate the existence of significant substantive constraints on EU policymaking, but also it implies—as we shall see below—that even if a common European "identity" and the full panoply of democratic procedures existed, it would be very difficult to induce meaningful citizen participation about issues of little salience.

The outcome is that public opinion and voter behavior in referendum campaigns tends to be volatile, with large numbers of undecided voters and large percentage changes in response to relatively insignificant symbolic events.[77] And it is unclear, even if the Irish were informed and coherent in

---

75. I am indebted to Professor Bonnie Meguid at the University of Rochester for access to her systematic dataset on issue salience in European democracies.
76. Jean Blondel, Richard Sinnott, and Palle Svensson, *People and Parliament in the European Union: Participation, Democracy, Legitimacy* (New York: St. Martin's Press, 1998).
77. To be sure, it could be argued that intermittent referenda, such as that in Ireland, help to educate the voters, but it is unclear whether this is worth the potential disruption. Even if it were in cases of treaty amendment (and states remain free to employ such procedures), such an argument certainly would not

their opposition, what notion of democratic legitimacy permits two percent of the European population residing in Ireland to dictate the path of European integration to the other 98 percent and to impose on them the economic costs of any failure to integrate. Lest this seem abstract, it is worth noting that long-term interest rates in East European applicant countries rose by 0.5 percent some months ago on the prospect that the Irish would reject the Nice Treaty a second time.[78]

In order to give individuals a reason to care about EU politics, it is necessary to give them a greater stake in it. The most compelling schemes for doing so rest not on the creation of new political opportunities—European citizens do not exploit the ones they have, despite clear poll data showing that they believe them to be effective—but the emergence of entirely new political cleavages based on intense interest. As in the past, the popular demand for new democratic procedures and human rights requires not just idealist commitment to certain institutional procedures, but intense desire for concrete policy change—a point often overlooked by those who debate the presence or absence of a "European demos".[79] A European demos could emerge swiftly, if there were clear incentives for citizens, interest groups, political parties, and political leaders to organize it.

Professor Philippe Schmitter of the European University Institute is one of the few analysts to appreciate the dilemma, and he has developed a concrete plan to inspire mobilization around Europe. He proposes that agricultural supports and structural funds should be replaced with a guaranteed minimum income for the poorest third of Europeans, national welfare systems should be rebalanced so as not to favor the elderly, and immigrants and aliens should be granted full rights.[80] With the EU acting as a massive engine of redistribution, individuals and groups would reorient their political behavior on whether they lost or benefited from the system.

(in the minds of most European voters) justify popular election of European judges, central bank governors, environmental regulators, or (perhaps also) Commission presidents.

78. As reported by the *Financial Times*, (London, England) October 21, 2002.
79. Jürgen Habermas, a social democratic idealist, tries hard to avoid this dilemma by invoking general social democratic ideals. But only concrete policy change will do. See Jürgen Habermas, "Why Europe Needs a Constitution," *New Left Review* (September–October 2001), pp. 5-26.
80. Philippe Schmitter, *How to Democratize the European Union...And Why Bother?* (Lanham, MD: Rowman and Littlefield, 2000).

Schmitter offers a coherent scheme targeted at precisely those groups most dissatisfied with European integration today, who are, broadly speaking, the poorer, less well-educated, female, and public sector populations. Yet its utter impracticality demonstrates the lack of a coherent alternative to current, indirect democratic accountability in the EU. Schmitter himself labels his Swiftian suggestions "modest proposals." To implement such broad-ranging proposals over the objections of most national citizens—including not a few social democrats who prefer to permit richer countries to defend their social democratic systems—would likely destroy the EU. And to insist that such issues be included in order to redress an abstract "democratic deficit" is to place the cart before the horse.

Conclusion

The preceding analysis suggests that the current system of EU policymaking, though it may seem an overly complex, cumbersome, unfamiliar structure, is in fact well suited to a polity as diverse as the continent of Europe. As we have seen, a complex system of institutional checks and balances keeps the system under tight control. This arrangement is democratically legitimate, even if it is not perceived as such, and no one has proposed institutional improvements that are likely to be both efficient and legitimate. The current mix is quite close to what European publics report they want.[81]

This is perhaps why the last decade, despite considerable public discontent, has witnessed the emergence of a stable institutional equilibrium that serves as a de facto constitution for Europe. The current division of labor—let us term it the "European Constitutional Settlement"—places market regulation largely at the European level; leaves educational, social, fiscal, and infrastructural policies largely at the national level; and suspends foreign policy in intergovernmental institutions straddling the two. The Treaties of Amsterdam and Nice have failed to alter its structure significantly.

The constitutional convention now underway, despite being turbocharged with Madisonian rhetoric, is unlikely to achieve much more. The most ambitious proposals still under serious discussion, such as incremental

81. See the public opinion data reported in Richard C. Eichenberg, "Europe and the United States in a Perplexing World," in Center for International Affairs, *Allies or Adversaries?*

expansion of qualified majority voting or flexibility, creation of a forum for national parliamentarians, and restructuring the European Council and its presidency, consolidate decade-long trends rather than launch new ones. Moves to deepen foreign policy, justice, and monetary policy cooperation appear to require only minor institutional reforms, and few other functional issues of significance are visible on the horizon. In any case, integration will probably advance more slowly, as the stock of desirable *grands projets* is depleted. Barring a severe crisis, this may well be the constitutional order that will govern Europe for the foreseeable future.

It may seem paradoxical that popular criticism of the EU should arise just at the moment when it has reached a satisfactory institutional equilibrium. Yet there is a deeper logic at work, for it is precisely when a polity is stable that its supporters trust themselves to become its critics. The generation of Paul-Henri Spaak would not have dared, even if they had been so inclined, to voice the criticisms we have discussed here. The current generation of Spaak Lecturers, on the other hand, considers it a civic duty. It is encouraging that debates about the future of Europe—like deliberations in the European Parliament—reflect the fundamental split between liberals and social democrats about the proper purposes of government. The EU is becoming a normal polity.

It is nonetheless surprising that the most intense criticism comes from pluralist liberals like Lord Dahrendorf, Ellemann-Jensen, and Ruggiero. One would have thought that they would be very pleased with what they see today. From the start—1957 at the latest—national leaders in Europe have been more pragmatic than they are given credit for, making decisions largely on the basis of concrete considerations of commercial and geopolitical interest. Thus, they constructed the EU through precisely the process of incremental "trial and error" that Lord Dahrendorf recommends. The result is a political system that is binding only where it needs to be, namely in enforcing a core set of market regulations and rather flexible elsewhere. It is an organization that, over the past decade, has deepened without encouraging protectionism, triggering excessive political conflict, slowing enlargement, undermining democratic legitimacy, or generating any of the other disadvantages often attributed to it. For these reasons and others, we must view with considerable skepticism the claim that European integration has gone too far—even as the EU reaches the limits of its economic and institutional development. Even as it has deepened over the past decade, the EU has become—perhaps in part due to the criticisms of liberals—much more like the flexible, open system liberals generally espouse.

In the end, perhaps it comes down to a matter of temperament. Some are very uncomfortable with ideological justifications for pragmatic policies—or elite management even when the public remains suspicious. It is therefore tempting, not least for the scholars among us, to side with Lord Dahrendorf's aspiration to justify Europe solely as "a matter of the head rather than of the heart," thereby "closing the gap between realities and aspirations."[82] Why not then just call the EU what it is—the world's most successful system of market regulation, without aspirations ever to be the United States of Europe—and leave illusions behind for good? Integration is slowing, and thus the costs of forgoing ideological justifications may not be great. To this, Lord Jenkins would have had a response. Broad public opinion is rarely swayed by complex technical arguments about optimal policy—to paraphrase Walter Hallstein, the celebrated founding commission president of the EEC—in the details lurks only the devil. Convincing European publics to accept fundamental EU reforms, such as the current round of enlargement, may often be—even today, in a Europe without illusions—a matter of the heart.

In the end the lessons of the past decade tend to incline toward Lord Dahrendorf's view. In an era where democratization has pacified Western Europe, talk of federalism triggers deep public suspicion, and technocratic planning (central banking excepted) has fallen out of fashion, Europe is nonetheless proceeding toward enlargement, monetary integration, and an ever-deepening Single Market. The critical constraints on integration today are not in the policies of countries where ideological justifications hold much weight, but in countries like Denmark, Sweden, Britain, and Ireland, where pragmatic arguments about Europe are the coin of the realm. There is an underlying functional reason why integration has continued in a measured way while ideological support is declining, namely the consistent increase in social support, above all from producer interests, for the economic integration of Europe. Over time, underlying socioeconomic developments and the prior success of the EU in achieving its objectives has created invested economic interests that are the major guarantors of its future stability.

From this perspective, are not the true "Euroskeptics" those who believe that the EU is fragile because it rests on fears of refighting World War II, hopes of realizing federalist dreams, the intermittent "political will" of national leaders, and the unintended consequences of prior actions? And are

---

82. Dahrendorf, p. 90.

not the true "Europeans" those who view the EU as a stable form of pragmatic cooperation deliberately tailored to the enduring, increasingly convergent national interests of European firms, governments, and citizens?

Part II

The Paul-Henri Spaak Lectures 1994–1999

1

The Disappointing Partnership Between British Governments and Europe

Why the Paul-Henri Spaak Tradition Rarely Embraces London

Right Honorable Lord Jenkins of Hillhead
October 1999

This is the first time I have spoken at Harvard since becoming chancellor of Oxford nearly eight years ago. The chancellorship of Oxford is a curious office, which as far as I am aware has no close analogue in any American university. It is old (1221), but relatively democratically elected with all the alumni entitled to vote provided they go to Oxford to do so, and much sought after mainly by ex-Oxonian politicians, of whom there have always been a great number. And contested elections rarely fail to have a former prime minister amongst the candidates, mostly the losing ones. It has the disadvantages of having no salary and very few perquisites except for pomp and circumstance. It has also become as weak in power as it is strong in dignity. I have sometimes compared it in miniature with the position of the queen of England in the heyday of Mrs. Thatcher's premiership. Its great advantage, however, which together with the illustriousness of the names of their predecessors makes it is so attractive to elderly politicians, is that it has no fixed term and no retiring age. The election is for life, and my two immediate predecessors, Harold Macmillan and

Edward Halifax, managed to last fifty-four years between them. No one since Cromwell, who first imposed himself and then his son on the university, has ever resigned.

Despite the non-existence in this country of an office analogous to mine and despite John Harvard's decision to found his college in a place called Cambridge (or was it the other way round—did he chose his site and then get the locality given what he regarded as a good academic placename?), I would regard our two universities as having at least as much in common as either does with Cambridge, England. I would not wish there to be any thought that the chancellor of Oxford had said in Cambridge, Massachusetts, or anywhere else, a word of disparagement of that fairly ancient seat of learning. I regard it as, at least in the century from 1850 to 1950, having lived nearer to the rugged frontiers of knowledge than did Oxford. I record Trinity College in that university as perhaps the greatest *college* in the world, with as many Nobel prize winners as the whole of France and its only rival as a *college* being here in its sister city. But Cambridge has one characteristic that is totally alien to Oxford, and I think, to Harvard. This is its desire to stand apart from metropolitan life and from government.

In our minuscule English geography, Cambridge is in immutable fact two miles nearer to London than is Oxford, fifty-one miles as against fifty-three. But psychologically, Oxford has been immensely nearer to London than has Cambridge for at least three hundred years. In contrast with that rough East Anglia fenland, it has enjoyed living in a lush river valley leading ineluctably to the capital and to the fount of glittering prizes. On every worldly score prime ministers, chief justices, viceroys of India, archbishops of Canterbury (putting them for the moment in the worldly category), it has always beaten Cambridge, which in turn has mostly won on the front of intellectual pioneers. About the only political exceptions have been in the past ten years, when a clutch of Cantabridgian politicians has dominated the middle ranks of the British government. The results do not suggest that Cambridge should be encouraged to bargain away the traditions of Keynes and Russell, Rutherford, and Dirac for a brief window of political eminence. The last Cambridge prime minister was Stanley Baldwin. We hope that the next one will not be Michael Portillo.

Oxford, on the other hand, stands unassailably on its record of having provided twenty-three of the fifty British prime ministers, beginning with Walpole. With as many as this they are necessarily a mixed bag. But if our last one was Margaret Thatcher, there seems a very good chance that our next will be Tony Blair. We have also recently filled in a few of our blank spots in our atlas of providing heads of state or government for other countries, including the presidency of the United States, an office which has previously eluded us. We have done better with the presidencies of major American universities.

I turn from these reflections on universities to the eponym of this lecture, and through him to my subject. Paul-Henri Spaak was of a generation that meant that although I saw him and heard him, I did not really know him. He died, in his early seventies, four years before I went to Brussels as president of the European Commission. But as he had started very young—he was prime minister of Belgium under forty and before World War II—he had a long period of influence, and was probably the most internationally known Belgian politician of the century. He was the second secretary general of NATO and indisputably one of the five founding fathers of the post–World War II European idea and of the institutions which it created. He was the only one of them who came from a small country and the only one who was a great orator. But I have always taken comfort, having no great gift of imitative ear myself, that, great internationalist although he also was, he was far from being a great linguist. He was a resounding orator in one language only—French—and his command over Flemish, now the somewhat aggressive majority language in Belgium, was so weak that I do not think he could survive in Belgian politics today. Nor was Spaak ever very convincing in English, despite his four years in the Anglophone because of American-dependent NATO. Perhaps because he did not weaken his mind by trying to express it in too many different tongues, he was, however, a man with a clear vision and sense of purpose. He was a key architect of both the ECSC and of the Treaty of Rome.

The other key animators (although one of them had gone by the time it came to the Treaty of Rome) were Robert Schuman of France, Konrad Adenauer of Germany, Alcide de Gasperi of Italy, and Jean Monnet, also of France but one who, partly as a cognac salesman and partly as deputy secretary general of the old League of Nations, had internationalized himself from early in life. Monnet was never an elected politician, although he was a very effective political operator. Despite his internationalism his roots were in *la France Profonde*, in the department of the Charente, which is about the furthest from a land frontier of any in France.

Three of the politicians, however, were all by a remarkable coincidence men who straddled the frontiers. De Gasperi had been born in the part of Italy that was in Austro-Hungary until the end of World War I and had as a young deputy sat in the Austrian Diet. Schuman had passed his first thirty years in Metz, which was in that part of Lorraine that was incorporated in

Germany between 1870 and 1918. Adenauer never lived under foreign occupation, except insofar as he regarded the Prussians as providing that, but he was a Rhinelander who looked so determinedly west rather than east that, when as mayor of Cologne in the 1920s he had to go to Berlin, he claimed that he never slept well after the *Schlafwagen* had crossed the Elbe into the unattractive pine forests of the east. Spaak, born and brought up in Brussels, was not exactly a man of the Belgian frontier, except to the extent that almost the whole of Belgium is on a frontier, and it is as much a crossroads as a country.

These men of the core of Europe were greatly buttressed from across the Atlantic by Marshall and Acheson, the twin if far from identical pillars of the Truman administration who left support for Western European unity as one of the most settled principles of United States foreign policy. This policy has persisted for many decades, substantially right through to the present day, although it is sometimes made a little more equivocal by the pressures of GATT negotiations.

To some extent support was also forthcoming from across the English Channel: from Churchill, who in his six years out of office between 1945 and 1951 made a number of European unity orations, and from Ernest Bevin, the powerful and pattern-setting foreign secretary of the Attlee government of those years, who was a key architect of NATO—an essential framework of security, without which the political and economic advances of the European Community could not easily have occurred. But the British attitude was always more equivocal than the American. To be fair to my compatriots, this was because the Spaak-Monnet vision of European unity in the 1950s posed far more difficulty for Britain's current view of its position in the world than for America's view about itself.

There was no suggestion that America should be a participant as opposed to an outside beneficent influence in European unity. Indeed to have done so would have been to nullify the whole concept of Europeanism. The United States could therefore be a most enthusiastic sponsor without calling into question its status as a power qualitatively different from the France of Monnet and Schuman, the Germany of Adenauer, the Italy of de Gasperi or still more the Belgium of Spaak. But this was precisely the dilemma that was posed for the early postwar British leaders. They, Churchill naturally above all but not uniquely so, wished to see themselves as the leaders of one of the triumvirate of victorious powers. This was understandable but unsustainable. It was also incompatible with a full British role in Europe, for that meant being willing to mingle on a basis of equality. Britain's position vis-à-vis Europe was essentially different from that of America because: three thousand miles separate us; full participation was open to and indeed expected of us, and; our economy and our currency were influenced and sometimes buffeted by what happened in the rest of Western Europe in a way that yours was not—your security was, but not, in those days, your economic performance or the strength of the dollar.

Out of all this sprang Britain's postwar ambiguity towards Europe. It was present in Churchill's speeches—it was never clear whether or not Britain was to be part of the unity he was urging on Europe. His successor, Anthony Eden, was the strongest anti-European influence when Churchill's words on Europe evaporated in the actions or lack of actions of his second government. Eden was willing to commit British troops to Germany until the end of the century, because that was American-style support from the outside, but not to contemplate joining the admittedly ill-fated European Defence Community, which foundered in 1954, because this involved full participation and some merging of sovereignty. He would accept heavy burdens as a buttress but not a role as a pillar, supporting from the inside. Equally Ernest Bevin as Labour foreign secretary a few years before. Because there was not much party difference on Europe in these crucial years of choice, both Bevin and Eden seized imaginatively the opportunity presented by General Marshall's 1947 commencement day speech in this university, but preferred a vast loss of influence in the developing heart of Europe to any foreign interference with the British coal and steel industries.

I have long thought the strengths, weaknesses, and dilemmas of Britain's leadership psychology of the time were vividly illustrated by two vignettes from the early days of the Marshall Plan.

First, the immediacy of Bevin's performance was splendid. Marshall spoke in Harvard Yard on June 5th. The ideas expressed were wide-ranging but also vague. Bevin heard them reported on the radio early the next morning, and then let no time go by before responding to one of Marshall's most pregnant sentences: "The initiative," he had said, "must I think come from Europe." Before the end of the month, Bevin, with the assistance of French Foreign Minister Bidault, had got twenty-two European nations (the Russians did not walk out until a few weeks later) assembled in Paris. So far, so very good.

Then the ludicrous and even pathetic aspect asserted itself. London led Europe on the issue. Yet having led it, the British government tried hard to separate itself from it. At a series of bilateral meetings with the Americans, a determined effort was made to argue that Britain should not be lumped in with the other European countries but (although a beneficiary) should also be a co-distributor with the United States of the aid to the other countries.

One meeting underlined the pathetic aspect. Will Clayton, as assistant secretary for economic affairs, was then I think equal to number three on the State Department hierarchy. Yet in London he was confronted in 10 Downing Street by a joint assembly of Attlee, Bevin, Cripps, and Dalton, the four most powerful men in a very notable British Government, who attempted to persuade him that Britain must be treated differently from the other European countries. Clayton quite rightly held firm. The British government did not, for they had no firm ground on which to stand, and to their credit, once resisted, cooperated enthusiastically on a basis they would not have chosen. The ludicrousness was that if you wish to show yourself a major power, superior to the neighbors amongst whom you are unfortunately living, you do not assemble the more powerful half of your government to argue (unsuccessfully) with one assistant secretary. The sadness was that the incident was a remarkable and depressing precursor of Britain's relationship with the continent of Europe throughout the 1950s and beyond.

So was the pattern set that led to Britain standing back from every European initiation for thirty years or more, but always subsequently deciding that we could not afford to remain outside. But we never seemed to learn, which was particularly unfortunate as our national habit was not that of striking out on a lonely path and sticking to it. This might, had it been sustainable, have had something to be said for it. But what we always did was to join reluctantly and late, almost a guarantee of getting the worst of all worlds.

Railroad metaphors have perhaps been overused in this controversy, but I claim copyright to one of my own. It is that of Britain regularly standing on a train station platform more or less benevolently waving goodbye to the European train as it pulls out. But having done so we do not stride out of the station, get in our Rolls Royce and drive resolutely off to the hills in the opposite direction. This is for the very good reason that there has not really been another direction in which to go—and perhaps because we do not have many Rolls Royces left either. Instead, we stand perplexedly scratching our heads on the platform and wondering whether we ought not to be on the train after all. So we end up running along the track and hoping that we can clamber aboard when it next stops at a signal or a wayside halt. Such a habit is conducive neither to comfort nor to national dignity. And when we do get aboard we discover to our own recurring surprise and resentment that all the seats in the dining car are already taken. In practical terms this habit guarantees that we never play an effective role in shaping the institutions that we subsequently join. And then we complain violently about their shape.

This happened with Schuman and Monnet's Coal and Steel Community in 1950–51, which we subsequently joined when we came into the Economic Community in 1973, twenty-two years late; with the Economic Community itself, when we declined to go to the formative Messina Conference in 1955 and subsequently stood outside the Treaty of Rome when it was signed by the Six in 1957, and which we were sixteen years late in joining; it also applied to the European Monetary System and its Exchange Rate Mechanism when they were put together in 1978–79 and which we entered in 1990, only eleven and a half years late. It could, I suppose, be argued that the degree of lateness was on a declining scale: twenty-two, sixteen, eleven and a half. It might have been expected to be seven or only five the next time round. Unfortunately, the date of entry into the Exchange Rate Mechanism (ERM) was not only late, it was also at the worst possible moment, because it was at an inappropriate rate and at a time when the deutsche mark, reacting to the strains of German reunification, rather like the dollar under the pressures of the Vietnam War during the turn of the decade from the 1960s to 1970s, had become a less than satisfactory pivot of a currency system.

During the 138 months that Britain was outside the ERM the system worked satisfactorily and quietly, bringing considerable benefits of stability in exchange rates, with no strains greater than could be accommodated by a few nontraumatic adjustments of central rates, to the eight countries which participated from the beginning. Of these months, at least 130, in my view, would have been better points of entry than the one that, largely for reasons of internal Conservative Party politics, was eventually chosen. The result was misfortune all round. The British repeated their experiences with the Economic Community. We then missed, partly through our initial hesitation and then through de Gaulle's exclusivity, the buoyant years of the 1960s and only came in for the difficult period beginning with the first oil crisis. With the ERM it was worse. Not only did we miss the decade and more of good years, but we came in only for two years of buffeting which ended in our bruised extrusion. It also left the impression in Europe that everything worked reasonably well until we arrived and messed it up.

Is there a curse on Britain's relations with Europe? As someone who has for forty years invested a great deal of political capital in the cause of Britain's adhesion to Europe, I have found myself forced in the past few years to ask myself that question. As has been apparent from the brief and somewhat tendentious history that I have given, there has been little to choose between the performances of the two governing parties. It was the Attlee Labour government that stood out from the Coal and Steel Community. It was the Eden Conservative government that did the same thing with the Economic Community. The Macmillan Conservatives who followed did the first sprint after the railroad train, which we had allowed to leave without getting on board. But the depth of that government's European conviction was never put to the test, because General de Gaulle stepped in, dismissed Britain as belonging to the *le grand large*, the open seas, and not to Europe, and brought the first negotiations for enlargement to a juddering halt in January 1963.

Harold Wilson, whose government followed in 1964, in fact did more for British Europeanism, more than any prime minister other than Edward Heath, although in a peculiarly uninspiring way. He twice led backwards into Europe. Having talked a lot of previous nonsense about the Common Market offering no more elevating a prospect than selling washing machines to Düsseldorf as opposed to the noble Commonwealth prospect of developing a hydroelectric scheme in the Great Snowy Mountains of Australia, he decided after three years of government that there was no other way for Britain, and skillfully converted the middle two quarters of his Cabinet—one quarter was much more committed than he was while the other remained intransigent to a sort of temporary Europeanism. Then, in opposition after 1970 and finding it impossible to support anything that Edward Heath did, he finessed back again and did his reputation great and unnecessary harm.

In government again after 1974, however, Wilson promoted the referendum on Britain's continuing membership of the European Community, gave deft if lukewarm support to a "Yes" vote, which was secured by a two to one majority, and consequently gave the most solid underpinning to the cause of British Europeanism that there ever has been. So far from using this result as a base from which to play a strong hand in Europe, however, he stood back for the few remaining months of his premiership from the Helmut Schmidt–Valéry Giscard d'Estaing partnership that was then dominant in Europe. His successor for three years, James Callaghan, although personally on better terms with them, did essentially the same. It was his government that alone of the then nine member countries refused to join the ERM of the European Monetary System. And at least one of the reasons for doing so was at once deeply symptomatic and ironic. I remember vividly at the Copenhagen European Council in April 1978, when the scheme which Schmidt and Giscard and I had worked out was presented, that the British delegation was frightened it would offend the

Americans. What the Americans wanted then, as fairly consistently over the postwar period, was that the British should get closer to Europe. What the British were looking for was some approach to an exclusive relationship across the Atlantic that would provide them with an excuse for keeping their distance across the Channel.

Then we come to the long Thatcher years. Her performance on Europe was curiously ambivalent. She has never had even a touch of Euro-enthusiasm in her makeup. "They are a rotten lot, except maybe for Schmidt," she graciously conceded in about the most favorable judgment I can ever recall her making. From the beginning she adopted her handbag-swinging technique at European Councils and seemed positively to enjoy being in an isolated position. And it was her Euro-intransigence, carried to a point that alienated all her senior colleagues, which eventually broke her.

And yet...The odd paradox is that by signing the so-called Single European Act in 1986 she signed away more national sovereignty than anything that was involved in the Maastricht Treaty, and nonetheless got it ratified without any of the parliamentary trouble that John Major ran into with Maastricht. As a result, the advance to the Single Market was the one major step towards integration taken in Europe in the past half century in which Britain was not left tagging along behind. Therefore, in substance if not in style, the objective record of Mrs. Thatcher, extreme Euroskeptic although she has now become, was more Europhile than that of Mr. Major, despite his initial proclamation that he wished to place Britain at the heart of Europe. He has been buffeted by his party difficulties into being just as frequently isolated as Mrs. Thatcher, and without any panache of intransigence.

From this somewhat depressing chronicle there arise several thoughts out of which a general theory can begin to be built. First, it was by no means a pure accident, the quirks of Mrs. Thatcher's personality apart, that it was the Single Market alone for which Britain was on time. The Single Market was a matter limited to packages, of the unfettered flow of trade, of trucks rolling unhindered across frontiers, and not of wider political considerations.

And the hesitant British view, in direct contradiction to the spirit of Paul-Henri Spaak (which saw Europe as essentially a political concept, although one that should use economic means to achieve the political end of a Europe that regained the influence it had so wantonly thrown away in its two civil wars of the first half of this century), was that Europe should largely confine itself to matters of packages. Thus the Single Market is acceptable, but a single currency is not, although a Single Market is half crippled without it, because a single currency raises far more issues of political control.

But Europe is about far more than packages. When Gladstone as a young man was made vice-president of the Board of Trade in the Peel government of 1841, he wrote a letter of bitter complaint saying that he had hoped to deal in the affairs of men, but found himself set only to look after packages. Packages are all very well in their way, and it is certainly desirable that they should flow freely rather than with hindrance, but they are not the ultimate purpose of human activity. Europe is and must be about men and women, and peace and politics and security, and art and life and buildings and ecology, and wider purposes than packages.

Second, it is not possible to make any very politically partisan case—not, at any rate, between the two blades of the Labour and Conservative scissors—out of the weakness of the hand that Britain has long played in Europe. Indeed the two governing parties have been like the old man and the old woman in those cuckoo clock-like weather houses; if one came out for a sunnier approach to Europe, the other went back in. Thus, Labour, which had traditionally been internationalist and against Conservative chauvinism and imperialism, cast the first stone against the Coal and Steel Community. The Conservatives in opposition voted for it, and then resiled in government. In the 1960s and 1970s, with Labour wobbling about, a combination of Heath's genuine European idealism and a defensive view on the part of the *hommes moyens* of the party that the relative free market of Brussels might protect them from an insular socialism, which the Labour Party still seemed strong enough to have the possibility of imposing, made the Conservatives the party of Europe.

Mrs. Thatcher and Monsieur Delors between them produced a gradual but dramatic reversal of alliances in the 1980s. The new right has become chauvinist and insular and the old left has come to think that there is more hope from Brussels than from Westminster of reversing the disastrously widening gap between the prosperous and the underclass. One of Mr. Blair's great tests, if he becomes prime minister, as I hope that he will, is whether he can break the unfortunate pattern of parties losing their European nerve in government. So far, the auguries are good, but this grave matter cannot by its very nature be put to the proof until after the next election.

It is not so much that one of the governing parties has played a more constructive role than the other on Europe as that the peculiar rigidities of the British political system have over the years bedeviled British policy on Europe. There has for at least twenty-five years been a considerable pro-

Europe majority in the House of Commons. But it has been a cross-party majority and party managers do not like cross-party majorities. Governments of neither party have been able to command support from pro-European policies within their own party strengths. As a result they have constantly weakened their policies in order to propitiate their Euroskeptic minorities. Except on rare and notable occasions, the true will of the House of Commons has thus been distorted by party games.

Equally, the British public, while far from brimming over with Euro-enthusiasm when given anything approaching a clear lead by their politicians, has been perfectly willing, as in the 1975 referendum, to assent by a large majority. The trouble with formulating an effective British European policy has lain much more with the politicians than with the people.

Nevertheless, they have between them managed to produce a consistency of hesitation, the government of Edward Heath excepted, which suggests something more than the weakness of individuals. This hesitation has now driven the present government into an extreme of illogicality, which threatens Britain's future adhesion to the European Union, an outcome that both the present prime minister and the present foreign secretary claim to find abhorrent. The British government believes in a Europe of "variable geometry," to use the current jargon, and it has given practical expression to this by securing its right to contract out of both the Social Chapter (dealing with common conditions of employment) and of moves towards a single currency. Yet, when as has recently been the case, the French and the Germans have talked about a "two-speed Europe," another current piece of jargon, with Britain and some others being confined to an uninfluential slow lane, this has produced a British reaction of indignation: it is intolerable and must not be allowed to happen. Yet, how you can participate only à la carte (a third piece of jargon) and refuse to join a move as central as that to a single currency and still expect to be a core member, I simply cannot imagine. This contradictory position is now causing sufficient long-term irritation as to make many in Europe doubtful of the desirability of Britain's future membership.

Moreover, it certainly does not promote Britain's national interest. There can be few political errors more elementary than to confuse nationalism and national interest. They are far from being the same thing, and indeed are very often the enemy of each other. I am not in the least against defending Britain's national interest in Europe; I just think it is ineffectively done, and that other countries, within a more cooperative framework, achieve a more effective result.

To take one example, the British government is strongly and sensibly in favor of the enlargement of the Union, both to the old European Free Trade Association (EFTA) countries and to at any rate the western rim of the former Soviet satellites. But without a strengthening of the decision-making process, a community of twenty or twenty-five members will be a protean mass without any sinews of command. So those who want a strong community think that deepening must go with widening. When Britain tries to make the one concept the enemy of the other, it arouses strong suspicion that it wants to reduce the community to a mere free-trade area, and thus frustrates its own policy.

What is the explanation of this persistent, self-defeating, semi-detachment? I cannot give a neatly encapsulated answer. Some would say it was nostalgia for empire, but although preoccupation with and liquidation of this legacy was a major distraction until, say, the mid-1960s, we have now had plenty of time to get over it. And the view that its more modern manifestation, the Commonwealth, might provide a satisfactory alternative orientation for Britain has died totally in the past twenty years. Then there is excessive Atlanticism: the view that, like a middle-aged virgin, we should keep ourselves intact for an exclusive relationship with Washington. But successive United States administrations could hardly have made themselves more clear that what they want is the reverse: a Britain which certainly helps to keep the Atlantic link in good repair, but does so by being promiscuous in Europe.

It is indeed my accumulated view that, even if the transoceanic world did not exist, Britain would still find its cross-Channel relations difficult. Some again might say it is because we are nationally such bad linguists that we do not feel much at home in a multilanguage community. But then the French are undoubtedly the second-worst linguists in Europe and yet manage to operate sure-footedly in the community environment. Moreover, we have a language that, thanks largely to America, with maybe a bit of help from the *Oxford English Dictionary*, is becoming even more dominant, whereas they have one which is internationally declining, even in Brussels.

Yet others, more highfaluting, would say that the trouble was semi-philosophical, a difference of methods of thought and expression: all Locke versus Descartes, all empiricism against general principles. Yet the Irish, who are certainly not notably Cartesian, manage to do very well in the community and to feel remarkably at home with its habits.

I am sorry not to give you a more definitive answer on the last point, but one cannot answer all questions even in a lecture as long as this one has been. But I hope that I have said enough to show that while Paul-Henri

Spaak was a great man and a great influence upon the very substantial European achievements of the past forty years, a statue to his memory has not yet been erected in London. Were such a proposition put forward, I would gladly subscribe modestly to the fund.

2

THE GLOBAL CHALLENGE
Opportunities and Choices in the Multilateral Trading System

Ambassador Renato Ruggiero
October 1995

I am delighted to be here today to deliver the fourteenth Paul-Henri Spaak Lecture and to honor the memory of a great European visionary and statesman. Spaak devoted his life to the cause of international cooperation, making his greatest contribution at a time when leaders the world over sought to redefine the global order, following the most generalized armed conflict in human history. It is entirely consistent that Paul-Henri Spaak was both a committed pan-European and an Atlanticist—these were interlocking pieces of the same jigsaw. In just the same way today, in our extraordinarily interdependent world, I do not think we can talk of international cooperation without taking a global view.

It is for this reason that I should like to focus on international cooperation in the broadest sense, and I am sure you will not be surprised that my emphasis will be upon the fundamental importance of the multilateral trading system to international growth and stability. I want to give you the sense of a system that is continually in evolution, just like the world economy it underpins. Let me start where Spaak did, in the struggle to rebuild a better world after 1945. I hope to show you as we move on that the challenges and the opportunities we face today are somewhat comparable to those that confronted the founding fathers of our system. Their vision is something we urgently need to recapture.

With the lessons of destructive nationalism and inward-looking economic policy fresh in mind, postwar international trade arrangements were designed to draw all nations into a mutual economic interdependence that would help safeguard peace and security. Trade was to play a central role in cementing relations among nations, in underwriting international harmony. From its largely American-inspired beginnings and transatlantic orientation, the GATT trading system has made a vital contribution to peace and prosperity over the last half century on an ever-expanding global stage.

The foundations of the system were rooted strongly in the principle of nondiscrimination and emphasized a solid rule-based contractual relationship among members. These two elements were the source of GATT's success. It is a success that is reflected in a thirteen-fold increase in international trade since 1950. More and more, economic opportunities rely on international exchange. In the United States, for example, exports amounted to only 5% of national income in 1960; by the early 1990s, the share of exports in GDP had more than doubled. Unfortunately, we lack good statistics on international trade in services, but we do know that it is expanding even faster than trade in goods and now represents some 20% of international trade flows.

As trade grows in importance, so does its contribution to the creation and the maintenance of jobs. In the United States alone, over sevenmillion jobs are supported by merchandise exports. Around one-third of all jobs created in the United States over the last tenyears or so are due to increased merchandise exports, and practically all new manufacturing jobs emanate from export activity. If we had figures for services, these numbers would be even more impressive.

Furthermore, international investment flows have also grown dramatically in the last few years. Foreign direct investment inflows to all countries averaged $50billion per year during the first half of the 1980s, and had risen to $194billion by 1993. There was a time when international business tended to see trade and investment as alternative means of securing access to foreign markets. Today, firms need to be able to both invest and trade on a global scale—and for this they depend upon open, and predictable trade and investment regimes.

The GATT presided over eight rounds of multilateral trade negotiations. In doing so, it gradually eroded tariffs, bringing them down to an average of less than 4% today, one-tenth of what they were in the immediate postwar period. As tariffs have been reduced, other trade-restricting measures have become more obvious. In later rounds of GATT negotiations, emphasis shifted towards nontariff trade barriers, generating an increasingly comprehensive and complex set of rights and obligations. At the same time, thus seeking to ensure that the system is equal to the task of managing international economic relations in today's world, negotiators have ventured into new areas of policy, outside those relating purely to trade in goods.

The recently completed Uruguay Round is the clearest example of how our agenda has expanded to keep up with the times. The Uruguay Round transformed the GATT into the WTO, putting the trading system on a coherent and solid institutional footing. A new, integrated dispute settlement procedure was created to guarantee quick, objective, and neutral adjudication when trade disputes arise between governments. The round also made significant progress in sectors where protectionist policies have been most resilient, notably in agriculture and textiles, and stronger disciplines were established on subsidies, state trading, technical standards, and licensing procedures, to name a few. The Uruguay Round was the first to address trade in services and intellectual property rights protection. This continuing commitment to trade liberalization and enhanced competition is a key contribution of farsighted governments to globalized economic activity.

Globalization, by which I mean a multiplicity of interlocking economic relationships among national economies, is a natural outgrowth of technological advances in communications and transport. It has also been encouraged by the favorable environment, which the rules and the market-access commitments of the multilateral system provide. Thus, supportive government policy and modern technology have induced businesses and entrepreneurs to operate—as most of them naturally wish—across frontiers in a manner that would have been very difficult twenty or thirty years ago.

The evidence of global integration is clear in the way trade growth has outstripped production growth year after year—each 10% increase in world production has been associated with a 16% increase in world trade. This trend is accelerating: last year's increase in world trade was nearly triple the growth in world production. Furthermore, by drawing attention to the fact that international trade has consistently shown greater dynamism than production throughout the postwar period, this rising ratio of world trade to world output not only shows the growing interdependence among nations, but it highlights the central role of international trade in postwar economic growth.

There are those who would like to put the clock back, to wish away the mutual dependence of nations. But no one can stop the course of history. Interdependence has made a huge contribution to rising incomes and peace among nations, and it is here to stay—and grow. The challenge that we face is how to make it work for all nations—and to make it work better.

This is a formidable challenge, it is true. But recent events also have presented us with an historical opportunity, a chance to define something different and durable in international relations. The long-standing and predictable political assumptions of the cold war have become irrelevant. North-South relations, dominated so often in the past by unnecessary polarization and a dialogue of the deaf, have also changed irrevocably. While the collapse of communism was vividly symbolized by the tumbling of the Berlin Wall, no such image drew attention to the changes that have taken place in relations among developed and developing nations. Yet these changes will prove just as momentous.

From the perspective of the multilateral trading system, then, what does all this mean? We face a dual task. We must extend the reach of the system geographically to make it truly global, and we must also ensure that it remains effective in the face of growing complexity in international economic relations. You will all be aware of the continuing debate within the European Union about choices between geographical broadening of the Union and the deepening of its substantive provisions. This is a politically charged debate, because broadening and deepening are often seen as competing alternatives. But for the multilateral trading system, these are not alternatives. We must press ahead simultaneously on both fronts, precisely because the WTO aspires to be a truly global and commercially relevant entity.

As far as geographical extension is concerned, we face a number of challenges. First, the dozen or more states created by the collapse of the Soviet Union have sought, or soon will be seeking, WTO membership. Russia's accession process is underway, as are those of several other former Soviet Union countries, including the Baltic states, Ukraine, and Armenia. Work on China's relationship with GATT has been underway for some ten years now. Bringing China, Russia, and other economies in transition into the WTO as full participants is a key objective for the coming months and years.

In the old days, centrally planned economies such as Poland, Romania, and Hungary were allowed to join the GATT in the absence of any serious economic reform effort. Instead, special accession protocols were drawn up, which recognized that trading opportunities would not be created by market forces. They were therefore based on import expansion commitments, and allowed discriminatory trading arrangements to persist. But the political expediency and limited economic relevance of those arrangements have no place in the WTO today, and the transition economies are engaged in dramatic and difficult economic transformations towards a market-based system. The terms on which they accede to the WTO must contribute to the reform process, and must be realistic. The sheer size and economic power that some of these countries represent also make it important to ensure that the accession terms fully support the integrity of the WTO trading system. The coherence of the system must not be sacrificed in pursuit of universality—even if universality is the ultimate goal—because a global trading system that excludes a significant proportion of the world's people is a contradiction in terms.

The other geopolitical revolution in the trading system is the leap in developing countries' participation. Over the last decade or so, dozens of developing countries have shifted towards liberal trade policies and greater reliance on international competition to generate income and growth. More than seventy developing countries have undertaken unilateral liberalization measures during the past ten years. That process has chipped away the old North-South divide. Many countries at quite different levels of income and development have put their faith in the WTO trading system for continuity, stability, and the promise of trade opportunities. This does not mean that the countries' interests and priorities are identical, however. While part of the WTO's job is to define commonality of interest where possible and to foster joint action, countries cannot be coerced; they must be brought along through the recognition of their own interest. Hence, as the WTO becomes a more inclusive and encompassing institution, it must accommodate a wider range of interests. This might be more difficult than in an older and simpler world dominated by a few like-minded countries, but we have to succeed, and success will be at least as rewarding.

However, as I have said, different developing-country WTO members have different interests While many continue to grow and modernize, generating enough wealth to make their people progressively better off, some developing countries are clearly not sharing in increased global prosperity. No society can participate effectively in the opportunities of a global market if many of its citizens lack the basic necessities of life and we carry a shared responsibility to provide the conditions for such countries to get themselves off the floor. As far as the trading system is concerned, we must do our utmost to see that developing countries are able both to diversify their export production and expand their export markets on a competitive basis. At the WTO, we are developing a special program for Africa that aims to help governments take better advantage of international trade and foreign investment opportunities. This is a modest effort, and more must be done, especially in collaboration with other multilateral economic institutions.

So much for the task we face in making the WTO trading system truly universal in a geographic sense. What about the deepening of the system? By pressing on with liberalization, by successfully providing a way forward in areas of trade where protectionism had long proved intractable, and by boldly addressing entirely new but very important aspects of trade, the Uruguay Round made a signal contribution to international trade relations. It was a landmark achievement to create the WTO. But following any birth, the offspring must be nurtured, and I see three major challenges facing our new institution in the years ahead. The first is to consolidate what we have done. The second is to give substance to our built-in negotiating agenda, which essentially constitutes unfinished business emanating from the round. The third is to meet the new challenges already gathering on the horizon. Allow me to say a little about each of these.

- First, consolidation, or *implementation*. The sheer range of subjects that were covered in the Uruguay Round is daunting for even the hardiest trade hands. The texts of the results comprise no less than nineteen Agreements, twenty-four Decisions, eight Understandings, and three Declarations. Some of these texts are obviously more important than others, but together they represent nearly 500 pages of carefully crafted language, replete with commitments. (Perhaps I should not mention the other 24,000 pages of specific market-access commitments.) For some countries, a number of these commitments will coincide with existing policies; in other instances, they call for change. A concerted effort is required by all WTO members to consolidate the Uruguay Round results and ensure full compliance. It is an open question whether phase-in arrangements for some of these commitments should be speeded up. For my own part, I cannot see why the benefits of liberalization in any country should be delayed one day longer than absolutely necessary. Even as they are, the commitments require steady, continuing work in national capitals and in the WTO on a day-to-day basis. It is activity that seldom catches the headlines, but it is essential to the proper functioning of the system.

- However, our biggest, short-term priority is to make sure the new *dispute settlement system* works in a legally and politically credible manner. When difficulties and disagreements arise, the WTO's consultation, conciliation, and dispute settlement provisions can be called into action. A willingness to abide by the dispute settlement procedures and findings is just as important as respecting the rules. With just nine months of experience under our belts, there are two reasons I think why we can already be encouraged already by the operation of the new system. First, governments are making use of it in a manner that demonstrates considerable faith in the WTO. Around twenty cases have come to the Dispute Settlement Body—a number far greater than in any single year of the GATT's 47-year existence. Second, the rapid automatic procedure, together with the knowledge that at its conclusion the system is enforceable, seems to be concentrating minds and encouraging quick settlements through the initial consultative process—the recent U.S.-Japan dispute on cars and spare parts is one of these cases. And that is the primary objective—to resolve trade disputes quickly primarily, to generate jurisprudence. Of course, many disputes will run their full course, and I have no doubt that we will be able to produce objective, clear, well-argued judgments which will command the confidence of governments and legislators everywhere. No one need have any fear of arbitrary conclusions or a lack of neutrality on the part of WTO dispute panels or the new Appellate Body.

- For all countries, new and detailed obligations have been created to *notify* policies and measures, so trading partners can be confident that they have full knowledge of each other's policies. Transparency is an essential ingredient for fostering mutual trust and encouraging respect for the rules. Indeed, one of the results of the Uruguay Round was the creation of a trade policy review mechanism, whereby the trade policies of individual WTO members are examined multilaterally by turn, and in depth. These examinations provide an opportunity for countries to hold frank and nonlitigious exchanges of view about each other's policies. They are a valuable contribution to transparency and help to raise awareness about policy issues among trading partners.

- In previous multilateral trade negotiations, unfinished business tended to reflect failure to agree on quite fundamental issues, such as whether to do anything about agriculture or textiles, or whether to redesign the rules on safeguard measures. This was hardly the case in the Uruguay Round. However, by the end of negotiations in 1993, it was clear that extra time would be needed in a few key sectors. This is clearest in the field of *services*, where we have already held post–Uruguay Round negotiations on trade in financial services and the movement of natural persons, and are in the midst of negotiations on the opening up of basic telecommunications and maritime transport services. We certainly did not achieve everything we would have liked in the financial services and the negotiations on the movement of natural persons, but we made progress. In financial services, in particular, some thirty countries undertook valuable, additional market-opening commitments.

- The negotiations on *basic telecommunications* are to be completed by the end of April 1996. They will open up significant new trade and investment opportunities. The negotiations coincide with industry trends towards liberalization, attributable both to pressure from user industries and rapid technological development. Nevertheless, there is resistance to the eradication of monopoly supply arrangements in many countries, and concerted multilateral action offers the best hope of securing far-reaching results. Success in these negotiations will mean that telecom operators should be able to offer a broad spectrum of competitively priced services in both national and international markets. The United States is in the vanguard of this negotiation, with one of the most liberal and low-cost telecommunications markets in the world. This is why its commitment to a genuine multilateral result is of vital importance. We need a strong result from the WTO negotiations if we are to make the vision of the global information society a reality—with all that it will also mean for revitalizing economies, transforming our societies, and empowering people.

- The negotiations on *maritime transport services*, on the other hand, deal with one of the most ancient means of exchange among peoples—one that retains its fundamental importance for the flow of merchandise trade. The prodigious improvements in shipping technology over recent years need to be matched by improvements in the policy environment in which these ships sail. This also is a negotiation where there are some firmly held positions, and it is essential that we keep on recalling that it is every bit as valid and important as the negotiations in other areas.

- Another part of the Uruguay Round's unfinished business is the *built-in agenda* for future work. This comprises several elements. WTO members have already established a mandate to enter into successive rounds of negotiations in trade in services, with a view to achieving progressively higher levels of liberalization. The first such negotiation must begin within five years. Similarly, in agriculture, members are committed to engage in negotiations aimed at further reductions in agricultural support and protection. The time frame envisaged is the same as that for services. These commitments and a number of others in the WTO Agreement clearly reflect recognition of the need for continual, incremental trade liberalization—a virtuous circle of global cooperative efforts that is the basis of an effective multilateral system.

  Then there is the so-called "*new agenda*"—those issues that, as the process of global economic integration continues, suggest themselves naturally as likely subjects for the WTO work program of the future.

- One "new" issue that is already in the WTO work program is the relationship between *trade and the environment*. At the heart of the matter is how we relate the rules-based multilateral trade system, continued trade liberalization, and further development of the global economy to environmental concerns and objectives. It is possible to envisage circumstances in which trade, unsupported by sound environmental policy, could involve damage to the environment—just as one can easily imagine environmental regulations that could harm legitimate trade. In such circumstances, careful judgment is necessary in weighing whether it is trade policy or environmental policy that must be adjusted. It is also not difficult to see how ill-considered international environmental agreements could needlessly frustrate trade and reduce incomes—and even put at risk environmental reform and improvement. At the same time, it is just as important to recognize the circumstances in which, by encouraging efficiency and better allocation of scarce resources, trade liberalization may support of an improved environment. I am optimistic that our current work on the subject in the WTO will contribute to a better understanding of the issues and assist governments in developing more coherent policies in this area.

- *Trade and investment* is a leading candidate for the new agenda, since one of the consequences of globalization is to lessen the distinctions among different forms of market access. In the GATT framework we used to think of market access simply in terms of tariffs and nontariff measures—reducing tariffs and eliminating other trade barriers at the frontier was the recipe for liberalization. But foreign investment was an altogether different matter. Indeed, countries often used to regard tariffs and other trade barriers as convenient mechanisms for inducing foreign investment, as protection of the domestic market offered attractive profits to foreign investors. This was the essence of the import substitution development strategy—a strategy that in large measure failed and has now been discredited. In today's world of international business, trade and investment are increasingly viewed as complements, not substitutes. Different parts of internationally based businesses can be located in several different countries. Increasingly businesses trade to invest, and invest to trade. The WTO cannot afford to concern itself only with the trade side of the equation—that would be to deny the reality of modern global business practices.

It is no coincidence that foreign direct investment flows worldwide quadrupled, to almost $200billion per annum, in the ten years to 1993. Indeed, the importance of investment was recognized in the General Agreement on Trade in Services negotiated in the Uruguay Round, where investment, or commercial presence, was one of the four modes of service supply in respect of which WTO members undertook market-access commitments. But I think we need a broader, or more horizontal approach to international investment rules. Such rules would build on the WTO principles of nondiscrimination and national treatment, and create a policy environment to encourage and safeguard foreign investment, whether in goods or services.

The OECD has already started work in this direction, but I believe governments will increasingly recognize the need for work on investment in a more global setting as well. Especially so since developing countries are not only the target of a growing proportion of international investment but are themselves becoming important overseas investors. I should note that the Uruguay Round Agreement on Trade-Related Investment Measures calls for an examination by members within five years of the case for developing provisions on investment policy.

- That same mandate refers to *competition policy*, which we will also have to examine as a possible candidate for further work. Of course, what we have done in the GATT and the WTO over fifty years in promoting a liberal trading environment is precisely the enhancement of competition. But if we have succeeded in getting the rules of competition between countries to work effectively, that very success requires us to go further and consider how the behavior of companies can serve to distort international competition. We will need to see whether there are any areas where either explicit competition rules or specific understandings are necessary internationally to complement the statutes that many governments already have on their books. I have no doubt that competition rules are essential to the proper functioning of markets—what we need to clarify, however, is how best to promote such disciplines, both nationally and internationally.

- Some WTO members would like to see the new agenda include the subject of *trade and social standards*. This is a highly controversial issue, and in the absence of a consensus there is no possibility that it could be brought into the agenda of the WTO. It is clear that what we need first and foremost is a comprehensive effort to bring some clarity to the many complex issues that are involved here.

The first issue to be clarified is the nature of the subject: Are we talking about the comparative advantage of developing countries, which comes from lower wage levels—as the issue is sometimes presented—or are we talking about human rights or labor standards? It is fundamentally important to clarify the terms of the debate as it relates to trade.

The second point is to identify key issues related to trade; for example, are we talking about child labor or trade union rights in terms of labor standards or in terms of human rights?

These are just some of the preconditions for opening a discussion on whether a useful debate is in fact possible on these issues.

Fortunately, we are not starting from zero. The debate on this issue in fact started at the Versailles peace conference and some of the principles involved have been reflected in ArticleXX of the GATT from its beginning. In the UN, in the OECD, in the International Labour Organization and in national administrations, the debate has made valuable progress and has even produced some practical measures. I would like to refer especially to the most recent work of the ILO, in order to identify some principles that could be important for any discussion in the WTO. These principles have been presented as "shared values" without any dissent from the ILO's membership.

One of these principles is that economic and social growth and development are, to a large extent, interdependent. When the economic situation is poor, the social situation is also likely to be poor. Correspondingly, where there is economic growth, social development is more likely to come too.

While no one should challenge the legitimate right of developing countries to use the comparative advantage of lower costs, and no one should use human rights and issues of social standards as an excuse for disguised protectionism, no country should deliberately deny workers' rights or attempt to generate artificially lower costs by forced labor, discrimination against women, exploitation of children, or other such abuses.

We should on no account allow this debate to reopen a North-South divide. Dialogue is the best approach to finding ways to improve the observance of labor standards.

Finally, the ILO has recognized the necessity of improving its means of acting on these issues.

I wanted to underline these points presented earlier in 1995 by the chairperson of the ILO's Working Party on the Social Dimensions of the Liberalization of International Trade, because I think that these shared values represent a possible starting point for a discussion of the issue. I also believe that in order to convince developing countries that no protectionist considerations are involved in the debate, it is essential to prove that all possible measures other than trade sanctions are being taken to alleviate the problems. One excellent example is the Memorandum of Understanding on the elimination of child labor from the garment industry in Bangladesh, which was signed in July 1995 by the industry, the ILO and UNICEF, with support from the Bangladesh and U.S. governments. This joint approach combines restrictions on child labor with the improvement of educational opportunities for the children involved. This is a targeted and constructive approach to a specific problem, and as such I believe it offers a useful model for future efforts. On the other hand, to simply restrict imports of garments from the industries concerned would have in all likelihood just worsened the situation of these children.

Let me sum up my thinking on this issue by repeating the need that I see for a wide-ranging and comprehensive consideration of the issues. Only in this way will it be possible to generate the necessary confidence to build consensus for a discussion on whether, and how, they relate to trade.

Last but not least, I should like to say a few words about two related subjects: reciprocity and the growth of regionalism in international trade relations.

- There are from time to time calls for trade policies based on *reciprocity* instead of the basic Most Favored Nation (MFN) principle. These are based on the assumption that the degree of liberalization already reached by certain countries does not give them any real defense in a multilateral negotiation vis-à-vis those countries whose liberalization process is much less advanced. Advocates of reciprocity argue that such countries have no real incentive to deeper liberalization, given their benefits from the MFN system.

  I would like to make a couple of points on this question. The first is that to present reciprocity as an alternative to MFN is a major departure from the trading system we have built up over fifty years, and it is just the opposite of what the founding fathers of the multilateral system envisaged.

  Second, I can understand that a nation or regional group that believes itself to be an open market has the right to fight hard to obtain from all its partners the greatest possible degree of liberalization. If this argument is used tactically and temporarily as a negotiating device, there is less need for alarm over its implications for the system as a whole. But if it becomes a permanent instrument of policy, then the risk for the multilateral system could become serious.

  Trade is technical in its substance but highly political in its consequences. Reciprocity as a structural alternative to the multilateral system equals bilateralism, bilateralism equals discrimination, and trade relations based on power rather than rules are the result. This would be a very dangerous departure from the success story of the multilateral system.

- The growth of regionalism is a more complex issue. There is no natural contradiction between regionalism and the multilateral system. This has been the shared assessment of the great majority of the international trade community. The real contradiction, it must always be emphasized, is between open trade and protectionism. Regional trade initiatives can certainly help to lower trade barriers and thus promote economic growth, but the relationship between regionalism and a multilateral system based on the MFN principle is nonetheless a complex one. The provisions of the GATT have sought to ensure compatibility by requiring regional agreements to cover substantially all trade among the partners and to promote trade policies that do not lead to higher protection or extra restrictions on the trade of nonmembers. In practice, however, it has been almost impossible to assess the consistency of regional agreements with the multilateral system under these provisions. Since the creation of the GATT nearly fifty years ago, one hundred and eight regional agreements have been notified: eighty existing agreements have so far been examined, and only six have been found consistent with the rules I mentioned above (the EU is not one of them). In recent times twenty new regional agreements have been notified and are waiting to be examined in the WTO. It will come as no surprise that inconclusive results are likely here as well. Clearly there is a need to improve the rules and the procedures under which the WTO's members can assess this crucial relationship. But it is also clear that the legal issues are only part of the story.

The relation between regional and multilateral liberalization in practice has been a different and generally more positive story. For example, successive enlargements of the European Union have been followed by multilateral trade negotiations, which have maintained a de facto link between progress at the regional level and at the multilateral level. These links are the reason why most people have seen regional agreements as building blocks for multilateral free trade.

Is the situation changing, and do we need to adjust this generally positive perception? Let me suggest some considerations.

Until quite recently, there was only one large regional grouping, and that was limited to a number of Western European countries. The U.S. historically opposed regionalism, but this situation has changed. Since the 1980s, the U.S. has begun to build its own regional agreements, through free trade with Canada, through Nafta, through Asia Pacific Economic Cooperation (APEC), and other international organizations. Now, almost all the WTO member countries also belong to a regional trade agreement. While the importance of regional agreements as a means of tariff reduction has declined (this is also thanks to the success of the GATT), they are becoming increasingly important in terms of trade rules and for the political weight they represent in international negotiations. These are elements that could break up the parallelism between regional and multilateral progress, and there is the risk that antagonism between regional groups could make progress in the multilateral system more difficult.

Furthermore, regional initiatives such as the suggestions for a transatlantic free-trade area could give the impression of re-erecting a discriminatory divide between the rich North and the poorer South.

The conclusion I draw is that we must be very attentive to strengthening the linkage that has existed up to now between regional and multilateral progress. What this means in practical terms is that regional liberalization initiatives must proceed almost in tandem with multilateral ones. What countries are willing to do regionally, they must then be willing to do multilaterally, so as to keep this parallelism between regional and multilateral commitments.

At the core of this relationship, there is the basic question of the kind of international system we want: a global system based on the principle of nondiscrimination embodied in agreed and enforceable rules, or a world divided into regional blocs with all the consequences this would imply for political stability and security.

Conclusion

To sum up, it is clear that the challenges facing the multilateral trading system are about much more than trade matters as they used to be defined. I know that for some people—and for some countries too—the pace of change is unsettling and even alarming. Whether in the challenges that the information revolution presents to anyone over thirty, or in the pace of economic globalization, there is an understandable reflex that asks the world to slow down a little. But we know it will not.

If we decrease our imports from the developing countries, we decrease their growth and our growth alike. And the growth of many developing countries will be the most powerful engine for growth in developed countries. At the same time, if we reduce export opportunities for developing countries, we only increase unemployment and poverty in these countries, and further restrict opportunities for their young people. And if we try to close our borders both to goods and to people, we will just increase instability, violence, war, and terrorism. So the only sustainable policy for us and for the developing countries is to continue a strong commitment to openness.

That is why we need to keep the multilateral system with its reliable framework of principles and rules in good repair: it is a firm foothold in a shifting world. Liberalization within the multilateral system means that this unstoppable process can be implemented within internationally agreed rules and disciplines. This is the opposite of a chaotic and unchecked process—change would indeed be a leap in the dark, without the security of the multilateral system.

At the same time, the multilateral system is becoming more and more a political issue. This is happening because its evolution increasingly concerns national regulatory policies more than cross-border obstacles, and because the challenges to the system are increasingly political rather than technical. In this context, it could become very important to consider the possibility of strengthening the institutional basis of the system—for example by enhancing the political dimension of its central institution, the WTO.

It is my profound conviction that the confluence of political and economic events of the last few years places us on the threshold of an unusual historic opportunity, that of establishing a truly global system for the conduct of international economic relations: a system that responds readily to change and to changing needs, and is one for which every nation will wish to claim ownership. Let us rise to this challenge, just as Spaak and the other builders of the postwar world did to theirs. Their achievements have shaped our present, and they should inspire our future.

3

FROM EUROPE TO *EUROPE*
A Story of Hope, Trial and Error

Lord Ralf Dahrendorf
October 1996

Twice in little more than half a century—thus in my own living memory—Europe emerged from the grip of dark forces of evil to the light of freedom. Hitler's barbaric onslaught on liberty and civility led through the hell of the Holocaust to a European continent in ruins in which, despite everything, the values so savagely attacked had prevailed. That was the challenge of 1945. Then, barely three years later, a large part of Europe was cut off from the new opportunities and enveloped in the brutal denial of rights and life-chances by Stalin's tyranny, which later turned into the gray oppressiveness of "really existing socialism." But this too did not last. In 1980, *Solidarnosc* took up the torch that had been lit and then quenched in Berlin in 1951, in Budapest in 1956, and in Prague in 1968. This time, however, the dictators were in retreat, until they finally had to let go of a communist Europe and leave it in the hands of "dissident" believers in democracy and the rule of law. That was the challenge of 1989.

I was sixteen in 1945 and had survived a spell in prison and in a Gestapo camp where anti-Nazi activity at school had landed me. Back in Berlin, we were now anxiously waiting for my father to come home from the horrors of the camps and, after his trial before the notorious *Volksgerichtshof*, the more orderly cruelty of a Brandenburg prison. When he came, he had already been appointed head of energy supplies for the devastated city of Berlin. From his prison days he brought with him the legacy of his Social Democrat friends who had not survived. It was a legacy of unity: unity of the labor movement to prevent a repetition of the political fratricide of the early 1930s, which in his view had helped the Nazis to power, and unity of Europe whose divisions had caused two great wars in our own century and several others, involving first Prussia then Germany in the century before. Both hopes of my father's were to be disappointed, at least initially and in the way in which they were conceived, before they eventually came to fruition in unexpected ways.

The unity of the labor movement met with resistance by communists whose leaders had returned to Berlin from Moscow believing that they could go it alone. But when they discovered how little support they had for their line of action, they began to force their plans upon the Social Democrats. This my father resisted in turn (as he always resisted force), until in the end he had to leave Berlin in a hurry, saved from Stalin's secret police (NKVD) by British friends who flew him (and me) to his native Hamburg. A decade later—my father by then had died an early death of exhaustion—it emerged that a revitalized Social Democratic Party (SPD) did in fact provide that unity which the resistance fighters had dreamt of, for there was no other party of social reform left to command the allegiance of voters.

However, in the early years postwar Germany's Social Democrats did not support European integration. In 1952 they voted solidly against the Treaty of Paris, which created the ECSC. My father was devastated and even considered leaving the party that had been his political home since he was eighteen, if not earlier. It took a decade for the German SPD to shed its curiously nationalist beginnings and become the party of Willy Brandt and later Helmut Schmidt, which was as European and Atlantic as Konrad Adenauer's Christian Democratic Union (CDU).

In fact, few of those who invented Europe after the war—a Europe of freedom and civility—came from the political left. On September 19, 1946, almost fifty years ago to the day, Winston Churchill, the British conservative, made a memorable speech in Zurich in which he called for reconciliation and European union. (His was a union of France and Germany, to be sure, with the Benelux countries and Italy involved, but Britain, still wrapped in delusions of grandeur, a mere "sponsor" along with the United States and, perhaps, Soviet Russia.) Those who pursued the idea were for the most part Christian Democrats—Alcide de Gasperi in Italy, Robert Schuman in France, Konrad Adenauer in Germany. They were, to be precise, Catholic politicians. Europe acquired a distinctly Roman flavor, all the way to the Treaty of Rome in 1957 to set up the European Economic Community (EEC), and this ultramontane quality did not necessarily commend it to more secular parties. Paul-Henri Spaak, one socialist among the founding fathers of postwar Europe (at least in terms of party allegiance), characteristically argued even during the war that Britain was essential for European unity, otherwise Europe "will be organized without and, as I dare predict, against England, and its dominant force will be, despite the defeat, Germany."

Not just Belgium, but several smaller countries of Europe have from the beginning played a special part in the process. Luxembourg certainly had more than its share if one thinks of Joseph Bech, the Prime Minister from Mondorf-les-Bains just across the border from Robert Schuman's home in Lorraine, of his later successor Pierre Werner, the author of the first project of Economic and Monetary Union in 1970, and of their two successors as Prime Minister, Gaston Thorn and Jacques Santer, who later became Commission Presidents. The Netherlands were from the beginning the most effective, perhaps the only force to combine strong support for European integration with insistence on its openness to the world and on democratic accountability. Joseph Luns—one of the few who could look de Gaulle in the eyes, for he was equally tall and he spoke without fear or favor—was but one of a long line of Dutch Europeans, many of whom emerged either from Dirk Spierenburg's foreign office or from Max Kohnstamm's Monnet Committee. Of the newer members of the European Union, the Irish and perhaps the Portuguese continue this tradition of small-country involvement.

But I must take up the thread of my story: my father's deep unhappiness with the anti-European stance of his party. In 1952, on a visit to Amsterdam, he heard of the SPD vote against the "Schuman Plan" for the ECSC and wrote an emotional paper full of foreboding. He remembered the time when in a German prison, he had his own thoughts about what would be after the end of Hitler Germany." How can Europe be brought into balance in view of the foreseeable East-West differences? He saw this as a great opportunity for democratic socialism—and as an obligation of Germany. But it would require more than recognition of Germany's collective guilt; what was needed was action, even perhaps "the internationalization of the Ruhr region" (with its coal mines and steel mills). The Schuman Plan is, if anything, a modest step in this direction, but it is "a political step in an economically decisive area which will lead to supranational solutions." Moreover, it prefigures a future that will attract hitherto passive young people to political involvement. How can Social Democrats, instead of forming the vanguard of this future, defend "national and other faintheartedness"?

Rereading such exhortations forty-four years later, one is struck by how much has changed, not least in the views then held by German Social Democrats—views which are now more likely to be found among British Conservatives. One is also reminded of the question. What is Europe—"supranational," or at any rate organized Europe—about? The answer is by no means obvious. In part (or so I have long thought) it is actually about small countries. Without joining forces with others they would be nowhere in this world of ours, and yet they have so much to offer. Moreover, since the larger European nations are not exactly superpowers, the experience of the smaller ones is relevant even for them. But this is just one motive. Another one undoubtedly has to do with the past. One must be allowed to wonder whether it was actually European integration that has prevented wars at least among the members of Europe's communities after 1945, though one impetus for cooperation was undoubtedly to put an end to the dismal past.

In practice this meant that since 1945 Europe was always about Germany—Germany as an acceptable partner, a Germany that is contained by inclusion. One cannot but admire the sentiments Churchill expressed in Zurich in September 1946: Germany's crimes (he said) are not forgotten. "The guilty must be punished. Germany must be deprived of the power to re-arm and make another aggressive war." But then "there must be an end to retribution." "There must be what Mr. Gladstone many years ago called 'a blessed act of oblivion.'" And then the famous passage: "I am now going to say something that will astonish you. The first step in the re-creation of the European Family must be a partnership between France and Germany. In this way only can France recover the moral and cultural leadership of Europe. There can be no revival of Europe without a spiritually great France and a spiritually great Germany."

Let us thus remember September 19, 1946, a mere sixteen months after Germany's total defeat! It did not quite turn out that way, of course. Not only is Britain hardly the "sponsor" of this Franco-German Europe, but also France is far from being its moral and cultural leader. Only the apparent need to "tie in" Germany has remained, *a fortiori* after the end of the East-West divide which so conveniently held the Western half of Europe together. Europe for many is about keeping Germany under control, and it is not just French politicians who feel that way. At least three German chancellors—Adenauer, Schmidt, and Kohl—showed a strong sense of the need for Germany's *Selbsteinbindung* (to use Helmut Schmidt's term); that is, for the country to tie itself to its European neighbors in order to prevent the recurrence of past aberrations. (The other three chancellors, incidentally, did not express such views, though each for his own reasons. They were of course Ludwig Erhard, Kurt Georg Kiesinger, and Willy Brandt). All the way to monetary union, one motive force of European integration has remained the desire to keep Germany within the fold.

Within what fold? For one thing, to be sure, the fold of the liberal democracies of the world. Not only was the Second World War fought and won in the name of democracy and the rule of law, but democracy at home is also as solid a guarantee against aggression abroad as one can hope for. As a rule, democracies do not start wars. Clearly, in this regard, the postwar hopes for Germany have been fulfilled, though one may doubt whether the role of European institutions in creating a firm social basis for Germany's democratic political institutions was more than marginal.

There is, however, another aspect of the fold within which Germany was, and is to be kept, and it is even more relevant after unification than before. A lingering concern remains whether Germany might not drift off once again to its Eastern destiny. *Ostpolitik* has heightened this concern, and unification may appear to give it a certain practical plausibility. Yet in this respect too, postwar changes have been remarkably successful. The success lay not so much in persuading Germany and the Germans of the values, institutions, and orientations of the West (important though this was), as in a much more fundamental and effective process. The German author Wold Jobst Siedler called it, perhaps slightly wistfully but no less convincingly for his regrets, the *Westverschiebung Europa*. The term is justly geological; we are talking about a kind of continental drift in which Europe itself has shifted to the West. "Europe regained is a Europe which looks to the West." The East is gone as an option. "Europe's East does not want to be an East" in the old, emphatic sense of the Slavophiles. Indeed, where are the Slavophiles now?

Timothy Garton Ash made this point in one of his remarkable *New York Review of Books* pieces years before the revolution of 1989. "Does Central Europe Exist?" he asked in 1986; he replied: Not yet. It was then still an idea, if a potent idea, the antithesis to the "imperial system whose main instruments of domination are lies, violence, the atomization of society." He described the alternative by "the imperatives of living in truth, nonviolence, the struggle for civil society—and the ideal of Central Europe." We rarely refer to Eastern Europe these days, and when we do, we mean the Ukraine and places further East. Actually they too want to be part of a Europe that is essentially Western in its values and institutions. The decline of the East, or so it appears, is terminal, and Europe's shift to the West irreversible. This, among other consequences, is the answer to the German Question.

It is not, however, as such the answer to the European Question. Those of us whose dormant liberal passions were reawakened, indeed redoubled by the collapse of *nomenklatura* communism in 1989 and 1990, have since seen some disappointments. Once again, great figures emerged to speak for their newly liberalized countries: Lech Walesa in Warsaw, Vaclav Havel in Prague, Arpad Göncz in Budapest, Zheliu Zhelev in Sofia, and others around them. A new Europe could have been built on their visions, but it was not. Their Western counterparts did not have the stature to live up to the challenge of liberty regained.

The disappointments of those of us in the old Europe who trembled and later rejoiced with our friends in Poland, Czechoslovakia, Hungary, and elsewhere are thus not the obvious ones. They are not due to the slow progress of the economies and civil societies of postcommunist countries, which was to be expected and continues to be a challenge to their own citizens and to those of us who are ready to help. Even the valley of tears through which people would have to trek before things got better did not come as a surprise. The key disappointment is the response by us, the more fortunate Europeans, to the needs of those for whom the idea not just of Central Europe but of Europe should now be real. Not to put too fine a point on it, Western Europe has betrayed its principles and promises when, instead of stretching out its hands to Central Europe, it has turned inward to its own so-called *approfondissement* á la Maastricht and even allowed the protection of ludicrous vested interests—in rationing imports of mushrooms and raspberries from Poland for example—to prevail over political imperatives. Institutionally at least, *EU*rope—the European Union, has failed Europe—the continent in need of cooperation and integration.

This then takes me from "hope," one part of the title of this lecture, to the other, "trial and error"; and worse, from reality to the arcane and rather uninspiring world of European institutions. Worse still, here I have to part company with my father who believed that a "political step in an economically decisive area will lead to supranational solutions." The company with which I part was, to be sure, distinguished. All the founders believed that the economic beginnings would, in the end result, in European union. Thus I have to part company with Walter Hallstein, the first president of the EEC Commission, and even with the patron saint of European integration, Jean Monnet.

Churchill's and others' dream first gained institutional reality when the Council of Europe was created in 1948. You may call this a Eurocentric statement for there was after all that other venture, the Organisation for European Economic Cooperation (OEEC) initiated here at Harvard with George Marshall's important address on June 5, 1947. The Marshall Plan was the greatest single stimulus to European recovery, but it did not unite Europe. The OEEC always kept its Atlantic flavor, though this did not detract from its success. Even today, the extended OECD, now an Organisation for Economic Cooperation and Development among the rich countries of the world, is an unrivaled source of socioeconomic information and coordination, but contrary to the Council of Europe, it was and is an intergovernmental—as distinct from a supranational—organization. This may be one of the reasons why it failed to meet the high expectations that accompanied its birth. Its most important purpose today is in the human rights field through the administration of the European Convention, particularly in the new member states in Eastern and Central Europe.

However, by the early 1950s it had become clear that other, more effective ways had to be found to bring the free countries of Europe together. The European Coal and Steel Community was one such way, more remarkable for its institutional arrangements than for its substance. On substance it is perhaps worth mentioning that a community founded to establish the joint governance of "heavy industries," which had given rise to conflicts for a century and more, soon found that it was in fact administering declining industries. One might surmise that this stubborn fact turned the community from an orientation towards the future to one towards the past, from a forward- and outward-looking to a protectionist institution—a virus that the European Union has found hard to shed. To return to institutions, however, the ECSC was Jean Monnet's first shot at supranationalism; that is, of national parliaments relinquishing sovereignty to a High Authority. By the same token, it set an example of how supranationalism makes democracy and even accountability more generally difficult.

However, in the early 1950s the ECSC was not regarded as the nucleus of a European Union. At that time, more directly political ways were sought, defined, and negotiated to the point of treaties. At that time also, France was clearly the driving force; the "leader" as Churchill had hoped. Rather, French governments played that role, both in the design of a European Defence Community (EDC) and in the proposal to create a Political Authority for a "European Community of supranational character" fashioned on the ECSC. But governments had rushed ahead of their peoples. The EDC failed in 1954 in the French Parliament, and the plan for political union was quietly dropped as a result. Instead, NATO was extended to include Germany, and in Europe an unfortunate process began which is with us to the present day: the process of trying to achieve political objectives by means of economic integration.

The facts are familiar. In 1957 the Treaty of Rome was ratified in the parliaments of six countries: Italy, the Benelux countries, France, and Germany (this time with the votes of some though not yet all German Social Democrats). The EEC began its life in 1958, along with the European Atomic Community (EURATOM). Ten years later, the ECSC, the EEC, and EURATOM were merged into the European Communities (EC). In 1973, the first major enlargement of the EC took place with Britain entering the scene. After the turbulent 1970s with the failure of the first project of monetary union, and the successful 1980s in which the Single European Act led to the completion not just of a Common but of a Single Market largely without nontariff barriers, the Treaty of Maastricht in 1991 mapped out a new program and involved renaming the creature the European Union (EU). From this time onwards, if not earlier, the EU went seriously astray.

The reasons for this lie deep in the history of the process I have described here. I hope you will forgive me for tracing them in a somewhat personal manner, not for autobiographical reasons, nor because one person's vexations in the European maze are of particular interest, but to give you a sense of the depth of feeling which Europe, and even more so *EU*rope, can arouse.

In December 1969 a particularly successful European summit took place in The Hague, and it was here that the French veto against Britain's accession was finally lifted. Major steps towards the deepening of European co-operation were also accepted. I was therefore pleased when, having been a Parliamentary Secretary of State in Willy Brandt's government, I was nominated as one of the German Commissioners of the EC beginning in July 1970. My responsibility for foreign trade and foreign affairs made the move all the more attractive. However, when I arrived in Brussels I knew little about the EC, its organization and culture. In the German Foreign Office it had been regarded as of secondary importance, a fact clearly indicated by the denomination of the most senior official in charge of European affairs not as under-secretary of the foreign office (a title reserved for the man in charge of general policy), but merely as under-secretary in the foreign office. However, I soon found out what was what, and I did not like it. To be sure, I did like my colleagues, notably the great European Altiero Spinelli, a victim of both Hitler and Stalin, yet an inveterate idealist; Sicco Mansholt, the stubborn inventor as well as defender of the Common Agricultural Policy; and also the shrewd future French Prime Minister

Raymond Barre, who was then in charge of the project of monetary union. But when it came to the institution itself I soon found myself a skeptic.

In July 1971, a year after my arrival, I could not hold my fire any longer. Under the pseudonym "Wieland Europa," I published a series of articles in the German weekly *Die Zeit,* entitled "Beyond Brussels: A Plea for a Second Europe." They turned out to be a bombshell. The thrust of my argument was simple. We have reached the end of the tether of the original treaties. The contradiction between its political objectives and the daily reality of the European Community has become abundantly evident. The supranational illusions of the European beginnings have turned out to be an obstacle rather than a motive force for real political cooperation. The illogical road to Europe has led us into a cul-de-sac: the logic which would force countries to move from a problematic agricultural policy to monetary union, and from economic to political union simply does not exist. All these points in my articles were also garnished with highly quotable—and soon much quoted—phrases like: "There are situations in which [the Commission] causes pity rather than respect"; or: "A democrat must be ashamed to see grown-up parliamentarians enact the farce which they have to play ten times a year in Strasbourg and Luxembourg."

My pseudonym did not stick for long, and it was disingenuous of me to believe that I could persuade the world between the author and the Commissioner Lord Dahrendorf. A Europe-wide outcry nevertheless did not lead to my resignation or removal from office. Parliament had a tense hour about "Wieland Europa" on September 23, 1971, in which only the Italian Communist member D'Angelosante supported my views. The Commission, however, was generous. Raymond Barre said that he would not do anything to cast a shadow on Franco-German relations, and Sicco Mansholt remembered that as a young man he had also done silly things. I apologized, and much was forgiven, though perhaps in those days the seeds were sown for my later English incarnation. I was reappointed to the Commission after the 1973 enlargement, but in the autumn of 1974 left Brussels to become Director of the London School of Economics. Since then I have lived in Britain, now not only a British citizen, but as Lord Lord Dahrendorf of Clare Market in the City of Westminster, a member of the Upper House of Parliament and of its European Communities Committee, on which I have acquired the reputation not of a "Euroskeptic" but of a "skeptical European."

I strongly believe that Europe matters and that Britain must be a part of it. My skepticism is entirely about the path which the process of European integration has taken—its inward-looking bias, its serious lack of democratic accountability, the increasingly unbearable gap between aspirations and realities, and then the fatal flaw of the theory that (to quote Walter Hallstein) "all politics is a unity," so that starting in one corner of economic policy will lead to a "chain reaction of integration."

Monetary union, the centerpiece of the Treaty of Maastricht, illustrates the fallacy. In the early 1970s, the first try failed because Europeans had set their calendar without regard to the rest of the world. When the convertibility of the dollar into gold was suspended in August 1971, a process began which swept away all of the well-laid plans of Pierre Werner and Raymond Barre. This may not happen again, though the invisible hand of "the markets" remains a threat even to the much more sophisticated plans of the late 1990s. But for all their sophistication, these plans have two serious weaknesses: they are irrelevant and they are divisive. The irrelevance results from the fact that monetary union fails to address what people rightly perceive as the real problems of the day, which are unemployment and supply-side obstacles to competitiveness. The divisiveness of monetary union has to do with the emergence of "ins" and "outs"—and even if the latter are, as the jargon now has it, "pre-ins," an inner core will move ahead and the European Union will for a long time be a two-tier arrangement.

The case for monetary union in Europe is primarily political. Chancellor Kohl certainly thinks of the day on which he overrode the views of all experts and pushed through the theoretically mistaken yet in practice inevitable decision to create German monetary union on the basis of a one to one exchange rate between East and West Germany. This feat, he believes, can be repeated in Europe and lead to instant unification. For France, monetary union means regaining some of the powers which are now lost to the *Bundesbank* and, of course, tying Germany in. Italy and Spain dream of both being in the First Division, and also of eternal stability. Britain, as all others accept, will continue to play cricket while they play soccer. But will political union really be the ineluctable result? Or will the whole plan founder on its political nonviability? Will the convergence criteria of fiscal policy lead to domestic unrest in France and elsewhere? Will there be shocks, asymmetric or otherwise, between the "irrevocable" decision of January 1, 1999 and the actually implementation of monetary union for citizens in 2002?

It is tempting to interpret the history of postwar Europe as one of political stabilization by economic growth and prosperity. Yet here as elsewhere one must beware of the elementary confusion between correlation and causality. The economic and the political miracles happened at much the same time, but it does not follow that one caused the other. More particularly, economic success did not stabilize democratic institution, even if people found it easier to accept the constitution of liberty at a time of increasing prosperity. Since 1989 we have learned that, if anything, the reverse of the Marxian theory of the primacy of economics—a theory now held mainly by capitalists—is true. The economic reforms by Leszek Balcerowicz in his brief but crucial period as Polish Minister of Finance were very important, but the institutional stability of the Polish state, despite changes in government, matters as much if not more. Where there is doubt in political institutions, economies do not flourish. The invisible hand cannot replace or create the visible hand, and healthy communities need both. They need functioning markets and reliable rules based on stable institutions.

The relevance of such observations for Europe is clear. If we want political union, no economic subterfuge will get us there. Money, it is true, marks the boundary between politics and economics. The stabilization of the zloty was itself an institutional accomplishment. Argentina's Economics Minister Cavallo may well have been right to enshrine the pegging of the peso to the dollar in the constitution of his country. But Poland and Argentina existed before, and would have existed even with highly unstable currencies; Europe does not. The next push for the EU has to be political, not economic. If we want to move forward, we shall have to return to the plans and ideas of the early postwar years. Reading the European Convention of Human Rights into the EU treaties might well give citizens more of a sense of allegiance than any amount of Brussels propaganda for monetary union. Even if there is no case for reviving the European Defence Community as long as NATO serves us well, the Western European Union (WEU), another relic of the postwar days, deserves a good look and perhaps some link with the projected Common Foreign and Security Policy. Even the plans for a Political Authority might be revived.

Europe matters. I have recently made the case in a little pamphlet (*Why Europe Matters: A Personal View*), which was intended to set the tone for a new Centre for European Reform in London. The Centre will provide ideas on which governments, and notably a government led by Mr. Tony Blair, might wish to draw. It defines Europe as a matter of the head rather than of the heart and aims at closing the gap between realities and aspirations. It does so in a constructive spirit, and in the hope of changing the tone of the British debate, which has become absurdly emotional.

In the year before Britain's entry into the EC, the political economist Andrew Shonfield was invited to give the prestigious BBC Reith Lectures. He spoke about Europe, of course. At the time he introduced a notion that in retrospect sums up the achievements of European integration better than any catalogue of directives and regulations. That was the notion of the "habit of cooperation." Europe has to develop this habit to become real, Shonfield argued. In fact, Europe has done so. Politicians, civil servants, and, alas, lobbyists have long discovered Europe as their preferred playground. But the habit of cooperation extends much further. Students and young people generally move easily across European cultural borders. Professionals consult naturally with their colleagues elsewhere. On the boards of foundations and charities, of nongovernmental organization of all kinds, the question is asked: What are our European partners doing? Traces of a European civil society are thus unmistakable, even if media and political parties and much else remain national.

Extending the blessings of this habit to the new democracies of Eastern and Central Europe is the next major task. It cannot be said too often: Widening is deepening because it expresses a common interest of those who are already "in." *EU*rope has to become Europe if it is not to fail its mission.

Where is all this supposed to lead? I have spoken of trial and error not in a critical vein but to indicate that the purposes of the European process are fundamentally open. Andrew Shonfield gave his Reith Lectures the title *Europe—Journey to an Unknown Destination,* which sums up my intentions, too. The entire debate about federalism and *Europe des patries* and the United States of Europe and the Brussels Leviathan, and even about the European Union is pointless. We do not know where European cooperation will end, but we can take the next steps in response to real challenges and expect an "ever closer union" to result.

We do know, however, what is not intended. There are two things: There is no point in Europe trying to opt out of the global marketplace, or of attempts to create universal political institutions. Protectionism and parochialism would be the end of a Europe that matters in the world. Once again let me quote from Winston Churchill's 1946 Zurich speech, which has put the case so well:

> There is no reason why a regional organisation of Europe should in any way conflict with the world organisation of the United Nations. On the contrary, I believe that the large synthesis will only survive if it is founded upon coherent natural groupings. They do not weaken, on the contrary they strengthen the world organisation. They are in fact its main support. And why should there not be a European group which could give a sense of enlarged patriotism and common citizenship to the distracted peoples of this turbulent and mighty continent?

The forces of globalization are so strong that perhaps the dangers of regional blocs should not be overrated. In any case, insofar as they exist at all they come from regions of another kind (which present the second undesirable perspective). The new world of global information and of the resulting financial and other markets is an uncomfortably exposed place for many. People seek shelter, and they seek it in smaller, allegedly homogeneous units. Far from wanting to be world citizens, or even Europeans, they feel that Italy is too big and diffuse for them and prefer Padania. They prefer Chechnya to Czechoslovakia, Wallonia to Belgium, Catalonia to Spain. The search for such mini-nations is understandable in a homeless world; yet it is also dangerous. It is an invitation to warlords and demagogues. It can lead to intolerance within, given that there are always minorities that do not "belong"; it can also lead to aggressiveness without, given that boundaries are precarious and the closest neighbors are usually perceived as the greatest threat. In such conditions Europe has a new, important mission. It is the balance of sanity for destructive desires. If it gets its act together and abandons reckless plans, which must lead to new divisions, a Europe of trial and error can even become a hope for liberty in turbulent times.

4

THE NEW EUROPE
How to Overcome Forty Years of Division

Uffe Ellemann-Jensen
October 1997

It is an honor to be chosen as the sixteenth Paul-Henri Spaak lecturer. I want to thank the Center for International Affairs of Harvard University and the Frank Boas Foundation for granting me that privilege. Since 1981 these Lectures have focused on U.S.-European relations. Coming from a small country in Europe that has—thanks to the joint efforts of the U.S. and its European allies—enjoyed freedom and prosperity during the four-decade division of Europe, it gives me a very special pleasure to address this distinguished audience at a time when we are facing a new and demanding challenge.

The challenge is this: to find the ways and means necessary to build new structures that will enable us to overcome forty years of division in Europe. I firmly believe that we will only achieve this end by exploiting those structures that have effectively safeguarded peace and liberty in Western Europe: NATO and the European Union. It is necessary now to expand these structures so that they include the new European democracies that have come into being after the collapse of the Soviet Union.

It is extremely important that Europe undertakes its full share of the responsibilities for fulfilling this task, and I see this as a precondition for a continuation of the close links between Europe and the U.S. Let's face the fact that we Europeans cannot solve these problems without the U.S.

However, let us also be aware that the U.S. needs relief because of its global responsibilities, and that Americans will not accept a situation where they feel that Europe is getting a free ride.

Consequently, we have to follow a parallel route on the two important tasks facing us: the enlargement of NATO, which is a shared task, and the enlargement of the European Union, which is a European task. The enlargement of NATO is decisive with regard to establishing a new European security structure. I believe it will be much easier to gain the necessary political backing from U.S. political leaders if Europe, at the same time, displays a willingness as well as an ability to solve its part of the joint task.

Thus, we come to my main subject today: What are we actually doing in Europe in order to overcome the forty years of division?

The Europe of the 1990s is a new Europe, but with deep roots in the old Europe. A look at the map shows us the dramatic developments of the last seven to eight years. First, the old division of post–World War II Europe, the iron curtain, disappeared—which for half a century formed a formidable barrier between different ideological systems. Then new nation-states started to appear, some known from a distant history, others as newcomers on the map, but with a background in old divisions.

The result was a new map of a new Europe, showing us the fragmentation of what used to be the Soviet Union, Yugoslavia, and Czechoslovakia, and the arrival of many new borders and new names. The process continues still, and I expect that in the next decade we may see new nation-states appear in Europe, altering the map even more.

Here, then, is the real challenge we face in Europe today, and the questions we have to answer demonstrate with chilling clarity these new circumstances: How can a more fragmented Europe avoid instability on a continent that recently experienced war again after nearly four decades of relative calm? How can Europe find its proper role vis-à-vis the United States, where attention seems increasingly drawn towards internal problems? How can Europe respond to the turmoil and instability in the former Soviet Union and the aspirations of its former satellite states to become part of the successful Europe—*our* Europe? And, finally, how can Europe maintain competitiveness against not only these new democracies on our own continent, but also against the many newly industrialized countries, especially those in Southeast Asia, that challenge the Europeans in all markets?

Completing this picture are the global headaches of regional and ethnic tensions, terrorism, environmental catastrophes, famines, refugees, the proliferation of nuclear weapons, and the inability to give the ideals of a "new world order" flesh and blood. In order to meet all these challenges at the same time, European unity is a must. There must be a strong overall political framework in place to give room to the growing number of European nation-states, without sacrificing the peace that has characterized Europe since World War II. I think this is obvious to all Europeans. I think it is equally obvious that the structures forming the European Union are the only answer, if we seek practical solutions to our problems. European integration is the way to overcome forty years of division in Europe.

Until now, European integration has taken place only in Western Europe, but that is going to change as the map of Europe changes. The process began eight years ago with roundtable talks in Poland, economic reforms in Hungary, and a new atmosphere in the many international fora that had been established to link East and West. Glasnost and perestroika set a new tune, and suddenly the Conference on Security and Cooperation in Europe (CSCE) became invigorated. We could discuss matters that used to be taboo, such as human rights, minority rights, and individual freedoms. In the summer of 1990 we had the so-called Conference on the Human Dimension in Copenhagen, where all European states from East and West, plus the U.S., Canada, and the Soviet Union, agreed on a new freedom charter, putting individual rights and minority rights in focus.

We witnessed the cracks in the Wall, when East Germans moved from Czechoslovakia through Hungary to Austria and freedom and, ultimately, the fall of the Wall and of one oppressive regime after another. Most were peaceful revolutions, with the exception of the overthrow of Ceaucescu in Romania. The Moscow Putsch in August 1991 was a brief setback, but with its failure came the restoration of freedom and independence in the three Baltic states and then the disintegration of the Soviet Union into a number of new independent states. Suddenly we had a new map of Europe. Created in a surprisingly short span of years, it brings us the important lesson that only fantasy sets the limit to what is possible in Europe. Nevertheless, this new era presents new challenges, and new dangers.

For half a century we Europeans lived in a Europe that was divided into two parts by the iron curtain. From where I grew up in a northern corner of Europe, crossing the iron curtain, only a few kilometers away, was always like entering another world with scary rules of life and an atmosphere of utter hopelessness and desperation. The nuclear threat was something abstract, but the rules of the game were simple and easy to understand, like in a game of checkers. Now things have changed and become far more complicated. Now we're playing a game of chess.

The threat of mutual destruction belongs to a misty past, but other threats have become much more present. Bitter wars were recently fought on our continent in the former Yugoslavia and in the Caucasus region. New actors appeared on the political scene, some with messages that I thought had been buried in the old bloody history of Europe—and certainly not relevant in *my* Europe, my *peaceful* Europe, peaceful in spite of the fact that a cold war had been fought for so many years.

Of course we should not forget that this new situation, confusing and dangerous as it is, has its roots in wonderful and positive developments which took place over a very short span of time: the fall of the Wall, the popular uprisings that dealt away with the old communist regimes, the introduction of democracy and market economies. We must remember that basically we are faced with a *positive* challenge and should deal with it accordingly.

In order to understand today's European Union, you have to understand its roots. In other words, you must know what really lies behind European integration. The process began after World War II when, for the second time in a decade, Europe had been torn apart by war between nation-states. On top of that, Europe was left not only in ruins physically, but divided between two opposing ideological systems.

Out of the despair grew the idea that a united Europe would make war impossible. European statesmen created a practical framework to give this vision flesh and blood. For example, the coal and steel union brought together old foes, Germany and France, in an effort to make the best out of combined resources.

These initial steps led to the Treaty of Rome and creation of the European Economic Community (EEC). The introduction of a political element transformed the EEC into the European Community and, eventually, the European Union. Although this agreement evolved from an arrangement initially dominated by economic issues to one increasingly animated by political concerns, the fundamental objective remained the same: integration should lead to peace and liberty. *That* was always the goal. Economic integration—pooling the resources—was always the means, not the end.

The Treaty of Rome states this concept clearly in its preamble, "pooling their resources to preserve and strengthen peace and liberty." It is very important to keep this in mind: *European integration is first and foremost a political endeavor*. It is so today, and it was so when the Treaty of Rome was signed more than forty years ago. The six founding member states, Germany, France, Italy and the Benelux countries, had indeed been at war with each other several times during the first half of this century. Today, war between member states of the European Union is not only unlikely and unbelievable, but also impossible for practical reasons. How could you establish your own "war machine" when your economies have become so closely integrated? This proves my point: European integration is, first of all, an instrument to preserve and strengthen peace and liberty.

Therefore, it is in full conformity with the original vision that the European Union is now going to be enlarged with the new democracies of Eastern and Central Europe. Greece, and later Spain and Portugal, were admitted when they had rather young and fragile democratic systems, but the purpose was to strengthen their democracies by introducing them to the political and economic demands and possibilities of the larger European integration.

From the original six member states, the European Community grew to nine in 1973 when the UK, Ireland, and Denmark joined. Later, Greece, Spain, and Portugal entered as full members. In 1995 the European Union grew from twelve to fifteen members with the addition of Sweden, Finland, and Austria, and negotiations will start in a few months with probably five to six new applicant countries from Eastern and Central Europe. More countries continue to press for membership, and within a decade or two we will probably have a Union with twenty-five to thirty member states.

To make this vision possible we have to deal with a number of practical and political circumstances—and, as always, the devil lies in the details. While fifteen countries currently comprise today's European Union, the Union exists with essentially the same basic structures as when there were only six members. This situation can greatly hinder decision-making, not to mention the practical problems of conducting business in eleven different national languages (and two alphabets, to make the babelonian confusion complete). As you can well imagine, the interpreters take up quite a lot of room in the bureaucracy—and in the budgets. Every time a new language is added, the increase in the number needed for simultaneous translations follows an exponential curve. Other practical problems include the number of commissioners and the rotation of presidencies. Should Germany as well as Luxembourg both be satisfied with having to wait thirteen years between presidencies in a Union of twenty-six?

There are also questions regarding the balance of voting powers. Presently, small countries have a much stronger relative voting power than big countries. As an example, my own country, Denmark, with only five million inhabitants, holds three votes in the European Council of Ministers; Germany, with eighty million inhabitants, holds ten. This means that one

Dane holds as many votes as five Germans. An enlarged Union will contain quite a number of small states, at least five of them even smaller than my own country, and this will create some problems.

We will have to resort more frequently to majority voting than we do at present in order to avoid paralysis and, if we continue with the present system, we will run into a situation where less than 50 percent of the population in the Union could control enough votes to establish a qualified majority. On the other hand, a group of small and medium-sized countries—for instance the new members from Eastern and Central Europe—could form a blocking minority and possibly blackmail others into concessions. Such a situation would, of course, not be acceptable and certainly not desirable, but you can imagine the trouble when the existing balance changes. We already have headlines shouting, "Big countries squeeze small."

These are all institutional problems, but they contain a lot of political dynamite. Such is also the case when you approach questions involving economic interests. To begin with the most difficult: The Common Agricultural Policy of the European Union needs reform as a precondition for enlargement with countries having exceptionally large agricultural sectors, like Poland and Hungary. Fortunately, the WTO has also called for an extensive overhaul in the Common Agricultural Policy. However, these demands have inevitably led to some resentment regarding enlargement, as have discussions of future structural policies of the Union in which Mediterranean countries fear losing out when new members also need access to structural funds.

Let me finally mention the many problems we are facing with the opening of borders and the need we have to establish an effective common framework to deal with international crime, drugs, terrorism, illegal immigrants, and refugees.

We certainly had a full plate in front of us when the fifteen governments of the European Union began a so-called intergovernmental conference two years ago to set up a new treaty to supplement the Treaties of Rome and Maastricht in preparation for enlargement. The intergovernmental conference concluded this past summer with the Treaty of Amsterdam, and, according to what was agreed when the whole process started, negotiations with the first group of applicant countries will start in January. The treaty was signed earlier this month, October 1997, and is in the process of ratification among member countries, a process likely to drag on until fall 1998. At least three countries are going to present the treaty to a referendum, my own country included, and we will of course have to face the risk that one country will not ratify it, a situation that may cause grave delays in the enlargement process.

We have a total of ten applicant countries from Eastern and Central Europe, but the European Commission has advised that negotiations are to be initiated with only five of them. There are two reasons for this decision: first, the Amsterdam Treaty has not prepared the European Union for enlargement by more than five to six countries at a time; and, second, the Commission has only wait-listed those countries judged unable to meet the criteria for membership within a time span that equals the expected negotiations. The group of countries that have received the green light from the Commission are Poland, Hungary, and the Czech Republic (which were also the first three to join NATO), plus Slovenia and Estonia. Cyprus is also on the list, but here we face a very special problem because of the conflict with Turkey and the de facto division of the country.

The five countries that are to be put on the waiting list by the Commission are Latvia, Lithuania, Slovakia, Romania, and Bulgaria. In the future we should also assume that other countries from the former Yugoslavia will be in a position where they can join the European Union.

It is, of course, most unfortunate if a situation arises where some countries feel they have been rejected. No one expected that all ten applicants could join simultancously, as they are at very different stages in their democratic and economic development. However, we must emphasize to these countries that they are part of a process, much like NATO enlargement, that will eventually lead to their full membership.

A special case in this context is that of the three small Baltic states, Estonia, Latvia, and Lithuania. Of all the countries applying for membership in both NATO and the European Union, they are the only ones that have broken free of the former Soviet Union into which they were forced during the early days of World War II. While it took them half a century to regain their independence, they are still vulnerable because of their geography as well as their history. These countries were not among the first of the old Warsaw Pact members to be invited into NATO, but at the Madrid Summit, heads of states and governments acknowledged that they should be regarded as "aspiring members."

It is hoped that NATO will find ways in which to increase the cooperation with these countries, while simultaneously avoiding a situation in which Moscow might regard the Baltic states as a "sphere of influence." That is where the danger lies—especially after most Western countries, including the United States, used terms like "internal affairs" concerning the war in Chechnya, contrary to both the letter and the spirit of the Helsinki process. It would be very dangerous for stability in Europe if false impressions were created in Moscow regarding the rights of the Baltic states as free and independent states.

With these caveats in mind, all three Baltic countries should be in the first group of new members to the European Union. However, at this point, only Estonia has received the Commission's endorsement. It is important that at least one of them be in that group, because it will "break the ice" and serve as confirmation that the rest of us will regard these countries as equal partners. I still hope that all three of them will be at the table when negotiations on enlargement start in January 1998.

As I have mentioned, the Amsterdam Treaty has not prepared the European Union for enlargement by more than five to six countries because the intergovernmental conference did not succeed in solving the difficult institutional questions I stated earlier. Therefore, the Amsterdam Treaty should be regarded as an intermediate station on the road towards enlargement. Nevertheless, they were able to achieve some progress:

- The new treaty remains committed to the fundamental principles of democracy, liberty, respect for human rights and fundamental freedoms, and the rule of law. These are not just empty words—if a member state violates these principles, it may lose its voting rights.

- The Union rededicated itself to act against discrimination based on sex, racial or ethnic origin, religion and belief, disability, age, or sexual orientation.

- Questions regarding freedom of movement, asylum, and immigration remain intergovernmental issues, but after five years these issues should be dealt with by qualified majority voting, allowing for much stronger and more effective cooperation.

- The European Parliament has been strengthened through a simplification of the legislative procedures.

- Greater openness has been established through enhanced access to documents and information about what is going on within the institutions.

All in all, we find some progress, but not much after fifteen months of work. In the European integration process we have to be content with small steps—as long as they keep us moving in the right direction.

We have certainly run into many unexpected delays and difficulties. Developments in my own country can be taken as an example. The Danes voted "No" to the Maastricht Treaty in 1992, causing much delay in the process, but other countries have also witnessed a growing popular discontent with the European Union. I believe the root of it all lies in the way in which the European integration process has developed over a much longer time span, and I believe that we should carefully search for these roots in order to get the process back on track. It will require that all European institutions live up to the most important challenge facing the Union now: the challenge of creating *an open Europe*—open to our own citizens, open to European states outside the Union, and open to the outside world. Openness is thus, as I see it, the key to the European integration process.

The concept of an open Europe has two aspects. First, the idea refers to openness towards the rest of the world, especially with regard to our closest partners in Europe and North America, and amongst the Central and Eastern European countries. Second, openness also speaks to development internally within the Union, so that democracy and transparency become crucial points. These issues rose to the top of the political agenda in 1992, when it became obvious that things were going wrong in the Community, in areas where we obviously failed to win the support of our citizens when the Maastricht Treaty was presented for ratification in the EC member countries in 1992.

We should keep in mind that the Maastricht Treaty was made during a dramatic change in the European political landscape—and that it was created in order to strengthen the instruments of the Community, making it better equipped to deal with the new situation in Europe. However, in June 1992, first the Danes voted "No" to the treaty, albeit by a very narrow margin, and then in France that following September the vote was "Yes" by an equally narrow margin. After these results, one opinion poll after another demonstrated that other EC countries would run into serious difficulties were they to ask their voters to support ratification.

The Danish and French referendums on Maastricht clearly showed that the people wanted information and influence on EC decisions, *not* that they were against a unified Europe. They reacted against what they regarded as an unacceptable development in the way the Community works. The debate in most other European countries revealed the same sentiment. It was widely believed that the Community had become too centralized, too bureaucratic, and too removed from the lives of ordinary citizens.

I believe something went wrong when we started to combine a number of national regulations as part of the Single Market process. Suddenly the EC was felt in the daily life of the individual citizen and the individual company, and it was often difficult to understand why national bureaucratic rules, which had become known elements in daily life, should now be replaced by silly rules from Brussels.

The speed of integration must be set by the political will of the participants, which reminds me of some clever words said in the very early days of European integration by one of its founding fathers, Robert Schuman: "Europe will not be built in a day, nor to an overall design; it will be built through practical achievements that first establish a sense of common purpose." It seems as though some of this "sense of common purpose" was lost when integration was speeded up in order to respond to the changes in Europe and has, I believe, promoted significantly the widespread notion of the European Community as a haven for bureaucrats and a centralized organization with too little democratic control.

That is why decentralization, participation, openness, information, and democracy have become key concepts in the debate on how to reform the policymaking procedure in the European Union. The lesson we all have to draw from the Maastricht chapter is that we cannot and must not lose the support of our peoples in the creation of a more unified Europe.

This statement leads me to another aspect of "openness."

We are now fifteen member states in the European Union—but more countries are knocking on our door. Enlargement of the Union with the new democracies of Eastern and Central Europe and the Baltic countries is at the top of the European agenda, but we have wasted too much time already in responding to the cries of distress from those regions' new political leaders. They feel that we have left them alone after the party was over, and who can blame them?

After the ecstatic days following the fall of the Berlin Wall, when distasteful regimes disappeared and great speeches were made, came the drab daily routine, with mounting problems and an increasing fear of the unknown. Unemployment, inflation, and a lack of social structures to ease the burdens for the most exposed groups have all led to the kind of anxiety that reminds me of an observation made by the Danish philosopher, Søren Kierkegaard: "Only free men can feel fear because they have to face choices, while slaves are not given that freedom." Suddenly that aspect of freedom became a part of daily life for the people of Central and Eastern Europe, to whom freedom to choose had been denied for half a century.

The verdict of history would be cruel and razor sharp if we did not respond to the challenges posed by the historical events of the last six to seven years. Indeed, I doubt whether our own ethics could survive such a stance. For years we encouraged these countries to cast off the yoke of communist regimes, and now that they have, we cannot back out and sell them down the river when they need our support.

We have to offer them access to our markets—even in sensitive areas like agricultural products, textiles, and steel. We also have to put real life into the prospect of membership in the European Union, including full participation in political cooperation, even before they have developed to where they can respond fully to the requirements of full membership. We have to do so, otherwise we will be trapped in a Catch-22: by withholding full membership until they meet all the requirements, we are ensuring that this situation will never occur.

If popular support for the political and economic reforms weakens, it will constitute a new threat to us all. A return to a totalitarian regime might not bring us back to the old days of East-West confrontations, with its threat of mutual destruction, but it could unleash the nationalistic forces buried in the soil of Europe. We are reminded every day that old nationalistic and ethnic feuds are boiling right under the surface in the former Yugoslavia, in the former Soviet Union, and in a number of Eastern and Central European countries. It is against this somber background that we will have to act in order to support these fragile democracies.

It will be expensive, of course, but we should regard it as an investment in our future. If we should face turmoil in Eastern and Central Europe with new massive movements of refugees and immigrants, the costs will be greater than those needed to prevent it.

One might ask the question: Is the European Union in a position to live up to this challenge? Can we find the political will necessary to handle these tasks, as well as the other looming item on the European agenda, the high and growing unemployment rates?

We have already seen how more immediate concerns have tended to undermine the political will to maintain a policy of free trade. We have experienced violent reactions from groups that have felt victimized by developments in markets—especially in agriculture, where our Common Agricultural Policy is under attack both by the realities of the markets and producers in other parts of the WTO system. There is every reason to believe that similar reactions will occur once we start opening up our most sensitive markets to competition from Eastern and Central Europe.

This is where we need political will—and leadership. It remains to be seen whether the political leaders of the Union can fend off the two big risks that will become obvious after the Maastricht Treaty is finally ratified by all member countries: an inward-looking Community, and a complacent Community.

Europe in the 1990s faces a number of challenges, and the way we respond to them will decide the destiny of our continent well into the next century. Opening up Europe will give us the opportunities to meet the demands that lay ahead.

The Union must not rest on its laurels, nor should the Atlantic Alliance, because "history is not dead." If we believe the reverse, then surely history will resurrect itself.

Let me end by illustrating that notion with a small poem, a so-called "Grook," by our beloved Danish poet and philosopher, Piet Hein:

We think of our age
as the age of all ages
when Man has grown modern at last.
But what other page
among History's pages
was so overburdened with past?

5

EUROPE AND THE BALKANS
The Role of Greece

George Papandreou
November 1999

Distinguished professors, students, ladies and gentlemen: It is good to be back...back to the institution that can be blamed for all the mistakes I have made in my recent political career. If we are to win the next election I might be willing to share some of the credit also...but until then, the blame it is.

All joking aside, it is good to be back at the Weatherhead Center for International Affairs. I've always believed that politics and politicians need to look at issues—at regular intervals—from a fresh and different perspective. Self-knowledge and self-assessment are part and parcel of a democratic process. My associates and I find ourselves in need of a new outlook in the form of constructive criticism. The greatest handicap in policymaking is when critique becomes mundane, routine, and too easy to anticipate. After a while, one tends to be prepared for it and is tempted to disregard it as soon as it hits the newsstand. I therefore cherish the prospect not only of sharing views but also of debating them in this Center after this address.

Today, I have been asked to raise issues about our geographical region and the initiatives Greece has taken within it. I shall not frustrate your expectation, but I would first like to spend some time "setting the stage"; in other words, describing the global situation as we view it from our part of the world.

The Stage

Profoundly significant events have occurred in the past nine months. I need not elaborate. However, allow me to offer you a glimpse of what we in Greece see happening around us.

We have had a war in the Balkans: one community in Kosovo was violently and cruelly forced from its home, in unimaginable conditions and numbers. Another country, Yugoslavia, and to a much lesser extent, Montenegro, was bombed so as to be systematically reduced to economic ruin. Neighboring countries' stability was tested to the full, and the economic and political consequences have engendered new tensions both within and among nations.

Systematic violence also occurred in East Timor. The international community watched in disarray and failed to address the problem until much havoc had been wreaked. Political and moral questions again came to the fore.

In a crisis, we, the international community, tend to revisit some of our most basic principles, and these developments have once again made us struggle with fundamental questions such as:

- How do we understand our world? What are our visions, ethics, and goals? And in this, what are the new roles, weaknesses, and strengths of international organizations?

- How do we view different regions and countries?

- What is the role of the sovereign state within its borders vis-à-vis each citizen and his or her individual rights and responsibilities?

The answer to these questions may differ. Our answers, however, express our view of our societies and our view of ourselves as individuals, as citizens, and as humans.

A few years ago, under the shadow of two world wars and the cold war, these questions did not seem provocative; their answers seemed repetitive and mundane. But today we review them under the light of a growing globalized structure. Economic globalization has been established, but continues to be a powerful ongoing process. Statements by the Chairman of the Federal Reserve do not only affect Greek fortunes invested in the New

York Stock Exchange, they affect equity investments in a Greek winery. Today, we take market relationships for granted.

The word for "market" in Ancient Greece—*agora*—has the same root as the concept of a public speech or speaker, *agorevo*. The speakers of the time, and in fact each and every citizen, could easily communicate with the *demos*, or people, by getting onto a large stone or a marble pulpit and speaking to them. But who is our *demos* in today's global market? Who are the communicators?

It is the political aspects of globalization that will pose the greatest challenges of the new millennium. A law passed in one country might affect the life of a citizen in another. Incidents of racism in one corner of the world might ignite fundamentalism in another. Political upheaval in the Far East might cause a government in Latin America to fall. Citizens of the so-called global village will wish they had a say in the coming U.S. elections; many Americans will instead choose to shun their voting rights.

In this global framework the questions posed above cease to have preset answers, because the role of individuals, citizens, and humans has profoundly changed. So then has the role of countries, regions, and international organizations.

The World Community: A Role for International Organization

Political globalization requires that the world community act consistently. It must be able to represent its global *demos* democratically; and I believe it must make the citizens of the world participants in the political and economic process of transition to a more integrated globalized world. This means, first of all, that international organizations, whether global or regional, military or economic, developmental or humanitarian, cannot respond to similar situations in disparate fashion. Second, in order to maintain global credibility, the international community must develop a set of global principles by which to evaluate and measure itself.

Let me give you an example where this has not happened. By bombing Yugoslavia, the international community, or at least a significant part of it, took a daring stand on an ethical dilemma: it stated that human suffering could not be subordinated to the sovereign state. This stand held the potential of becoming a global principle. Have we followed this principle in other regions? Certainly not. By imposing sanctions on the Federal Republic of Yugoslavia (FRY), the same community reversed its stand. For the purpose of deposing an authoritarian ruler, human suffering was subordinated to other political objectives. The global principle was gone and so was a good portion of the community's credibility. East Timor and Cyprus present clear proof of inconsistency in stated global principles.

Other issues before us present equal if not greater challenges: human rights, mass migration, fetal organ trafficking, cloning, developments in the field of biotechnology, the information society, brain transplants, child pornography. The international community cannot possibly hope to deal with these issues on a national level. They are global issues and require global principles and global institutions. To establish global principles the international community will have to act consistently, collectively, and certainly democratically.

International organizations have often been used to spread democratic institutions, to globalize democracy. I believe they should also be used to democratize globalization. Can you visualize such a role for the United Nations and the International Court of Justice? Can we expand the flexibility of the Security Council? What is the role of the General Assembly—do they not need more of a say? Can we control abuses and waste in FAO, UNESCO and other organizations? Can you picture a truly democratic NATO? If not, then we will fail in stating and protecting global principles.

The Region: The European Union and Southeastern Europe

The need to "democratize globalization" is universal. However, we believe that a regional approach to this goal presents a viable strategy, and that the European Union is itself a regional effort to democratize globalization.

Historical obsession with imposing national authority in Europe is signified by the continuous shift of borders, the number of lives dedicated to defending those borders, and the amount of resources wasted for the purpose of securing an added kilometer of sovereign territory. Almost every one of the member countries, at one time or another, has tried to impose its political will. The resulting devastation has made us change our political objectives.

Today, we in the European Union do not try to change our borders. As much as it may "hurt" our national pride, we have decided it is wiser to live with the ones we have. However, we have made them so permeable that they have ceased to become obstacles, allowing our citizens to "pursue happiness" on either side. Predictably, the resulting multiethnic, multicultural community of the European Union has amplified the potential of the continent.

The breakup of Yugoslavia and the current political situation in Southeastern Europe remind us of the absurdity of our past behavior. A community strongly united by a common experience is now being deeply divided by ethnic hatred. While walls fall in Europe, walls are being raised in the Balkans.

Division after division of Yugoslavia was meant to re-create "secure" historical borders. Today in Kosovo, discussions focus on the division among ethnic minorities. Is this the best solution the international community can muster? Divide each village, each neighborhood, until no ethnic Albanian shares their community with a Serb, until no Christian shares their school with a Muslim? And when we do this, how long will it be before the Albanian clusters around the Balkans dream up Greater Albania again? How long will it be before we dig up dreams of Greater Macedonia, Greater Bulgaria, or Greater Serbia?

Greece has the privilege and responsibility of being a part of several communities of nations and several regions. We belong in Europe and in the Balkans, we belong among the countries of the Mediterranean and the Black Sea, and we are a member of NATO. Our role in all these communities has allowed us to evaluate systems, strategies, and approaches to peace and prosperity. We care about the unification of Europe and have invested our resources in this effort. We care about development in the Black Sea and play a leading role in the Black Sea Corporation. We care about peace in the Middle East and have expanded our role in it through the Athens dialogue. In NATO we have consistently supported its quest for a new identity and believe it can prove to be a force of reason in the coming century.

Etien Balibar writes, and I agree, that wars today require the "demonization" of the opponent, often for marketing purposes. The Yugoslav authorities demonized the Albanians, while NATO governments demonized the Serbs. The problem with this approach is that once this message becomes deeply ingrained among people, the only true end to conflict comes with the extermination of the "demon." The absurdity of this approach results in an even more absurd standoff between an authoritarian ruler and the world community. With Saddam Hussein and Slobodan Milosevic, our record is impeccable: two for two. We, the international community, not they, will appear in history as responsible for the resulting human suffering.

In a continent where the word "extermination" still sends shivers down our spines, we have learned that any form of ethnic "demonization" is unacceptable. So we stopped the violence, stopped the redrawing of borders, and decided to respect them so profoundly that they seem as if they do not exist.

The Individual: Human Rights and Civic Responsibility

Ethnic cleansing, whether brought about by the annihilation of minorities or the redrawing of borders, is often rationalized by the need to protect other individuals and their rights. In several countries, reference to human rights and individual rights laws is used to fend off criticism about weak human rights records. Are we to assume that imposing the same law in two different countries creates the same level of protection of rights? I have found that the level of respect a community shows to its individual and human rights is directly related to its citizens' sense of civic responsibility.

In communities where teachers place the value of education above the value of national identity, girls and boys learn to live in peace. In communities where priests place the value of spirituality over the value of church popularity, Christians, Muslims, and Jews learn to respect each other's greatness. In communities where journalists report the truth, people learn to respect each other's "realities." In communities where doctors exchange blood irrespective of ethnic affiliation, ethnic purity ceases to be a virtue. And in communities where rescue teams are willing to cross borders to save lives on either side, as happened recently between Greece and Turkey, friendships develop. I could add to this list business leaders, service providers and tradesmen, musicians, painters, and filmmakers—every person who affects the lives of others.

I believe the message is simple: Human rights laws cannot alone provide for human rights. Civic responsibility and democratic institutions provide for human rights. Whether in government agencies or nongovernmental organizations, schools or churches, businesses or newspapers, heightened civic responsibility and democratic conscience are the essences behind a civilized society.

In this world, which is moving towards global integration, we need to create structures that will go beyond the democratic deficits of a global market. We need to create regional cooperation, which will allow for the democratic aspirations of the peoples of each country to be expressed, and we need to teach our citizens and societies to make this process their own by redefining their own roles and identities.

Celebrated economist and Nobel laureate Amartya Sen has conclusively shown that no substantial famine has occurred in a democratic country. We believe this is only the beginning of the virtues of democracy and democratic institutions. They stand in the core of our policy.

Southeastern Europe

Having worked and studied in these distinguished halls, you might find what I have stated to be obvious. That has been my objective. For if you judge what I have so far stated as obvious, then I might persuade you to also consider our policy in Southeastern Europe and the greater region around us as obvious.

Our part of the world has always been a center of civilization, democracy, and resistance to totalitarianism. However, it has also spawned great and destructive wars, not least of which was World War I. It is a region of contradiction. While it could be a model of multiethnicity, it has generated some of the most extreme forms of nationalism. A large part of it belongs in Europe, both historically and culturally, but it has yet to prove its will to absorb and embrace the rule of law and the welfare state.

Nevertheless, as people deeply tied to the region, we have learned to be optimistic. Despite successive wars and the appalling crimes and devastation that have swept through much of the Balkans, we sincerely believe that through tragedy new opportunities can arise. These recent testing times have proven a rite of passage to greater wisdom, moderation, and, it is hoped, cooperation. We have emerged from this crisis—and it is not entirely over—with a sobering commitment to cooperation among us. In a place where we still know all too little about each other, or know only our stereotypes, we have been forced to break through them and become much more familiar with each other and more honest about our fears and shortcomings.

These have thus become times of great change in the region. They are also times when Greek foreign policy is moving towards a proactive stand on regional stability and development. The management of our foreign policy in the past crisis, balancing our obligations as members of NATO and the European Union with the reality of belonging to the region, offered

Greece a new role as interlocutor in often-difficult moments. We intend to build on this. How? I will outline our objectives, our principles, and the actions we have taken or intend to take in order to assure our objectives are achieved.

Objective:
A Truly United Europe

Before I state our central foreign policy objective, however, let me explain the standards upon which it is built.

First, we believe that stability in our region is the prerequisite for Greek security, and we define stability to mean the practice of democracy, the strengthening of institutions, the reduction of economic inequalities and the rule of law. Our security lies in being members of the European Union and of NATO. We also believe that the institutionalizing and intensification of genuine democratic practice is the surest way of securing the rights of minorities—the lack of which is one of the greatest threats to international security.

Finally, we believe that these principles apply in our immediate geographical vicinity as much as they do in a global framework. We have strengthened our participation in the international community and thus expanded our interest—from the Middle East to the Baltics, and from Russia to the western Mediterranean. Yesterday, on November 3, 1999, Canada's Foreign Minister Lloyd Axworthy honored our country by offering us a chance to participate in the Human Security Council, a small group of nations including Canada, Iceland, Ireland, and Switzerland, committed to peace and security. We intend to take our message even further.

Our guidelines might sound like dreams. But they are tempered, as is steel, by the fire of living in a region that has seen too much blood spilled in this century and where we have witnessed all too often that saddest of sights, mothers who are condemned to outlive their children. This reason alone, ladies and gentlemen, calls for a radical vision for our region. And our vision for our immediate region is this, and it is simple: Europe will once again be united, in total.

This vision stands as the guiding light in our foreign policy's foremost objective: Every country in Southeastern Europe, from Cyprus to Croatia, from Albania to Turkey, join the European Union with "all rights and all responsibilities pertaining thereto." We see one, sole and unifying path:

from totalitarianism to democracy, from violence to peace, from poverty to prosperity. Each country in Southeastern Europe might stand today on different ground, but they should all be heading in the same direction. There is only one path to becoming part of Europe, and each country should be working with the same objective in mind.

To those of you who think our vision far-fetched I say: "So was a united Europe." We know all too well that to achieve our stated objective we need to do some hard work, but we have no other option. We are prepared, and we have begun.

Principles: The Total Balkan Approach

Before I present you with a detailed strategy for achieving our objective and some insight to the things we have done, I need to emphasize the one basic, overarching principle that we uphold: We believe in what I have often called a Total Balkan Approach—a regional approach to democracy, security, and prosperity.

A Total Balkan Approach requires two conditions. The first is that the international community develops one coherent, consistent, and comprehensive approach to Southeastern Europe. The countries in our region are badly served by mixed signals and, trust me, there have been several mixed signals in our histories. I am thinking of two countries in particular where the international community and especially the European Union and its Northern Atlantic allies are currently acting inconsistently: Yugoslavia and Turkey.

We cannot talk about a Total Balkan Approach and exclude the Federal Republic of Yugoslavia. The country lies in the center of the region and the well-being of its neighbors is interrelated with its own well-being. If we turn our back on its population—and there are healthy parts of the population—we will either break their hopes of becoming part of the European family or, in the worst-case scenario, we will encourage other powers to reach out and help them. This will isolate Yugoslavia for years to come.

Several countries, including officials in the U.S., believe that the European Community must provide Turkey with candidate status—not a candidate status of substance but one of empty promise. They hope that such an event will deter religious fundamentalism and still manage to keep Turkey's Muslim population at a manageable distance from the European continent. We do not share this sentiment. We believe that such a move is designed to preserve a status quo that is unhealthy and vulnerable. Only true democratic institutions and real respect of human rights will deter any religious fundamentalism, and that is why we support a full candidacy for Turkey with all the rights and all the responsibilities attached to it.

The second condition for a Total Balkan Approach is that the countries in the region approach the international community as a region. We need to think beyond borders, with our neighbors' best interests in mind. Their security and prosperity will lead to our security and prosperity.

There is a tendency in many countries of the region to think bilaterally. By this I mean that they search first for the security of a relationship with such centers as Washington or Brussels, often at the expense of building regional relations. This tendency is further nourished by the manner in which multilateral institutions like the EU or the World Bank tend to manage their programs on a country-by-country basis. The long-term risk is that the so-called Balkan policies of these institutions could potentially further Balkanize our region. We need to turn this on its head. We must encourage strategies that create incentives for investment in initiatives and programs that bind the region together indissolubly.

Strategy: Democracy, Security and Development

In Greece we started thinking of regional reconstruction while the war was still ongoing. Unless a plan was put in place for the rebuilding of the region, unless a vision and a strategy were shaped, the population would all too soon return to chaos, fanaticism, and violence. We shared our plans with our counterparts in the European Union. The product of our deliberations is the Southeastern Europe Stability Pact: a comprehensive plan for getting the region back on its feet.

The stability pact addresses three main areas of concern: democracy, security, and development. All too often people tend to focus on development and assume that the other two areas of concern will subsequently improve. This is not going to be the case in our region.

We must first ensure that the fundamental institutional bases of all our societies are strengthened, harmonized, and democratized. Not only must we strive to build effective business communities, we must also standardize the supervision of financial systems in all the countries of the region. The media must not only be strengthened to provide credible reporting to the public, but should be strengthened in such a way that the reporting crosses frontiers and is used by our neighbors' media. Judicial systems are equally in need of such efforts. Unless we start the long process of building strong democratic institutions today, all our efforts will fail, as citizens of our multiethnic communities will continue to feel excluded from the process of developing the region.

Second, we must be aggressive in ensuring that all forms of likely threat to security within and among our countries are dealt with directly, openly, and with vigor. The question of minorities is of fundamental importance. I would warn those who believe that the solution is a redrawing of the Balkan frontiers to suit ethnic boundaries that they are taking the lazy approach. It will have tragic consequences. We live in a region where minorities are abundant. The answer does not lie in new frontiers, but in securing the rights and protection of minorities within democratic systems in existing frontiers.

Security also lies in developing a degree of cooperation among the countries of the region, which will enable them to stave off the explosive consequences of uncontrolled ethnic aspirations. Dreams of "Greater This" or "Greater That" should not be allowed to be fuelled by weak leaders operating in weak democracies. Only if the path to democracy and security is assured will we be able to proceed in the development of the countries in the region.

I do not suggest that we wait until democracy and security are achieved before we proceed with development, but I cannot stress enough that development should not ignore the basic principles I stated above. And so I repeat them:

- Development should focus on projects that benefit the total region;
- Development should focus on projects that promote interregional cooperation; and
- Development should go hand in hand with the building of democratic institutions and the security of the populations in the region.

Implementation: Efforts and Initiatives

I have walked you, admittedly in much detail, through each guiding principle that shapes Greek foreign policy today. Why? We believe that particular stands in a principle-based foreign policy need few explanations—they flow effortlessly from the guiding principles. Even if I do not spell out a particular stand on a particular issue in the region, you will probably be able to infer it by referring to our principles.

We have a stand on Cyprus: we want the country united, peaceful and democratic; we want it multicultural; and we want it to join the European Union.

We have a stand on the Former Yugoslav Republic of Macedonia: we want the country united, peaceful, and democratic; we want it multicultural; and we want it to join the European Union.

We have a stand on Yugoslavia: we want the country united, peaceful and democratic: we want it multicultural; and we want it to join the European Union.

We have a stand on Turkey: we want the country united, peaceful and democratic; we want it multicultural; and we want it to join the European Union.

I think you get the pattern. We have one message, a good and virtuous message, and we support it in every country in our region, for every community in our region. We focus our efforts around the protection of security, freedom, human and minority rights, within the framework of existing borders and international law. We want to help convert the kaleidoscope of races and minorities in the region into an instrument of solidarity, stability, and multicultural cooperation.

We do not see differences among us as a source of fear. We do not see our differences as a trigger for the clash of civilizations. We see them as a fertile ground for the dialogue of civilizations—a dialogue for peace. We work for the day when multiculturalism will inspire creativity in all fields of social life.

We are intensifying our cooperation with all parties, both on bilateral and multilateral levels. Our goal is to ensure that the stability pact is an effective mechanism that will benefit the entire region and, by extension, the whole of Europe. In this context we are developing a number of institutional reforms and proposals. These include the joint appraisal of the individual needs and problems of each country in the region, the establishment and development of mechanisms for interregional cooperation, and the appropriate coordination of these various activities in order to minimize overlap and maximize overall benefits.

In terms of economic objectives, Greece has prepared a comprehensive Plan for the Reconstruction of the Balkans, based on the potential involvement of both the public and private sectors. It focuses on social infrastructure (education, healthcare, housing), economic infrastructure (transport, communications, energy), and production (industry, investment, culture, and trade). We have invited all countries involved to meet and discuss these initiatives, and we are applying pressure on the relevant international organizations to be generous in their support of the economic reconstruction of the region.

It is no coincidence that Thessaloniki, Greece's northern "capital," has been chosen as the administrative center for the stability pact. In the eyes of the people in the region and our European counterparts, Thessaloniki is not only the financial, business, and trade center of the region, it is also a city in a country that took an active, balanced, and fair stand during the turmoil.

Admittedly, even though our message is simple, its practical applications are not. Each country in the region, each community, poses a unique challenge. I will close my address by taking you through some of the major challenges we are actively involved in and the stands we have taken.

In Cyprus, which is well on its way to becoming united with Europe, we are working on building communication between the Greek and Turkish communities. We have no tolerance for the last remaining "Berlin Wall." We want it destroyed not because of our historical association with the island but because it represents an era long gone. It is the last remaining relic of the cold war and has no position in a globalized community. The island's path to the European Union is bound to benefit both communities and to help them build their common future. Our ultimate goal is the island's unification and demilitarization.For Bulgaria and Romania, we act primarily as allies on their path to a united Europe. We help them meet European criteria for membership by sharing our experience. Through bilateral as well as trilateral efforts, we contribute to legislative reforms, the strengthening of democratic institutions, and the promotion of regional cooperation. Our investments in these countries are substantial; through them we help build the open economies that these countries seek.

For Albania and the former Yugoslav Republic of Macedonia, we have initiated several efforts to bring the countries closed together. Minorities' issues have brought them at odds with each other and this has often been explosive. We have begun trilateral meetings and have taken active stands in supporting their economies through private and public investments. We work with them to build democratic institutions, to secure peace within and among them, and to do our best for their economic development.

Our relations with the former Yugoslav Republic of Macedonia are better than ever. We have sided together in most issues during the conflict and have worked together in order to modernize the country's economy. Greek companies have made tremendous investments in the country and have purchased a wide variety of companies such as the largest bank and refinery.

We are working with Albania to help the country develop into a welfare state governed by the rule of law. Albania urgently needs a functional institutional system that will protect the property of all citizens, crush the Mafia-style power structure, and protect foreign investment.

In Yugoslavia we have taken a strong stand against Milosevic's authoritarianism and support the forces of democracy. We provide these forces with everything necessary to build functioning, local democratic institutions. We know the country's shortcomings and we know its capabilities. We know because we were there before the bombs landed, and because we stayed there while the war was going on. We have made a commitment to work hard to keep its population, especially the healthy majority of its population, close to Europe.

We work to guarantee a multicultural society, promote democratization, and support financial development in Kosovo within the structure of the Federal Republic of Yugoslavia (FRY). We believe that a further breakup of the FRY will provoke new conflicts that will destabilize the entire region.

If we do not take precautions to protect the population of the FRY from starvation and poverty, especially as winter approaches, there is a real danger that the coming year will bring another flood of refugees, perhaps in even greater numbers than before. This may well create fertile ground for criminal acts of mass terrorism. We believe that the West should take bolder initiatives and support the European prospects of the FYR—provided, of course, that the country carries out essential democratic reforms and demonstrates the will to follow such a course.

When we speak of a European trajectory of Southeastern Europe, we include Turkey. Naturally, Turkey must "win" a European role for herself. She must make real progress in terms of democratization at home, and show a spirit of cooperation that will enable us to resolve the long-standing issues of Cyprus and the Aegean according to international law.

We believe that our differences with Turkey should not be characterized as bilateral differences. The rule of law, respect for international law, the protection of minority rights, religious and educational freedom, the presence of armed forces on another candidate country's territory—these constitute the basic differences between the democratic ideals of the EU and present-day Turkey. Obviously, these differences concern the EU also.

In the course of the conflict, Greece and Turkey were confronted by the need to communicate on a wide variety of issues. Out of this process emerged a warming between our governments, which led to a dialogue on a number of relatively uncontentious issues such as the environment, tourism, culture, and security and business cooperation. In the last months relations have been given a further impetus by the heartwarming reaction of our two peoples to each other in times of tragedy. Their reaction, which spelled "We want and we can live in peace," is a strong message to both governments. We are trying hard to build on this message.

There have indeed been profound historic differences between Turkey and Greece, and the cycle of reciprocal suspicion has become both paralyzing and dangerous. I believe we are in a new phase. This is not merely a function of circumstance; it fits with our overall principles on which we base our foreign policy. Communication is better than silence: dialogue with substance must substitute for the dialogue of the deaf. The road to that achievement is a long and arduous one, and it requires the profound political courage to take significant steps to meet the stringent requirements of membership in the European Union. We encourage Turkey to engage in this process.

In other words, Greece is calling for a real—not a virtual—candidate status for Turkey. As Turkey fulfills her obligations to the EU, Greece will be in the forefront helping Turkey along in its aspirations to become part of the EU family.

Conclusion

Ladies and gentlemen, there simply is no truth in the saying that we in the Balkans are trapped, that we "have produced more history than we can consume" and that we are prisoners to past conflicts and hatreds. History is not duress unless one makes it so. The challenge to every new generation of Greeks, and the challenge to our neighbors, is to learn from our history—not become slaves to it.

In halls such as these, people have labored over great visions. If promoted by a practical strategy, these visions have helped make the world more democratic, safer, and a little less painful to those in need. In Greece and our extended region, similar aspirations, sometimes great and universal, and more often smaller and local, are helping to build democratic institutions, cement peace, and pave the way to prosperity.

We are building a new vision for our region, slowly but surely. We look forward to the day when Belgrade and Pristina will be an easy bus ride away, when Tirana and Skopja, Athens and Ankara, and of course the two parts of divided Nicosia, will no longer be separated by fear and suspicion, but be joined in peace. Perhaps that day is still far away, but as a Chinese proverb has it, "A journey of a thousand miles begins with one small step."

This step we dared take this year. We dared to imagine the world at the end of a thousand miles. Rigas Fereos, a prominent Greek revolutionary wrote in a constitution for the Balkans more than two centuries ago: "All should be equal with equal rights without prejudice in the Balkans: Christian, Muslim and Jew, Albanian, Slav, Romanian, Bulgarian, Greek, Turk, Armenian, from Bosnia to Arabia."

Today, sixty days before the next millennium, we commit ourselves to keep walking in this direction of a new hope and vision for our world.

PART III

CONFERENCE PROCEEDINGS

6

TRANSATLANTIC RELATIONS
One Year after September 11

September 2002

Session I

Etienne Davignon (Chairman): I would like to begin this meeting by first welcoming Frank Boas, president of the Frank Boas Foundation, for without his generosity and support of the Spaak Lectureships, our continued exploration of European-U.S. relations would not be able to occur.

I have a friend who for the last thirty years teases me each time I give a seminar. He asks, "What are you going to speak about?" I respond that I am going to speak about relations between Europe and the United States, to which he replies, "You have been doing that for the last thirty years; can't you find another topic?" I expect one could, but I believe that over the years the subject has remained topical. With regard to our conference today, the only regret I have is that it is perhaps a little too topical. There's more on the table than any of us would like to consider, and I expect the discussions will reveal a degree of general uncertainty that has never been as high.

Frank Boas: Thank you for your very kind words, Stevie. It's certainly a great pleasure to be back here in Brussels, where I spent nearly twenty-nine years of my life and have so many wonderful friends, many of who are in this room today.

Mr. Chairman, I would like to also thank you and the Spaak Foundation for making this conference possible and for your very warm and, as usual, very good Brussels hospitality. And I would like to also make a very special mention of thanks to François Danis, the secretary-general of the Spaak Foundation, who has worked very hard to make sure that all these wonderful arrangements that we are taking for granted really have happened. You all probably know that François is Paul-Henri Spaak's grandson, and we are very pleased that Antoinette Spaak, who is Paul-Henri Spaak's daughter, is here with us today.

I also would like to thank the Spaak Lecturers for making their original trips to Harvard, not just for a *discours d'occasion* but to present their thinking in a public forum and to interact with professors and students of the Harvard community. I want to extend special thanks to those Spaak Lecturers who are here with us today and who will join in our discussions. I want to thank all of the participants who will animate these discussions. And indeed, a very special thanks to Professor Moravcsik for the excellent paper that he will present to us. For me, this presents a real sentimental occasion because Andy's father was both a classmate and a housemate of mine at Harvard, so I am delighted that he is here.

Mr. Chairman, I would like to suggest that this conference, the preceding ones in 1985 and 1991, the Paul-Henri Spaak Lectures at Harvard, and the publications resulting from these lectures, are in my view a very fitting tribute to Paul-Henri Spaak, a great statesman. As we all know, Paul-Henri Spaak was one of postwar Europe's founding fathers. He devoted the last thirty years of his life to the unification of Europe and its alliance with the United States, and it is fitting that he was often referred to as "Mr. Europe." I have very fond memories of accompanying Fernand Spaak, Paul-Henri's only son, to Harvard in April 1981 to inaugurate the Paul-Henri Spaak Lecture Series. Fernand, following the footsteps of his illustrious father, was a true believer in a United Europe and spent his entire career serving its emerging institutions. Little did we know that his eloquent lecture at Harvard, followed only two short months later by his tragic death, would in effect constitute his intellectual testament and parting thoughts on the partnership between Europe and the United States.

It was Fernand's lecture that set the standard for the tone and the quality for the lectures to follow. I shall always remember that he ended his lecture with the ringing words "Europe Now." As we left Harvard in a taxi to catch our respective flights home, I turned to Fernand and I said, "You know, I think your father and my father would have been pleased with what happened at Harvard here this week," and he replied with his warm smile, "I think you're right." That was the last time I saw my friend.

Mr. Chairman, it is my hope that the next generation of leaders and scholars on both sides of the Atlantic will maintain an interest in European-American relations, which these lectures, conferences, and publications have attempted to encourage and foster. I look forward to two very stimulating days. Thank you, Mr. Chairman.

Etienne Davignon: Thank you, Frank. It is quite clear that perhaps no major historical event has so depended on the contributions of certain individuals and on diplomatic relations between individuals than European-American relations. My European colleagues here know how true that is. Why did something become possible at one moment, when it was impossible thirty seconds earlier? The situation did not change, nor did the arguments, but somehow the chemistry between the decision-makers changed. I think it is also true in the relationship with the United States. If one were to revisit the historical record, there has never been as benevolent a major power in the world in terms of its relations with some of its partners.

It is my pleasure to turn our attention to Professor Andrew Moravcsik's paper that we have in front of us, which is fascinating to read. I think it would be best if Professor Domínguez would be kind enough to speak first and then we will carry on.

Jorge Domínguez: Thank you, Mr. Chairman. On behalf of the Weatherhead Center for International Affairs, I want to express my gratitude to you personally and to the Spaak Foundation for inviting us to be here as well as to the Frank Boas Foundation, and of course in particular to Frank Boas for his generosity and his foresight in organizing these activities and particularly this conference, "Transatlantic Relations One Year After September 11". I would like to add just two comments: one about the Center for International Affairs, the other about the context of the Spaak Lecture series.

The Center for International Affairs was founded in 1958 by Robert Bowie and Henry Kissinger. It was founded to a large extent on three certainties. They were certain that the world was uncertain and that fundamental research was therefore an important feature of helping to prepare ourselves for the circumstances in which we live. Second, they were certain that the relationship between Europe and the United States and the issues within Europe were also of fundamental importance. Thus the Center at its founding was both Europeanist and Atlanticist. And third, they were certain that research and thinking on international affairs was too important to leave to academics alone. This conference is a very appropriate part of that tradition as is the Fellows Program that brings a number of very distinguished practitioners of international affairs, some of whom are in this room, to the Center for a year. The Spaak Lecture series is also particularly salient in that context, as it brings distinguished Europeans to speak at Harvard. The Spaak Lecture series was noteworthy at the time it was founded, and the circumstances of the early 1980s—as Frank Boas just said—are extraordinarily pertinent today.

Let me invite you to recall some of the circumstances of U.S. relations with Europe in 1981 and in the early 1980s. There was a new president of the United States, a Westerner, the Republican governor of a large state who enjoyed wearing cowboy boots and was proud of not being an intellectual. There was renewed salience with regard to military issues and discussions between the United States and the governments of Europe. Relations between the Social Democratic chancellor of Germany and the president of the United States were difficult personally and politically. The prime minister of the United Kingdom was engaged in a balancing act between the Atlantic Alliance and Britain's relations with Europe and enjoying European solidarity in 1982 at a moment of war with Argentina. The United States launched a preemptive military attack, on the unilateral authority of the president of the United States, without the consent of Congress, without any prior authorization by any international institution (certainly not the United Nations Security Council), on a country we have all forgotten—Grenada. The details differ between then and today but the analytics of the issues are really quite precise. The president of the United States labeled a major adversary an "evil empire," a word that has now reappeared in the diplomatic vocabulary of the president of the United States, and there was more than a whiff of war in the air. There was a process of weak, difficult consultation at best between the United States and its European allies other than the United Kingdom, and the question of the impulses of the United States to act alone and to act militarily was very much on the table.

The world today is of course not the same as it was in 1981: the cold war has ended, the European Union has both deepened and enlarged, the North American Free Trade Agreement has significantly changed the international economic relations of the United States, Canada, and Mexico, and September 11 has occurred. Yet the question of the propensity of the

United States to stand alone or to act alone is now quite long-standing. It was an issue in World War I; it was an issue on the eve of World War II; and it was an issue in the immediate aftermath of World War II, as we thought through the questions of the Atlantic Alliance again. How to engage, how to harness, and how sometimes to contain the United States for its own good as it acts internationally are questions that have persisted and therefore justify continued discussion. It's significant for Europe; it's significant for the United States; it is at the heart of what the Center for International Affairs has attempted to do under my predecessors and now; and it is essential for the better world that we hope to construct for our successors. Thank you, Mr. Chairman.

Andrew Moravcsik: Thank you very much. It is a privilege to present to you an exceptionally distinguished set of politicians and public intellectuals, the thirteenth through seventeenth Spaak Lecturers: Lord Roy Jenkins, Lord Ralf Dahrendorf, Uffe Elemann-Jensen, Ambassador Renato Ruggiero and George Papandreou. I take particular pleasure in doing this in honor of, and in the city of the legendary founding father of modern European unity, Paul-Henri Spaak.

You will find in your packet a lengthy paper containing a detailed analysis of those five Spaak Lectures. Today, I propose only to highlight some broader points taken from them that might help spark a transatlantic discussion here in this room, and to focus on one issue that I think is close to the heart of each of those papers. That issue is this: In an era when the ideology of European Federalism is now weaker than it has ever been, how are we to justify European integration? I don't mean to imply that European integration itself is in a crisis—Europe has probably never had such a successful decade as the last, but the *belief* in European integration does face a crisis. That's why both the talk and the paper are entitled "Europe without Illusions."

In reading and rereading the five lectures in this spirit, I am repeatedly reminded of the saying, "It's tough to make predictions, particularly about the future." Let me say parenthetically, being a scholar doing due diligence, that there is a revealing transatlantic paternity dispute about who actually first said, "It's tough to make predictions, especially about the future." Now, if you ask any red-blooded American who said this, they will immediately answer that it was the baseball player Yogi Berra. For the Europeans in the room, Yogi Berra was the catcher for the New York Yankees from the 1940s to the 1960s and one of our greatest twentieth century vernacular philosophers. Dozens of his sayings have passed into common wisdom. But ask any European who said, "It's tough to make predictions, particularly about the future," and what you'll hear is that it was the famous Danish physicist Niels Bohr. I am not sure whether it was the Italian-American sportsman or the European intellectual. (Though as a scholar, I think the Europeans have a better case.) Maybe they both said it. In any event, let's call it the "Berra/Bohr" principle, which this paper will amply illustrate. It captures the need to be modest about assessing the transatlantic relationship in European integration in any point in time. It's changed considerably over the years and predictions are always risky. I think if Paul-Henri Spaak had been here to see the twists and turns over the last fifty years, he would have been repeatedly surprised by the workings of the Berra/Bohr principle.

One sees this principle at work first in the topics chosen by the Spaak Lecturers between 1994 and 1999. They capture something of the European mood in the late 1990s, and are quite different from the topics addressed by speakers from 1981 to 1994. Previous speakers focused primarily on transatlantic relations—itself a change from the first five lectures in the early 1980s, which focused almost entirely on the EU. One can see this in Manfred Woerner's lecture in 1992, which focused almost entirely, as one might expect, on the future of NATO, the need to adapt out-of-area disputes, and similar issues. He categorically states (demonstrating the Berra/Bohr principle) that Europe and the United States will now come together in the Atlantic Alliance as never before and stay that way.

Secondly, whereas the Spaak Lecturers preceding the 1990s focused on security matters, as was normal in the cold war, the five speakers we are discussing here gave more balanced attention to social and economic interactions. Ruggiero's contribution is an example: he examines the economic relationship between regional institutions like the EU and the multilateral system. None of them could predict (again the Berra/Bohr principle) that September 11 would suddenly put security issues back onto the agenda and that the resulting tensions, as Professor Domínguez accurately described, would resemble those of the cold war.

I am sure that transatlantic relations will be the topic of much discussion today, but I am going to stick to the more European-centered focus of the lectures we are discussing. Most striking in that context is the way these five speakers approach the question of European integration. Each quite sincerely professes to be European, and yet all are to a greater or lesser extent hypothetically or concretely critical of some aspect of European Union policy. Lord Dahrendorf and Elemann-Jensen are quite fundamentally critical of what Europe is up to. Neither could be called Euroskeptics, but the fact that they dared to fundamentally criticize Europe is something new. For fifty years, respectable politicians, at least of the center and of the six original EU members, never questioned the legitimacy of fundamental elements of European integration to go accepted, whereas these lecturers focus on it immediately.

This was perhaps in large part because over the years many saw geopolitical imperatives—be it the democratization of Germany and Italy, the communist menace at home and abroad, the armed presence of American military power—create a kind of unspoken permissive consensus of public and elite opinion about Europe, which permitted the political parties that favored Europe to move forward with narrow or economic issues of interest to producer groups. The future of Europe was left to prominent statesmen, Spaak being a noble example, who dealt with the various problems more quietly. But this quiet, elite-driven style of EU politics came to an end a decade ago. The old fundamentals of European integration were questioned in the context of referendum, Constitutional Court decisions, and public opinion. That is what you see reflected in these five Spaak Lectures.

Taken together, these lectures cast doubt on almost every core belief of the generation of Paul-Henri Spaak: the necessity of integration to prevent war in Europe, the need for Europeanism as a defense against foreign extremism, the inevitability of spill-over into ever expanding areas, the destiny of the EU to become a centralized federal state, the conception of EU officials as impartial administrators of common interest, and the general existence of a higher purpose that justifies the EU's lack of traditional democratic accountability via elections and a strong parliament. All that is called into question by one or more of these speakers. It would not have been, nor was it, called into question by these kinds of speakers ten or twenty years before. Again following the Berra/Bohr principle, I think Spaak would have been quite surprised by the depth of the current discussion in Europe about the legitimacy of European integration.

In a widely read book, Oxford don Larry Siedentop asks, "Where are the Madisons for Europe?" But a more appropriate question would be, "Why are there so many Madisons in Europe?" Everybody in Europe is a James Madison—including most major politicians, commentators, philosophers—and political scientists as well. There is no other place and time in the world history where there has existed as rich and as lengthy an elite debate about constitutional reform as what we have seen in Europe over the past decade. This debate has revolved around the issue about how European integration can be justified in an era where the reflexive political assumptions of anticommunism or European federalism do not hold. One might even call them myths or illusions—hence the title of this presentation, "Europe without Illusions."

Perhaps even more novel than the need to justify, and difficulty of justifying, European integration, it is striking that among these five Spaak Lecturers are notable liberal figures, notably Lord Dahrendorf and Elemann-Jensen, who are uncomfortable with the EU as an institution aimed at "ever closer union." They are concerned about the future of the EU not so much because they are afraid it will stop but because they are afraid it will move forward. They think integration has gone too far too fast and perhaps too far, and they believe that if it continues to deepen the resulting stresses will create inefficiency, spark conflict, deepen the democratic deficit, derail plans for enlargement, and perhaps even trigger a collapse. Dahrendorf goes so far as to hold the belief in political union a fatal flaw, an obstacle rather than a motive for real political cooperation.

Looking back today, five to seven years later, I think we have a number of reasons to be more optimistic than these prognosticators were—again illustrating the Berra/Bohr principle at work. Now that historians have access to the primary documents and confidential records for the period of the 1950s and the 1960s, an era when the European project was getting started, they are learning more about the motivations of those that started it. Historians generally find that European politicians have always been more pragmatic and more focused on commercial and economic advantages than was previously thought, and less concerned with promoting democracy, preventing another Franco-German war, creating a bourgeois coalition against domestic and international communism, or realizing the ideal of a united Europe.

This pragmatic turn in European integration started, I believe—and here I speak as a historical scholar of integration—quite early. The old conception of European unity primarily to prevent war or to oppose communism was already in trouble in the mid-1950s. Fifty years later, it is easy to forget what a decisive break occurred between the European Coal and Steel Community (ECSC) of 1952 and the European Economic Community (EEC) of 1957. When discussions began in 1955 about a customs union, Spaak and Monnet were much more interested in carrying on in the spirit of the ECSC by regulating major strategic sectors that could support warfare, notably transport and atomic energy. Within a matter of days, European economic and business leaders, who had resented the meddling of the ECSC from the start, had vetoed any such proposal.

The proposal for the customs union, which actually came from the Dutch Foreign Minister Willem Beyen, was accepted by Monnet and Spaak with great reluctance as a quid pro quo to keep these other more political, more geopolitical projects going. Spaak, as ever, adopted quickly. Monnet did not, and secretly visited Adenauer several times between 1955 and 1957, desperately begging him to kill the customs union project. Monnet did so not just because he believed (steeped as he was in French domestic politics) that it was politically difficult to achieve the customs union, but also because he thought trade liberalization—as opposed to working on strategic sectors that were highly regulated—was by its very nature apolitical and would not contribute much to the broader goal of political union.

Again we see the Berra/Bohr principle at work: One never knows what the consequences are going to be. In the end of course, both Spaak and Monnet reluctantly supported the EEC—and Monnet was even instrumental in securing its passage through the French parliament. Transport cooperation and atomic energy cooperation persisted in only symbolic forms, then died a quiet death. Yet the customs union was a great success. Why? Because it turned out that a more market-oriented and less political conception of integration was in fact more viable. Because politicians were pragmatists through the years. Because the EU as it emerged was the only arrangement acceptable to major economic interests. And, above all, because once in place, the customs union and later the single currency have created vested economic interests that assure continued support over time.

We see the same lesson—pragmatic economic concerns are more important than ideological or geopolitical motivations—time and time again in the history of European integration. Historians now acknowledge that Macmillan chose Europe primarily for commercial reasons. We know also that De Gaulle vetoed the British bid not so much to make a transatlantic point about NATO or Anglo-Saxon dominance, but above all to protect French farmers. We know that the Single European Act of the 1980s was as much or more the result of concern about economic "Euro-sclerosis," in fact so brilliantly set forth in the Commission by Davignon, more than the federal schemes of Spinelli. And so on down the line to the present.

So, my broader historical point is this: We learn from the Spaak Lecturers and from recent historical literature that broad political claims for European integration and the ideologies about them—about the role of European integration in promoting democracy, overcoming centuries of warfare, opposing Soviet expansion, and bolstering centrist political beliefs—may have been exaggerated. They helped to create public support, but they were not essential to the European project.

A stress on commercial interests is often viewed as a sort of covert Euroskepticism, but in fact is a sort of Eurooptimism, because it means that the basis of European integration is solid and permanent even in the face of a certain amount of ideological skepticism about the broader European project. One might even say that the real Euroskeptics are those who believe that the EU is built on idealism alone. The *true* believers in Europe, among whom I would include myself, are those who believe the EU has become so ingrained in the decentralized interests of European civil society that European nations can no longer walk away, even if their publics wanted them to. And there are promising, substantive, practical, functional projects to move ahead today. One example, I think the most promising one that people speak of now, is in the area of former Third Pillar activities: immigration and police powers. Another is the coordination of non-military and low-intensity foreign policy instruments. Such proposals make a lot of practical sense after September 11 and even though these are politically delicate issues, European countries appear to be moving ahead in a modest way.

But back to the Spaak Lecturers. All are skeptical about these kind of projects, not just because they read the history in a different way than historians do, but because they also have a different analysis of what's going on now in Europe. And again, Dahrendorf and Elemann-Jensen in particular, and at times Ruggiero, believe that there may be contradictions between a specific direction that the EU takes in deepening and broadening European and Western values, especially free markets, deeper cooperation, and democratic legitimacy.

Let me present and address each of their challenges in turn.

The first potential disadvantage that concerns the Spaak Lecturers is whether Europe deepening will raise the prospect of greater European protectionism. Viewed from Ruggiero's prestigious perch in Geneva, there is a potential conflict between regional integration and global trade liberalization. He points out that up to now integration has been relatively benign, although he does note that of the 108 regional agreements to have been reported to GATT over the years, only six are consistent with GATT rules, and the EU is not one of them. He does suggest that deepening could push Europe in the direction of there being a stark choice between regional and global cooperation.

With the passage of nearly a decade since Ruggiero's prognosis, however, this tension between regionalism and globalization seems a bit overdrawn. The Single European Act and the single currency have been implemented with minimal disturbance to global trading and financial systems. Agriculture policy is now, as then, a problem, but there is every sign that a new trade round may actually address some of these issues. So, again the Berra/Bohr principle: If these lecturers addressed reasonable concerns from the perspective of the mid-1990s, it now seems that Europe has surmounted at least some of the worst prospects of protectionism.

There is, however, a second concern: fragmentation of the EU. A number of the lecturers worry, as do many Europeans today, that differentiating among states within the EU, with deepening cooperation only among those who are already in the Union, may create conflict and undermine the overarching project of enlargement. Dahrendorf is again the most concerned: he fears political nonviability shocks derailing the transition to the EMU and massive domestic unrest. My distinguished Harvard colleague, Martin Feldstein, went so far as to predict the prospect of war as a result.

It's true that in Europe we see more and more open and flexible arrangements; meaning effectively that countries singly or in groups can opt in or out of policies in the social, monetary, foreign defense, environmental, immigration, air transport and agricultural areas. Long transition periods will exacerbate this when enlargement comes about. It's striking that fifteen years ago, these kinds of flexible policies were anathema, uttered only by Margaret Thatcher. Today they are Euro-orthodoxy, with nice names like "flexibility" and "enhanced cooperation." (What would George Orwell have thought of this barely noticeable rhetorical reversal?)

Yet, surely the massive disintegration and exclusion that Dahrendorf predicted have not come to pass. Indeed, this sort of harsh critique is simply not viable. A year before the governments are likely to decide on a "big bang" enlargement of five to eight countries, it appears that deepening and widening can be and have in fact been reconciled to an extent that I think surprises most people. Even the single currency, the domestic political problems in Britain and Denmark aside, now appears rather benign and conflict free, and the number of members has increased—even if we have to wonder whether it is wise public policy.

To summarize, the first two concerns are protectionism and fragmentation—and neither seems warranted.

Yet there is a third concern, which I think we need to take more seriously: this is the threat of popular discontent. A number of lecturers and many Europeans today complain that the deepening of European integration exacerbates the so-called "democratic deficit" in Europe. Democratic legitimacy is of course the major issue in Europe today. It's the primary reason member states gave for calling a Constitutional Convention, and thus it is fitting that my discussion of these five Spaak Lecturers should close with a discussion of it.

Today, the EU is widely viewed as democratically illegitimate, and it's not hard to see why. Only the relatively weak European Parliament is directly elected and its elections are desultory affairs. At the powerful European Commission in Brussels, Eurocrats appear to rule. One does not need to be an anti-globalist or a Tory Euroskeptic to have misgivings about a system run by travelling technocrats always on a train back and forth to Brussels. This odd form of governance gives rise to fears of "bureaucratic despotism" by a super state in Brussels, as Larry Siedentop, a don at Oxford University, recently put it in a much celebrated book.

Ultimately, however, I believe the threat of democratic illegitimacy, like the threats of protectionism and fragmentation, is misleadingly exaggerated. It is exaggerated because it fails to point the EU in a broader context. When compared to the member states with which it shares power in a symbiotic relationship, the EU is in many ways a very limited polity, the opposite of a "super-state". Just consider the following: The EU has no power to tax and its spending is capped at three percent of national levels—with no prospect for more. All the policies that voters care about most—social welfare, pensions, education, decentralized infrastructural investment—remain almost exclusively in the hands of national governments. If "taxation without representation" defines tyranny, as the American founders had it, then European institutions with such limited fiscal means can hardly be criticized.

The EU has a similarly meagre administrative capacity. It has no autonomous police or military, and it employs fewer officials than a modest European city. EU regulations must ultimately be reformulated and administered by national authorities. Democratically elected national governments dominate EU policymaking, and no legislation is possible even under the most permissive circumstances without at least seventy percent or so of their weighted votes, which is nearly the majority you need to amend the American Constitution, which, I remind you, has happened only twenty or so times.

Policymaking takes place under the scrutiny of fifteen governments, each jealous of its prerogatives, and that makes it transparent. Furthermore, without fiscal discretion, politics in Brussels remains much cleaner and more transparent than most, if not all, European states. The exception proves the rule: Madame Edith Cresson had a long career in France, but she did not last long in Brussels.

While European officials enjoy exceptional autonomy and some confidential prerogatives on a narrow range of issues—central banking, constitutional adjudication, civil prosecution, oversight of certain safety regulations and perhaps trade negotiations—such functions are those that are commonly left to technocrats in many countries, who are viewed as more expert, impartial and representative of the common good. I would therefore argue that it is a mistake to think that Europe should try to become more democratically legitimate by publicizing and opening up its activities to democratic participation. Of the five most salient issues in Europe—health care provision, education, law and order, pension and social security policy—none is primarily an EU competence. By contrast, the issues in which the EU specializes—trade liberalization, monetary policy, nontariff barriers, and the possible exception of environmental policy—tend to be areas that do not inspire electorates. This may help explain why European citizens fail to exploit even the limited opportunities they have to influence EU politics.

If the EU does not deal with salient issues, then the real question underlying the "democratic deficit" debate is this: If there were real European parties, real European elections, real European debates, *what would they be about*? I think that is a more difficult question to answer than most people who promote democratic reform in Europe believe it to be. Recent experience with referenda and parliamentary elections in member states give us an answer. If you ask citizens to make complex choices on the basis of issues on which they do not have strong substantive interests, one encourages an informationally impoverished and institutionally unstructured deliberation, which encourages unstable plebiscitary politics. In short, you get political chaos. And a typical result is the recent Irish referendum on the Nice Treaty in which public opinions swerved by a large margin (10-15%) at the last minute in response to a minor incident in the Commission. The implications are clear: European integration is likely to remain an elite process for the foreseeable future. Existing EU institutions, even without a transcendent geopolitical and idealistic justification, are healthy and legitimate. If it isn't broke, don't fix it!

Let me conclude by defying the Berra/Bohr principle and advancing my own prediction. While the stock of *grands projets* that are both desirable and feasible is perhaps depleted, substantive cooperation in areas like Third Pillar matters is likely to advance incrementally. This means that, without any fundamental functional impetus to reform, the current constitutional order of the EU is very likely to be the constitutional order which governs Europe for the foreseeable future. The treaties of Amsterdam and Nice failed to alter its structure significantly and, despite the attempt to turbo-charge the Constitutional Convention with Madisonian rhetoric, few believe it's likely to achieve a lot more. It might seem paradoxical that popular criticism of the EU should arise just when it seems to be so successful at generating policy outcomes and it has reached a satisfactory constitutional equilibrium. But I think there is a deeper logic at work here, because it is precisely when a polity is stable and healthy that its supporters trust themselves to become critics.

The generation of Paul-Henri Spaak would not have dared, even if they had been so inclined, to voice the criticisms we have been discussing here. The current generation of Spaak Lecturers considers it their civic duty to do so. It should be encouraging to us that debates about the future of Europe, like deliberations in the European Parliament, reflect fundamental splits about the proper purposes of government—often splits between liberals and social democrats, as the diverse Spaak Lectures make clear. This suggests that the EU, as Paul-Henri Spaak would have hoped, is becoming a normal mature polity. And that, ladies and gentlemen, is the most promising trend of all. Thank you very much for your attention.

Etienne Davignon: Thank you very much, professor. I think you have confirmed another truth, that the best analysis on Europe usually comes from the United States. I think we will first get the reactions from Frans Andriessen, Jean François-Poncet, and Renato Ruggiero, not for intellectual reasons, but simply because of the practical reasons you mentioned.

Frans Andriessen: Let me first say that I would like to express my thanks to Professor Moravcsik for his excellent analysis of the situation. I have to admit that my Spaak Lecture dates from the time that we had "Europe with Illusions," and now we are living in a Europe without illusions. Nevertheless, at the end of your presentation, you offered some encouraging remarks on what could be the further development of the European integration process. It was not my intention to go deep into internal European matters, but to say a few words on transatlantic relations.

I have to say that while I finished my Spaak Lecture in 1990 with some optimistic words on the relationship between the United States and the European community, if I had to give the lecture today, my finish would be perhaps less effusive than it was at that time. The reason for this is that it is my personal conviction that the relationship between the United States and the EU is in a very critical state—perhaps even more critical than we believe when we look at the many diplomatic meetings and institutions we have created since the 1990s, and when we see how consultation has continuously developed.

But the world has completely changed since the early 1990s. That time was characterized by two superpowers, and the European community more or less in between, with some promising prospective changes. For instance, the Comicom was coming to an end, and the Eva countries were trying to fit in the economic constellation of the European Union. Moreover, the countries of Central and Eastern Europe were trying to find their place within the democratic institutions of Western Europe and had begun to discuss the letters of enlargement and accession to the European Community. We even had the question of whether *glasnost* and *perestroika* really were compatible with the authoritarian system in the Soviet Union. I raised these issues in my lecture in 1990. The European Union was in between. We negotiated with the United States at that very moment of the first transatlantic declaration, rapidly followed by a more or less comparable declaration with Japan and Canada. With the Soviet Union, we were negotiating an agreement of cooperation and economic development, which positioned the European community between the world's two main powers.

None of that exists anymore. We are living now with one superpower, and it is perhaps due to that fact that the situation is unbalanced. There is no reason, it seems, for dialogue. There is one main power, which is invincible, but after September 11 not untouchable or invulnerable. I think that these two elements, the fact that we have one superpower and the uncertainty of our very existence, provide one of the reasons why relationships between the United States and its former allies are changing or have changed fundamentally. And I don't believe that we on this side of the Atlantic or those in the United States appreciate what has happened since September 11.

We are now living in a world with one mega power—the European Union being to a certain extent an economic superpower but in political aspects a dwarf—and I was a bit surprised that your analysis didn't mention the lack of the political development in the European Union. When you consider our reactions to what the United States is doing now with the International Criminal Court and our reactions to the ongoing discussions over Iraq, you see that instead of the commitment of consultation between the European Union members, every country is taking its own position. That did not exist in the 1990s. But that balance no longer exists, and there is now this unknown and undefined global power—terrorism—which is a dangerous element in our international relationship.

As far as Europe is concerned, it is important to note that we are enlarging at a very rapid speed. Some people say it is too rapid, that we are not sufficiently prepared to absorb all the elements and all the implications of such an unprecedented enlargement. We will have to redefine our relations with our neighbors. And we will have new neighbors. Russia, Ukraine and Belarus will be neighbors. I do not know whether Belarus will have a great impact, but the other two will. Turkey is now a member candidate, which means we will have neighbors in the Middle East. We have not yet defined the implications of that enlargement in geopolitical terms, and I am not sure that others in the world are making the analysis either. It is quite clear that in redefining our relationship with countries such as Russia, there will also be a redefinition of our relationship with the United States—not necessarily in a negative sense but perhaps in a more conscious sense, in a more European sense. I think that the Europeans and the Americans will have to recognize how this will affect the future relationship between the United States and the EU. I finished my lecture in April 1990 on a very positive note saying that the U.S. and the EU were not drifting apart, but drifting together. Now I see a risk that we might drift apart.

Etienne Davignon: Thank you, Frans. In the European methodology there is a need for a special balance between Germany and France, and the need for leadership. What strikes me in what has been said so far is the absence of competition inside Europe for the European leadership. Is this due to a lack of vision, a lack of ambition? I don't know, but it is one of the factors we have to reckon with.

Jean François-Poncet: Thank you. I am not going to comment on the brilliant presentations of the previous speakers, especially Professor Moravcsik, because it deals with internal developments in Europe. I will instead limit my comments to the relationship between Europe and the United States.

If I had to summarize transatlantic relations, I would say that they are very strong—practically indestructible—but troubled. They have remained troubled over the decades but they have recently become fragile. It goes without saying that Euro-American relations during the cold war were dominated by the threat from the Soviet Union and, because of that, the alliance appeared to be indestructible. Everyone on both sides of the Atlantic was aware of the fact that there was no alternative. Regardless of the bones of contention—and there were quite a number of them—safety and freedom for Europe inevitably prevailed because they also meant safety and freedom for the United States. That situation changed fundamentally after the end of the cold war. The Berlin Wall fell in 1989–1990 and everything changed. Has September 11 introduced a change, too? Personally, I don't think so.

I think that September 11 simply highlighted a change that started back at the end of the cold war and has been with us for some time. What has changed is that safety and security in the United States does not necessarily correspond with safety and security in Europe, where Asia has replaced the EU and China has replaced the Soviet Union as potential adversaries. Nevertheless, the alliance has stood because of the good will on both sides of the Atlantic. Nobody wanted to put an end to the alliance; although it had lost its purpose but everyone thought it should be sustained. The American military presence in Europe was kept to a minimum, but Western Europe still relied on that military presence, as was demonstrated by the war in Yugoslavia. We could not have done anything without the Americans.

With regard to defense in Europe, the United States did not oppose these initiatives, provided that they took place inside NATO and under its leadership. Mr. Andriessen previously mentioned another concern of the United States, which was to have greater influence in Russia in order to have a say in the fate of the former Soviet Union's nuclear arsenal.

Against this backdrop appear a number of disputes between the Americans and the Europeans, and they have become more serious. Economic disputes include the European agricultural policy, the aeronautics industry (civil and military), and the competition policy of the EU. In terms of political disagreements, the Middle East has always been a bone of contention between the United States and Europe, including the Declaration of Venice draft. The same can be said about the differing policies with regard to Iraq and Iran, as well as the various positions on the death penalty, abortion, and energy. Despite all these conflicts—drug trafficking, Islam, and nonproliferation—there is still a convergence of interests between the U.S. and Europe, which has kept the alliance alive.

Now I'd like to turn to another question: Has September 11 really changed things?

The first response is that it is far too early to tell. Yet I think we can make some initial observations.

In the wake of September 11 we witnessed something rather important: the immediate reflex of solidarity that was felt all over the European population. I am the chairman of a small township in the South of France, and everyone on our staff had two little flags—an American flag and a European one—and we had five minutes of silence in remembrance of this day. This solidarity was also expressed with a proposal made to the United

States; The American reaction to terrorism has been to eradicate terrorism by force, pursuing al Qaeda networks all over the world, and destroying their financial assets. But terrorism has deeper roots—racist, philosophical, and economic—and if we don't tackle the roots, we will never be able to eradicate it. This implies that we have problems in the Middle East, where the geographical roots of terrorism are to be found.

Europe is also concerned about the tendency of the U.S. toward unilateralist positions. Unilateralism is too close to isolationism, which is unacceptable in today's world. This raises a whole series of problems, like the International Criminal Court and the nonratification of the Comprehensive Test Ban Treaty. With regard to Iraq, this is another area in which a crisis is emerging between the United States and Europe. Everything will depend, of course, on the way the Americans act. Numerous voices in the United States have asked the president to turn to the United Nations Security Council first, and to ask for a new mission of experts to be sent to Iraq. But is the president going to follow their advice? I don't know. I think it will be difficult for him not to, but he could perhaps just ignore their advice. Whatever the result of these inspections might be, we see that his aim is to change the regime in Iraq. Henry Kissinger wrote in a *New York Times* article that this represents a radical change. Kissinger noted that this change is not inevitable, rather it fits on a continuum starting with the Treaty of Westphalia, which stated that the basis of life for Europeans was in noninterference in other countries' affairs. We had already accepted that Protestants were to remain Protestants, and that Catholics were to remain Catholics.

Davignon mentioned that France has been both the bad pupil and the good pupil in Europe, depending on the times. But the bad pupil of the Atlantic community is Germany! One shouldn't forget it. This has been one of the reasons of a conflict between Germany and France. When de Gaulle proposed a bilateral treaty between France and Germany, its purpose was to make fun of Great Britain and the U.S., who had refused the proposal for a directory of three states—France, the UK and the United States—which de Gaulle proposed just after he came back to power. So today we see something surprising. We see that Germany refuses any participation in an American operation in Iraq, even if NATO or the UN agrees. This is not the case with France.

The break, if it occurs, is entirely unexpected. I think it would be dramatic and it is the last thing that I would ever hope for, but there is a growing divergence of sensibilities and attitudes toward international actions between the Americans and the Europeans. If I were to try to summarize these differences conceptually, I would say that Europe is becoming Wilsonian, and America is becoming Bismarckian. Is this a good development, or not? I would say that it is perhaps not all that bad, because these two concepts represent both sides of Western sensibility or sensitivity and they are complementary. The world needs both policemen and diplomats. I think that the American political scientist Robert Kagan, is right when he suggests that Europe is becoming Wilsonian which is proof of its weakness. Europe would like to be a superpower, but it doesn't have the means. When you are a political dwarf and an economic giant, you opt for multilateralism.

Renato Ruggiero: I would like to say something to Professor Moravcsik. I've worn several caps in my professional life, and with each one, I have seen a different perspective, but now is the time for synthesis. If I appeared to be too regionalistic when I was in the World Trade Organization, it was due to my job there. Today it's different. I've always believed that European regionalism should not be opposed to globalization because it is of a completely different nature. Listening to the previous speakers, I wonder whether we are going to speak about transatlantic relations or Europe? And then I realized that both questions are intertwined; in order to appreciate transatlantic relations, one needs to also question what is taking place in Europe, and where is Europe going.

I don't want to repeat the arguments that have already been put forward, but I would like to provide some analysis of what a new Atlantic relationship based on a more realistic and equitable balance would be like.

When I read the paper of Professor Moravcsik, I realized that Europe must have both its heart and its mind working properly. One of the reasons we've had fifty years of major success in the Western world is due to the fact that after World War II we set up a new world order based on heart and mind. Together, we had a vision of what should be done from an institutional point of view: the Atlantic Alliance, Marshall Plan, setting up of major international bodies such as the United Nations, World Bank, GATT, IMF, etcetera. At that time, Americans and Europeans shared a number of common values. The transatlantic formula of the past fifty years really became an incredible success, and I believe that a number of us can be proud of what we achieved. We reshaped utopia and dreams and made them into realities. Who could have imagined that on a continent devastated by two major world wars, we would create an island of peace? If everyone is drawn towards European construction, it is because everyone recognizes the fact that we changed a continent dominated by rivalries and wars into a continent where we live in peace and democracy. This was the basis for European construction.

But all this took place because we had the combination of heart and mind. We had the vision, the instruments, and the interests that led us to achieve what was in fact achieved. But everything I've listened to shows that there is now a difference. Where does that difference reside?

After September 11 occurred, I was then Minister for Foreign Affairs and like all my colleagues, I got on the plane. I went and visited Iran. Jack Straw and I were inspired by Colin Powell to go and see how Iran and Syria were faring. Everyone was pro-American. All the reactions were pro-American reactions, but all that changed very quickly. Why? Well, the list of things that make our relationship with the Americans what they are is very long and was mentioned previously by Jean François-Poncet and Frans Andriessen. I think that the main reason why transatlantic relations are now difficult is that we no longer share the same values. We no longer have one single enemy—we have a whole range of adversaries that are completely different. Terrorism differs from poverty, even if there is a link between them. The problem of ecological balance, the problem of drinking water—all these are challenges and adversaries that we face, but our approaches are different. As François-Poncet said, this explains why transatlantic relations are in such a difficult plight.

If the challenge in the last fifty years was how to guarantee proper governance in a divided world, the challenge today is how to ensure governance in a world that has become interdependent. These are entirely different situations. My response is that there is no possibility for Europe to really influence the United States if Europe remains divided and we do not make progress towards a true European defense and foreign policy. If we look at what happened at the level of the European construction, only those men with a vision won—never the Euroskeptics!

I was Lord Roy Jenkins's spokesman when he launched the idea of the European Monetary System. Nobody believed in it. Maybe a few did, but they were the exception. But he sold that idea to Valéry Giscard d'Estaing and Helmut Schmidt. I remember when the European Council decided upon that European Monetary System and two days later Lord Jenkins called me and other members of the cabinet and said it was a major victory, even though he told us never to say that our aim was a single currency. But it was already at the back of his mind, and it emerged much later. So, there is no limit to what we can achieve. We can encounter problems, but if we could have a president of the European Council appointed for four years, this could have a strong influence on institutions and the political landscape in

Europe. The European Parliament and the Commission should see their powers reinforced, and the national parliaments should also play a greater role. I think all this will take place, perhaps more slowly than those who are really interested in this would like, but perhaps more quickly than Euroskeptics wish.

When the United States realizes that Europe is moving forward, that there is someone at the level of heads of state and governments to represent the image of Europe and speak on its behalf that might change things. If Europe's nature today is multilateral and therefore weak, I don't think we should lose that multilateral aspect even if we are to become stronger. But we can only influence the United States if we are stronger, so we must make sure that this is what Europe becomes. I'm an optimist, a visionary; I think that this is possible, and that we will see it.

Michael Palliser: Before discussing how I see the current state of relations across the Atlantic, I want to make one comment to Andrew Moravcsik. I thought it was a marvelous introductory paper. I disagree with him in only one respect. But I think it is quite an important one because we tend to differentiate between the political and the economic, depending on whether we're in the economic field or political field. In fact, these are two sides of the same coin and it's a great mistake to put them in separate compartments. At the beginning of what Professor Moravcsik was saying about the different Spaak Lecturers, he implied that the early Spaak Lecturers were much more concerned with political concepts and the notion that Europe was being rebuilt in order to prevent war amongst European powers, whereas the Lecturers of the 1990s were rather more realistic and thought in more sensible, economic terms. I am distorting what he said, but only to underscore his point. One has got to remember the reasons that underlay the thinking about why America is unpopular in the world. What are the underlying reasons?

Well, what were the underlying reasons for World War II? In my view, they were essentially economic, and not political. In 1945, I was serving in the British army in Germany after four years of war when we had the postwar election in the United Kingdom. To fairly universal surprise, Winston Churchill was rejected by the electorate, which voted in the Labour party. I was not in the least surprised and indeed would have been very surprised if Churchill had been re-elected. Why?

Because in my battalion I'd spent a number of years with young men, mainly from Yorkshire in the north of England, a number of who were completely illiterate. They were splendid men and they fought splendidly, but they weren't educated. A number of them came from families that would have been desperately poor throughout the 1920s and even more in the 1930s, and I would have been very surprised if they or their families had voted for the politicians whom they blamed for that. Perhaps "blame" is a bit unfair, but there it was, and I thought that the election result was absolutely inevitable. I only cite it because we tend to forget that Hitler was elected—but he was elected by an electorate that was in a desperate economic condition; the middle classes in particular had suffered appallingly in Germany in the 1920s, and one can't really separate out the economic underpinnings for something from the political. Of course there were political reasons (and military and security ones) for the war, but that's really the one substantive comment I wanted to make to Professor Moravcsik.

Unlike François-Poncet, I did actually dig out the Spaak lecture that I gave in 1985. Its title was "The Nature of the Power of the United States and the Influence of Europe," and in many respects it is fairly relevant to some of the problems we're looking at today. In that lecture I drew a distinction, which I've always thought an important one, between "power" and "influence." And, in a number of places, I made the point that power is the prerogative of the powerful. That sounds like a real statement of the obvious, but in a sense it's also relevant to what Renato Ruggiero was saying a few moments ago. Influence is often the weapon of the weak, and the two are quite distinct, but I also made the point that a recent exercise by the United States of its power had not necessarily increased its subsequent influence on the situation in question. I think that this distinction is one that is worth making and one we have to think about.

The other point that I emphasized was something that my father-in-law, Paul-Henri Spaak, had written in *Foreign Affairs* soon after the Suez crisis: "Europe can no longer do without the U.S." Although this fact is now uncontested, the United States would make a terrible mistake if it were to think it could do without Europe. In spite of the difficulties, are the best friends of the United States in Africa, in Asia? No, they are in Europe.

Like François-Poncet, I am still a temperamental optimist after thirty-five years in the British diplomatic service, which, as far as I was concerned, was characterized by a devotion to the thought of a united Europe, not in terms of a sort of a super-state, but simply in terms of Europe pulling together and acting together instead of fighting with each other. This service was also devoted to friendship with the United States. Time and again, people said to me or said to others like me, "How can you reconcile these things? You can't be both a passionate European and a passionate pro-

American—these are incompatible." Well, I have always argued these are complementary positions: America needs Europe, Europe needs America, and that is the reason why in spite of all the problems at the moment, and God knows there *are* problems, I think that our interests almost force us to work together.

Etienne Davignon: I hope we will have some comments and reactions from the Harvard contingent. I would also like to add an additional question. In the present situation there seems to be contempt for those who disagree when a case is presented as having only two choices: "good" and "evil." When I was in the U.S. just before the holidays, I was struck by this phenomenon. People said to me, "You French don't want to do anything that could hurt the Arabs because you have so many Muslims in your own country and you don't know how to deal with them." Is the economic importance of Iraq being greatly exaggerated? If you look at the figures percentage-wise, economic interests in the region are totally meaningless.

Charles Maier: First, I would like to thank Frank Boas for having included me in this wonderful opportunity to hear the preoccupations of Europeans first hand. Peter Hall and I represent another Center that also likes to think about Europe, the Center for European Studies, and this rift between the U.S. and Europe has really become very preoccupying. As everyone of you knows, opinion in the United States is very divided as to what Frank refers to as "the debate." The images of the World Trade Center are quite indelible, so it has been difficult to mobilize a meaningful debate. Those of you who follow the Council on Foreign Relations know that it's moved its agenda almost totally to terrorism, which I think is short-sighted.

That being said, since I am a historian, I will speak for a few minutes about the historical analysis of the present situation. Not only is the future hard to predict, it is hard to predict the past, as Marxists used to say. Historians say that the way we see the past will always change as we travel beyond it, like some mountain that keeps changing its appearance as you draw away from it. I think it would be helpful today if I briefly propose a way of thinking about the past.

It is not only the end of the cold war that has changed the world. For fifty years, Europe and the United States faced an agenda, which I believe they have largely resolved. We can call it roughly "the agenda of redistribution." It involved the relationship of labor, workers and capital, which was expressed in the balance of the welfare state and it involved farmers versus the city, which has been frozen into the structure of the European Union as a way of keeping farmers happy. I think this is the way I would read Professor Moravcsik's paper. In a sense it says: Look, the European Union was a wonderful success in solving the problems on the agenda of redistribution. In that sense, the European Union is almost like the postal service: you don't have to ask to the same extent about democracy as you would if that were its only agenda—it's run by a group of devoted, farsighted civil servants who have shed their nationality in many ways and it's produced, thanks to many of you, a really functioning institution. Moravcsik's paper points out that in some ways it is such a success because the institution has been limited: the amount of public spending it can take and spend is very small. In that sense, the lamentations about the democratic deficit may not be as acute as they would be otherwise.

But the point is that in the last ten years the vital agenda is no longer a redistributive one. It is a question of who is in a political community and who is outside a political community. Now, that affects us internally by virtue of questions of migration in both our societies. It affects us precisely in the questions that were evoked here by François-Poncet: Is Turkey in or out? Will Russia be in or out—as Europeans, as Westerners, or not? And finally, is the United States to be in or out? I think our present world civilization is beset by questions about those who belong and those who do not. In the European Union, this is what gave rise to the Schengen Agreement: it is a question of the frontier of inside and outside and who you wish to admit across the frontier. It is the Third Pillar, which is in a sense even more fundamental to politics than redistribution. I don't think that we've resolved this question, and I think that in this sense we have not developed the institutions. I think democracy may or may not be more important for resolving this set of questions than the questions concerning redistribution.

As far as terrorism, I don't think we've thought enough about terrorists or how they exist.

There is a great debate in the U.S.; many Americans don't feel we need Europe. We have sufficient military force, without European contributions. This has an impact—as Michael Palliser said—politics and economics are deeply intermingled. Europeans are "wimps" when they plead about the *cause profonde* of terrorism. I share this sentiment to a degree. Who knows whether we will ever remove the *cause profonde* of this phenomenon—we have to worry about what happens next week. But as we think about the difficulty of these issues, I think we should think about them in the perspective of a whole new political agenda that encompasses the very basis of what belonging is in the modern world, and where frontiers are and what they mean. It's no accident that the U.S. looks more and more like an empire and that this language is becoming more and more open. In the *Financial Times* of the last week there was an interesting letter which said, "Well, we had our empire, the Romans have theirs; look, the United States has its." There was another letter from a correspondent in Trieste, who said, "Well, Europe must unite and it must unite against the United States."

James Cooney: I want to share one story that occurs to me today and then extrapolate it to our present context. But first let me make one comment: it's a little bit tongue in cheek, but I think it's relevant. I'm actually quite grateful for the continual crisis that we have between the U.S. and Europe, and I suspect that all of us around the table should be grateful. After all, it's what keeps us in business, it's why people are willing to pay us or invite us to these kinds of conferences, so let's not solve all the problems today. Here is the story that occurs to me, I will then extrapolate it to the present.

This comes from the mid-1980s; I think it originated with Jane Kramer in the *New Yorker*. She was trying to explain the European reactions to Ronald Reagan's suggestions for the Strategic Defense Initiative. She said, "if you look at the British, they say in public, 'We agree with the U.S.; this makes real sense.' As soon as they're in private with the American administrators, they say, 'For goodness sake, what are you talking about? This is crazy, you can't possibly do this.' The French in public say, 'This is a stupid idea, we can't understand why the U.S. would do this'; in private they would say, 'This isn't such a bad idea; we can go along with this. Let's just be careful about how we express it.' The Germans, in the mid-1980s would say in public, 'Yes, we think this is a good idea; we go along with the U.S.' In private, when they were talking with the American officials, they would say, 'Yes, this really does make sense; we can go along with it.' But when they got back to Germany, they would say, 'What are we going to do with these crazy Americans? We don't know what to do!'

So if I extrapolate this to the present and look at the European Union, here's what occurs to me: The European Union is growing comfortable with being willing to disagree with the U.S. in public. There is also a unity behind the scenes where officials talk with one another. Furthermore, there's no question that the Europeans now have the confidence to tell the Americans that they're crazy when they don't like the policy. The problem is the Americans aren't always willing to talk to the Europeans in private for those conversations. So my critical comment about the U.S. is that we should give the Europeans a forum for these discussions, that we should give them the opportunity for consultation. In the U.S. today, there are many who say there should be consultation because the Bush policy may be correct. Let's at least make certain we have the consultation.

Jorge Domínguez: I already had some opening remarks, so I don't want to extend myself too much. I do think it's worth emphasizing that I began with the continuities in U.S.-European relations because I had expected that our panelists would so thoughtfully emphasize circumstances that have changed.

Let me take this moment to pick an intellectual theme, which has also a long-standing political tradition in the U.S. and that for the reasons that we've heard has become more salient around this White House. First I want to emphasize that these are *not* my views, nor the views of the U.S. government, which is rather more important. But it matters for those who have not heard it put in the way I'm about to say.

It isn't just that the Alliance is complicated, it's not just that there're differences, or as Charles Maier said that some in the U.S. may think that it is unnecessary. For the Critics, the Alliance is wrong and is undesirable. It is counterproductive militarily, because when the U.S. goes to war, the Europeans are not militarily up to it. They are no longer capable; they are not in effect inter-operable, and U.S. military commanders have to spend a great deal of time babysitting the Europeans. Again, I'm trying to use a language that is deliberately intended to communicate many of these increasingly deeply-held feelings, though not by a majority of you. Secondly, the Alliance is politically counterproductive. The effect of the Alliance is to give the Europeans a veto on U.S. policy. It adds what the economists call "transaction costs." It is *much* more effective for the U.S. *not* to have this Alliance. Thirdly, and Mr. Chairman you already alluded to it, the Alliance is morally wrong. We know what is right, and we do not need to debate the nature of evil.

Next, Mr. Chairman, are the Alliance's counterproductive diagnoses. There is all this silly babble about deep roots. This *is* a military problem. Men and women are dying, and a military problem necessitates a military response.

And then the last item to be mentioned is one that has shifted even in the relatively brief period of the Bush foreign policy team, as those of you who follow the U.S. closely know. In the presidential campaign in 2000, Condoleezza Rice, now the national security adviser, wrote a very interesting article in *Foreign Affairs* criticizing the nation-building policies of Bill Clinton. This policy perspective has flipped; the word "empire" has been resurrected. Not only is the U.S. acting in ways that now resemble nation-building, but it is acting consistent with the themes that I indicated previously in my brief reference to Grenada. In the part of the world I study, which is Latin America, U.S. military action, in the unilateral decision of the president, without the consent of Congress and without the prior authorization of *any* international institution, is the norm. Grenada 1983, Panama 1989, the Dominican Republic in 1965, and so on. The word "empire" builds on this tradition, which from its own intellectual perspective is successful and works. The world is therefore now being treated in a fashion to which the near-neighbors of the U.S. have long been accustomed. Your surprise is that you are not accustomed to that treatment.

Participant: So you're saying to Europe, "Welcome to Latin America."

Jorge Domínguez: Yes.

Jean François-Poncet: I think that everything that has been said so far is extremely useful. Building on what Maier was saying, I want to focus on trying to explain some of the trends that people have pointed to in the last couple of hours.

My first point concerns American policy and the increasing divergence with Europe. It is fairly straightforward that the greater a nation's power, the more likely it is to be unilateralist, because there is less need for compromise and less need for multilateral institutions. We have seen that in the U.S. for nearly one hundred years now.

Second, if there is some sort of balance in great powers' foreign policies between military deterrence and economic engagement, it follows that if Europe is an economic giant and a political dwarf, then the U.S. is a military giant, and while it is not an economical dwarf, it is economically less powerful than it is militarily. That gives it a preference for military deterrence over the effects of economic engagement that Europe does not have.

Third, if foreign policy relates to rules, norms, international institutions, respect for sovereignty and reciprocity, the greater a nation's independent power and influence, the less it will be likely to rely on those good things. The U.S. again follows along from this expectation. In other words, there are logical explanations for the different attitudes of the U.S. and Europe towards multilateralism, the balance of military and economic influence, and attitudes about sovereignty and international institutions. I think there are reasons for these divergences, and we should expect them to continue.

The second set of things I wanted to point out, however, goes in somewhat of a different direction. And that is, while there is a commonality to American policy, there is also a striking division within the U.S., as Maier pointed out. When Domínguez was saying at the outset that there were many similarities in U.S.-European relations between the present era and 1983, twenty years ago, I think back further and say that in 1973 you had John Connally thumbing his nose at the Europeans, and if you go back even further, to 1923, you had the U.S. pulling out or never joining the League of Nations. There is a long-standing history of American unilateralism and even isolationism with regards to Western Europe and there is a commonality among all the dates I mentioned: they have all been dates of Republican presidencies, and the exception, that of Eisenhower, really wasn't an exception. Eisenhower could have run as either a Democrat or a Republican. He chose to run as a Republican. The attitude of the Bush administration is very much in the mainstream of one hundred and more years of mainstream Republican foreign policy thinking, going back to Teddy Roosevelt and through to the Taft Republicans. The immediate postwar period is an aberration: there was a short period, maybe twenty years or so, in which the Republican Party signed on to a kind of centrist consensus in favor of multilateralism, internationalism and commitment to Western Europe. But there has always been a very powerful segment of opinion both in the U.S. and particularly within the Republican Party which has been uncomfortable with multilateralism, uncomfortable with economic and political internationalism, uncomfortable with the commitment the U.S. made after World War II, and much more favorably inclined toward the kind of unilateralist positions that were common in the U.S. before the 1930s and that in fact dominated its foreign policy before the 1930s.

I would say that the mainstream of the Republican Party is somewhat reflexively protectionist, is unilateralist, tends towards isolationism and—where engaged—tends towards military and not economic engagement. Regionally, it focuses very heavily on Asia and the Caribbean basin and perhaps Latin America. Again, you can go back 120 years and find a common thread from Teddy Roosevelt through the 1920s through to the present day. One could argue about what the source of this stream of thinking within the Republican Party may be. For my purposes, I think it is useful to point out that it is highly regional in its basis, (Midwestern, Southern, Southwestern). Its economic coordinates are also fairly straightforward: it is not based in the Northeast, it is not based on the economic sectors that are highly international, and it is very politically powerful within the U.S. So I state this, not because I approve necessarily of the position, but because I think it is important for you in Europe to understand that there is a powerful stream of thought, of interest, of attitude in the U.S. for which this is the norm of American foreign policymaking.

What are the implications? I don't know. One could engage in whatever the U.S. version of Kremlinology might be, like back in the bad old days of the Soviet Union, when you would look at the Kremlin and try to figure out who the softliners were and who the hardliners were and then argue over what was the best way to influence them. That's too complicated for me to carry forth very much, but I think there are implications to the notion that there is a systematic and consistent point of view being expressed by the U.S. administration that goes back many years. It has been brought to the forum by the end of the cold war, but it is not the result of the end of the cold war. It has deep roots in U.S. society and political economy. It is not going to go away. It is amenable to influence from outside, but it is an important component of the U.S. political economy. I think that's an important thing to highlight.

Peter Hall: I want to take up some of the thoughtful remarks of François-Poncet. I will begin by agreeing with some of his points. I think the fundamental rupture did come in 1989 with the fall of the Berlin Wall—and not on September 11. Although September 11 was a national trauma of extraordinary proportions for the U.S., the fundamental problems go back to the end of the cold war. The key point is that nations on both sides of the Atlantic face common dilemmas, and the characteristic feature of a dilemma is that neither side is sure just how to resolve it. What we see in U.S. and European policy in recent years is a process of experimentation marked by debate. François-Poncet refers to the implicit debate between Bismarck and Wilson—I think you said that the U.S. has become Bismarckian and Europe Wilsonian. Woodrow Wilson is the only political scientist ever to have been elected president of the United States, but he was not universally regarded as an effective president or successful leader in the realm of international relations. So I think this remains a very open debate.

My colleague Joseph Nye contributed to it some time ago, by distinguishing between "hard power" and "soft power": hard power being primarily military and occasionally coercive economic force, soft power being the power to persuade (often focused on groups beyond governments). Much of the current debate is about the relative capacities of hard and soft power to resolve these common dilemmas. In that debate, I think that neither the U.S. nor Europe has a clear-cut position, notwithstanding the arguments that can be made for a natural division of labor between them. I think it was Dominique Moïsi who said, "the U.S. fights, the UN feeds, and Europe funds." But that is not invariably true. Just a few years ago, after Somalia, we were wondering if the U.S. would ever fight again, and Europe does not fund as much as it might. So the debate is very real and we are in an era in which governments are experimenting and learning. During the last presidential election campaign, it was striking to hear George W. Bush say, "We will not engage in nation-building." But, of course, that is just what the administration is currently doing in Afghanistan, because in some sense it is the only way forward. Something is being learned here.

In that context, it might be useful to categorize the issues that divide the U.S. and Europe and to remember that the two continents have always disagreed from time to time. I see three different types of issues today. There are issues that might be called "normal items of disagreement," such as steel tariffs, agricultural subsidies, and issues of the sort that inspired the "chicken wars" of the 1970s. Then there are "items of unusual importance," because they represent opportunities that might be missed. I would put the Kyoto Protocol and the International Criminal Court into that category. However, these are still items on which reasonable people can disagree. I happen to think that the U.S. should have signed the Kyoto Agreement, and I do not think the International Criminal Court is a good idea, but we could have a debate about these issues on which there are two reasonable sides. Notice that such debates are rooted in common dilemmas rather than conflicts of interest. The problem is how to accomplish a goal on which there is broad agreement, and the arguments are more about means than about ends.

Finally, there is a third category of issues into which the question of what to do about Iraq would certainly fall. It covers issues in which debates about means begin to shade into conflicts of interest, raising questions about whether unilateral or multilateral approaches are most viable for addressing an urgent problem, how useful soft power is compared to hard power, and how important allies are to the exercise of soft power. Even on such questions, however, one can find proponents for both sides on both sides of the Atlantic.

Part of the problem today is that this argument is conducted though the medium of domestic politics, and that makes a huge difference on both sides of the Atlantic. Certainly partisan politics has had an impact on the tenor of the American debate. François-Poncet referred to sensibilities, and many of us in New England feel the difference in sensibilities to which he referred quite acutely. However, Gerhard Schröder is now running against

George Bush because he has found him a more tractable opponent than Edmund Stoiber, showing us that domestic politics matters in Europe as well. When our sensibilities are offended by some of these debates, we should remember that domestic politics is often the factor mediating the overtones, if not the substance, of policymaking.

Etienne Davignon: I would first like to thank Professor Domínguez for clearly indicating what in my view is a very clear question on the type of power exercised by the U.S. If you agree with what François-Poncet said, that historically the U.S. has found it easier to deal with the problem militarily, does that mean that it is necessarily a good idea? The Alliance and other institutions become bothersome and even counterproductive in this scenario. And if you add a moral tone to it, and play this out in domestic politics, you are on safe ground until it backfires. Your guys can end up being sniped for another five years. No one wants to be detested and both individuals and countries like to be loved, but there is a real debate about the counterproductive nature of existing agreements that deter the efficiency of the military. Why does this pose a fundamental problem to the Europeans? If you set aside the significant influence that the Soviet Union had on the rebuilding of Europe—and it is logical to leave it aside because of its specific characteristics and the fact that it led to the division of Europe—European unification has not been directed against anybody. It hasn't been directed against its member countries—or any one of its member countries. Even in difficult times no one tried to formulate a policy saying, "We are going to construct this policy against that few." Instead of pretending that we are in a period of adjustment, because circumstances have changed, I'm in favor of arguing that things having changed.

What is the credibility of the institution? I remember when Andriessen and I were together at the Commission trying to restructure the steel industry through inventive steps. We asked ourselves what would happen if the Court of Justice froze our case out? Would we be the first to say that we should not apply the decision of the Court of Justice? In a certain sense, these types of institutions only have the value that the people or other institutions are ready to give them. If you just say that you look the other way, what happens? Nothing, except, and this is my fear in relation to Iraq, as François-Poncet indicated, force has to be dealt with through a procedure, however hypocritical that procedure might be.

Renato Ruggiero: Being an Italian, we have experience fighting terrorism, and we saw very clearly in our country that to do so we certainly needed power, police, and certain instruments. But the main political instrument against terrorism was to isolate it. So our job was to isolate it from the workers' movement, and from the political parties. If we look at what happened after September 11, we see that the U.S. strategy was on the one hand to prepare a military operation, and on the other to isolate Al Qaeda and the terrorist movement. That was a great success, and for a while it seemed that Al Qaeda was isolated both militarily and politically. At that moment, though, there was a black spot, perhaps due to the Middle East conflict. All efforts pointed to saying that this is the moment in which to oblige Israel and the Palestinians to settle their differences. And what happened? At a certain moment: Iraq!

This is something that is not really clear to me: Why, in a moment when we had the impression that all the cards were in our hands and especially in U.S. hands, did the Americans change the game and focus all the attention on Saddam Hussein?

Etienne Davignon: I think that there are many answers to this question, but I would like to hear what our American colleagues think.

Charles Maier: This is a purely personal observation as a newspaper reader and someone who is interested in our politics. It seems to me that we do not know which is the cart and which is the horse. After the outrages of the café bombings inside Israel, and after some of the retaliatory remarks, the time I felt most sympathetic with George W. Bush is when he said, "This has got to stop," and he talked about both sides at once. It's not the same thing, but when children quarrel and you finally can't take it and you say, "I don't care who's right, just go to your rooms."

In the U.S. press about terrorism, I think Americans sometimes feel that Europeans are not as sympathetic about the outrages about suicide bombings. It was easier to get outraged about the World Trade Center; it was huge, dramatic and happened in U.S. territory. I was in Israel in the spring. People are desperate there and I think that Americans sometimes believe that this desperation was not felt. But it's true: the U.S. administration backed away, because there were people in this administration who felt that Iraq could be solved, whereas Israel and Palestine are intractable. That's why somewhere in those weeks, in late spring, there was some decision to put one problem ahead of the other because it seemed to be easier. That's the way I observed it. I'm not an insider, I have no ready accessibility, and there may be others who follow this issue more closely. But I saw a moment where our policy flipped.

Andrew Moravcsik: Just one sentence. No politician in the U.S. will press Israel hard in an election year. Period.

Jorge Domínguez: The team that came into office with George Bush had a concern about Iraq that was left over from Bush I. Some of it is personal and some of it is professional. It includes a set of people who, a dozen years ago, wanted to march into Baghdad and who believed all along that not to do so was a mistake.

In the aftermath of September 11, there is a clearing of the decks in domestic politics in the U.S. This group made its case effectively to the president, and so, this agenda advanced not because of domestic politics but because there was no domestic political debate.

This allows me to make a connection. Both Hall and Davignon made a point with which I ordinarily agree, namely, that domestic politics in the U.S. makes the conduct of U.S. foreign policy much more difficult. Certainly Ruggiero knows that, in trade negotiations, domestic politics is an enormous obstacle. In this case, however, and this is only a matter of the very recent past, it has worked in the opposite way. This is not quite the way François-Poncet put it, but he almost did it this way, which is that Brent Scowcroft is representing the foreign policy of France in the domestic politics of the U.S. As domestic politics reappeared in the Iraq debate after a long absence, the result has been a debate inside the Republican Party.

The interests of the French government are being advanced, albeit inadvertently, thanks to a domestic political process in the U.S., whereas ordinarily we would say that the domestic political process makes U.S.-European relations more difficult. In this case, it just makes such relations slightly easier. Similarly, with the reassertion of Congressional power, the president has just agreed that he will go to the Congress to seek authorization prior to war, though he had refused to do so. Once again, a domestic political process is facilitating the U.S.-European relationship.

Finally, one of the features of this debate is the insistence of some in the Republican Party and the Congress that the president ought to go to the UN Security Council. It is very rare, as you know, to find from within domestic U.S. politics an argument on behalf of multilateralism. Given that everything I said this afternoon was so gloomy, I did want to make this modest optimistic point because this is unusual. It may be transitory, but it is also new.

Jean François-Poncet: It has been a very interesting discussion. I would like to try and propose an answer to Ruggiero's excellent question, which

I think is central. I will try to make my answer in defense of George Bush as I visualize what the reasons could be. Whether my analysis is right or wrong, I don't know. I think you have to start with one preliminary remark that the situation in the Middle East is the crux of whatever happens in the world in the next ten years. Maybe after that the crux will be China, but for now it's the Middle East. Now, could it not be that those who advise Bush have come to the conclusion that, given the situation as it is, there is no way out of the Middle East problem. The proof of that is the failure of something we thought was about to happen, which was the peace agreement between Israel and the Palestinians, with heavy American intervention (Clinton, Taba, and so forth). But after this long march towards peace—difficult, but going from one success to the other—it finally failed. Couldn't then the answer be that you have to change something fundamental in the Middle East? What you have to change is the balance of power: with Iran as it is, Iraq as it is, and the Saudi Arabia which we have "uncovered" (everyone who's followed Saudi politics and the money they've thrown all around the world to help Islam develop, it's no surprise, but it came as a surprise to the U.S.). The situation is such that while there is an overwhelming Israeli military power, there is sort of a political stalemate, and changing Iraq, nation-building, trying to produce the first real democratic state in the Arab world, could, in effect, be the key to some sort of a solution. After all, it was after the Gulf War that the Madrid conference happened. So, let's do it all over again, just a little better: let's go to Baghdad and we will build a peace solution. It seems to me that that is the best justification for Iraq. My guess is that Iraq can be done away with quickly, and some knowledgeable Americans believe that is the case. I spent some time this summer in a remarkable U.S. institution called "Bohemian Grove," where I met some of the Republican establishment. They predicted the invasion would be over in a week and would require no more than 60,000 men. If the U.S. can accomplish this—nation-building in Iraq—if they stayed ten years, if they convert Iraq with a federal constitution to democratic… I'm dreaming of course, but if it becomes so, maybe we will be thankful. We've been critical of Reagan, but who criticizes Reagan today? He did seem to be a simplistic cowboy, but in fact that's probably what the world needed when he was there. Maybe his Star Wars was one of the factors that got the Russian leadership to quit in the end, without shooting. The Europeans of course think that what I'm saying is nonsense and that basic feeling is exactly what Davignon has said—you do not solve political solutions by military means.

But there is one thing you said that was very intriguing, Professor Hall. You said Schröder is running against Bush. I think that's a very good way of putting it, if I may borrow it. I think it is a good remark, and a dramatic one: If you can win an election in Germany by running against the American president, then something is broken in the Atlantic Alliance.

Renato Ruggiero: I'd like to add one personal recollection to this discussion. I think it is something I can say, because President Bush's father mentioned it publicly many times. I asked him why he stopped and did not go on to Baghdad. His answer was very simple: We organized Desert Storm on the basis of a large international consensus and a UN Resolution. When the U.S. liberated Kuwait, the authorization ended. So the alternative was to go ahead, alone, and break the political alliance, or to stop and to save the political alliance at the same time the U.S. saved Kuwait. He chose this second alternative. It is striking that this attitude is completely different from the attitude his son now seems to be taking.

Benoit d'Abboville: I'd like to come back to what François-Poncet said. The distribution of roles between Americans and Europeans as described by Kagan, which has been mentioned repeatedly, saying that the Europeans chose multilateralism and influence by default because they don't have the power. Don't you think that this could quickly change? Following what's going on with Iraq, we saw in Afghanistan the present administration refuse nation-building, stating that it would be there for three months, which turned into six months, and now it will be closer to three years.

An awareness of realities is beginning to emerge even within this Bush administration. On the U.S. side, they're beginning to realize that they need allies, even for less noble tasks like logistics. You need Uzbekistan to reach Afghanistan and you have to pay the price for that. Tomorrow you might need Bulgaria to set up an anti-missile infrastructure.

So I believe that beyond oversimplification by a certain elite, we will very quickly go back to what was the strength of U.S. foreign policy and transatlantic relations: the search for a bipolar relationship. After all, the Western world was reconstructed in 1945 on the basis of multilateral institutions by the U.S. at the service of the U.S. Sorry, the U.S. foreign policy doesn't boil down to the domination of an ideological group inspired by religious right-wingers who think that we're back in the border period when the settlers had to defend themselves against the Indians.

Dominique Struye de Swielande: I felt that there was a shift at the end of our discussion, and it is more as a former ambassador in Germany that I'd like to make a comment. People said that Schröder could win the elections based on a form of anti-Americanism. On the contrary, if there is one country that is very pro-American in Europe, it is Germany.

One does not win an election, one loses an election, and if Schröder were to win the election it would be because Stoiber loses it. Schröder is a good tactician and he's trying to diversify the political debate. He knows that on economic grounds, his efforts have been a failure, so he is not really striking a chord of anti-Americanism; he is simply following the noninterventionism strain that the Germans adopted after World War II. I don't want you to go home believing that there are anti-American feelings in Germany.

Jean François-Poncet: What I find striking is the fact that Stoiber, who started criticizing Schröder's positions, finally endorsed them, and since he did, it's surely because he believes that Schröder's position will benefit from an election point of view. You're right when you say it's not anti-American feelings. In France there is no anti-American sentiment. It's the position of the French intelligentsia, but it's not the position of the people in general because they want to maintain good relationships with the U.S. But it is a very serious development in Germany and it is making Franco-German relationships much easier, so I'm not going to lament that. I thought that what Professor Hall said had to be emphasized because its exaggeration shows something new in Europe and in transatlantic relationships, and it is a very important element for our American friends to take on board.

Luc Frieden: I'm the minister of justice in Luxembourg and a former scholar. Let me add a few brief remarks, not as a historian, but as an actor of European construction, especially in recent years. First of all, I'm rather surprised to hear the emphasis being placed on divergences and problems between the U.S. and Europe, rather than on what we have in common, especially after September 11. In my own experience, for a temporary period at least, September 11 consolidated the relationship between the U.S. and Europe, especially in the fields for which I'm politically responsible, and it has also given a positive push to European integration in the field of domestic affairs and justice. Without the terrible pictures of September 11, we would never have come to an agreement for a European arrest warrant and a common fight against terrorism.

I entered the government four years ago, and I have seen a number of U.S. colleagues and the attorney general on a number of occasions. Ashcroft will visit the justice ministers next Saturday in Copenhagen, and he will come to Luxembourg the week after. If we could forget Iraq, which of course we can't, it is this idea of strengthening of relations that would prevail.

Now on Iraq, one word based on my personal experience. When I accompanied our prime minister, Mr. Jean-Claude Juncker, during his official visit to the U.S. a few months ago, Iraq was already one of the topics tackled in our talks with high-ranking U.S. officials. At the time, we were surprised. I refer back to what was said by the Belgian permanent representative to the UN: we, and the public, could not understand why intervening in Iraq was so critical. Certainly the Germans have concerns about any intervention involving German citizens, and a few days before elections Schröder could oppose intervention in Iraq knowing that public opinion was not in favor of it. That, however, doesn't mean he is anti-American in talks with other ministers throughout the world.

Nobody mentioned this afternoon the problem of the euro and the rebalancing effect it could have vis-à-vis the dollar and the U.S. The impact of that will appear quite clearly in the mid term and the long term. It's still in its infancy, so it's too early to say more about this, but sooner or later, maybe ten years, the positive impact or the rebalancing impact that it will have in our relations with the U.S. will clearly appear. Europe still needs Europe, and Europe still needs the U.S., as Paul-Henri Spaak said years ago. It's true for our relations with the U.S. and also for the European construction: it will unite us, even if we have to go through troubled waters.

Frans Andriessen: The conclusion I take away from this session is the fact that unilateralism, which has been emphasized by many of our American friends this afternoon, though not necessarily defended by them, is a fact of life in the U.S. And this seems to me a serious danger for the relationship between the U.S. and Europe. My question is, what can we do about it?

This is not simply a matter of solving a trade dispute. This is a mentality that in my view is directly linked to the fact that the U.S. is a superpower, and it occupies an isolated position, from which it does not feel the need for consultation.

There was a time when we in Europe were unilateralists in world politics. But these empires are gone and we shouldn't try to reestablish new empires. Europeans have for the last one hundred years or so tended toward multilateralism. We know that's what we need; otherwise we can't survive as an entity. The U.S. does not have that need. How can we bring these two different cultures together? I am a bit discouraged about the possibilities of how we can establish future relationships that will really contribute to peace, the state of law, human rights and a better division of the welfare in the world.

James Cooney: I apologize to the Germans for mentioning their case again as this session draws to a close, but I think that this example is particularly pertinent to the problem we've discussed this afternoon. I was in Germany all week, and the newspapers there were warning that Schröder had taken some very serious steps. This is the first time that a German chancellor has introduced this kind of anti-American tone into the elections. It is not anti-Americanism, but it is an anti-American tone. Frankly, I think it will disappear after the election, and I don't think it's a long-term problem. It is, though, a gamble that makes me a bit anxious and it probably makes Schröder and his party a bit anxious, too. In defense of the Germans, I think that the German ambassador to the U.S., Wolfgang Ischinger, actually spoke very effectively last week on the Sunday morning TV program *Meet the Press*, where he was asked what happened to this famous German unconditional solidarity that was promised last fall? He answered very well and he said, "Yes, we did promise unconditional solidarity, and we still promise unconditional solidarity regarding the war against terrorism in Afghanistan. What you are doing in Iraq is something else very different, also important: it deals with the issues of weapons of mass destruction. That needs to be addressed too, but unconditional solidarity for the war against terrorism is not a blank check for everything that you want to do."

Session II

Etienne Davignon: This morning we have circulated the text of Mr. Michel[83] from last evening, and in the discussion this morning we will stress economic matters a bit more. I am saying "a bit more" for an obvious reason: yesterday we noted repeatedly that the distinctions between the various fundamental elements that have promoted the development of European integration and Atlantic relations are as closely linked as ever.

It would be appropriate, before even starting today, to give our American friends an indication of our ideas about the Constitutional Convention. François-Poncet in his introduction yesterday already men-

---

83. The text appears at the end of the conference proceedings on page 186.

tioned this point and it weighs on European development significantly in the coming months.

There are three or four elements that we can perhaps put forward. Yesterday we stressed the importance of individuals on events. This is perhaps an incorrect assessment, but the fact that Giscard d'Estaing is the chairman of the Convention is not insignificant because of the importance he gives to this task and because of his role as a prominent actor in the field. A second factor is that the Convention has established a presidium, which also will have an impact on the Convention. Can we really achieve a sufficient consensus within this presidium so that it may be added to the weight of the presentation of the chairman at the end of the Convention? Well, the answer to this question is rather ambivalent, due more to circumstances than to deliberate will. This consensus that is developing within this presidium is to prepare a constitutional text, even though the contents are not agreed to yet. Today, the idea is to have a constitution-like text. I say "constitution-like" because there is a margin for interpretation on the contents of these constitutional texts.

The second element that seems worth considering is the absence of the Blair-Chirac-Aznar logistics. To be simple and clear, this emphasizes the importance of states for future developments. The institutional structure will matter, and Europe may need an institutional structure that does not necessarily have the Commission as the leader and that is not necessarily based on mere coordination between states. In this framework, questions of foreign policy and defense will be at the very core of this discussion. How will these topics be discussed?

My summary of yesterday's discussion is as follows: How can we achieve sufficient power for the European entity? The one option that should be discarded is for Europe to be committed to nothing. The third element, which is appearing slowly, can now be seen in the developments of Giscard d'Estaing's statement. As soon as you have an institutional discussion, that institution needs to be able to act. There is still the comparison to be made with the original club of six, and the emerging union of twenty-five members. We tend to think that the enlargement process is a precise mathematical adaptation to a multiple membership structure, but we will also have to rebalance power as a consequence of this change. There is still disbelief about whether these countries might be able to do something. It is important to consider the importance of the actions of the Commission. I will just cite as an example the latest declarations of Giscard d'Estaing in which he says that the right of initiative to be granted to the community institutions is something fundamentally necessary.

So, this entails the question of the diversification of the institutional structures according to the topics that need to be solved. Mr. Solana cannot be at the same time the person in charge for the European Council and the Commission. But one should not exclude that we will probably end up with something close to that anyway.

I think there are three things that bear upon the Convention. First of all, the present situation: What is going to happen in the coming months in our world? What is going to happen in economic terms?

There is a second element to consider: the economic impact of poor management on the present political crisis and its consequences. Russian oil reserves could perhaps replace the North Sea as far as a provider of energy in a future crisis.

A third element, which is difficult to assess, is the lack of public interest in all that is happening at institutional levels. European public opinion will probably try to abstain from anything political in the short and medium term. This Convention may be viewed by historians within fifteen years as a procedural trick in order to gloss over those issues for which we have no solution. I think that the Convention will have to consider both problems and potential solutions in order to try to come to a consensus.

I was trying to say that it is impossible at present to determine what the results of this Convention will be. The Convention's chairman should perhaps consider that they will need to do the utmost to avoid having their work rejected by the member states who would say, "OK, now, you children have played long enough, so let's take up serious matters on our own." I think that it will be rather difficult to start from scratch and we should not expect this Convention to come up with an appropriate solution.

Jean François-Poncet: I do not have much to add because my analysis is in line with yours, Davignon. But I would like to come back to one issue.

My remarks might have indicated that I do not expect much from the Convention. If that is the case, I should correct this impression because it is not what I believe: I think the Convention is a great opportunity. I cannot see why an intergovernmental conference would end up in something different than Nice. I think there is a new element playing a part there, and on the eve of an enlargement that is going to paralyze Europe if no reform takes place, the Convention represents a big hope.

My second comment underscores what Davignon said about it not being an accident that d'Estaing is the president of the Convention. I have worked with him on a daily basis for five years, and he has several strategic assets in his possession. The first of these is that he is very smart. He also has the ability to simplify matters: he can pinpoint the fundamental elements. He has also another quality that qualifies him as one of the statesmen of his generation: he has perhaps the best contact with the media. When it comes to blowing his own trumpet, he is a world champion! The advertising around his own person and around the Convention are one and the same. He will do whatever is necessary to make sure that it is spoken about, and that it will be a hindrance to some governments.

This being said, I would like to come back to the term "constitution". The European treaties, starting with the Treaty of Rome, have a constitutional value: they are *above* national legislation. Without that, there would never have been any European construction. So that is not going to be the feature distinguishing the new Convention from the previous treaties. The idea is to prune the texts that exist and present them in a coherent way. That is what the Convention will be about. It is going to be an extraordinarily difficult exercise: the Treaty of Rome is a patchwork, it is far from obvious to understand what it is all about, and the idea is to come up with a new text that would outline a few principles. I do not know how many articles there will be included in that, but in my view, Giscard d'Estaing will draw up such a constitution. It is an attractive exercise, but also a threatening one. The idea that Europe can only break new ground is an idea that should keep us on our toes, in particular the principle of subsidiarity: everybody is for subsidiarity, and that is my case. If the matter concerns which animals you can hunt during which season in the South of France, I do not want the Danes to decide on that! Which issues should remain of national importance? I spoke about hunting as an anecdote, but there are far more important topics to which we should pay attention.

The idea of a constitution is a good one, but let's keep an eye on it. We can of course discuss the order of importance of the various topics. Professor Moravcsik, in your paper, there is a very interesting development on the democratic deficit, and I agree with your conclusion: there is no democratic deficit. It is not a democratic deficit—I would say that there is no European public opinion—but rather isolated public opinions. In my eyes, the main problem is the European executive. Today, 350-380 million people, and perhaps 500 million after the enlargement, will have a problem with the European executive. In my opinion that is the crux of the matter. Whether we like it or not, there are two schools of thought behind this, and they have existed since the EU's inception: the Jean Monnet approach, which is something original and does not exist in national constitutions, and the traditional approach, which gives power to the various states. I think there will be a fight between these two schools of thought. I am convinced that Giscard d'Estaing will try and make sure that his text is not brushed under the carpet by the various governments.

On the other hand, in order to avoid having his text dismissed, he might go too far in the direction the governments want. So he should strike the right balance. Personally, I am convinced that the Commission remains a fundamental element. The other element is majority decision-making. Governments cannot take part in the executive unless they abide by the majority rule. Experience has shown that this in itself is not sufficient and that intervention from the Commission is necessary because it is upon proposal from the Commission that a majority comes out—without the Commission's intervention, it is very often impossible. So I think the Commission has a fundamental role to play.

Rightly so, Davignon mentioned the initial model, the one that existed at the time of the six founding members. I still clearly remember the way we arrived at the weighing rule in the Treaty of Rome, and that was because Spaak put his foot down—I can still hear his voice, I can still hear him say to the French, the Germans, the Italians, "You all belong to big countries, you can accept this system without any worries, but put yourself in the shoes of Belgium, of the Netherlands! We have reasons to fear decisions imposed upon us, and that is why Luxembourg was given a voice, and a bit more voice was given to Belgium and the Netherlands." I told you yesterday that I preside over a small general council where the population is the same size as that of Luxembourg, and I often think I could organize a war of secession to become a member of the EU, and I can tell you that the level of subsidies received by my constituency would be much greater than what we get from France. I am not saying that the Treaty of Rome was unbalanced, but to take that model and extend it to a community of thirty countries where all newcomers have the same population as France or Germany, except for Poland, have populations much lower than those countries, will create problems. If these problems are not solved, it will generate difficulties. All the more so, because the countries that become members and have less than ten million people are the poorest, and the most populated countries are the richest. The richest are afraid they are going to be exploited by the poor, and they are reluctant to accept that. I think that we are wrong to believe that we can do without the Commission.

My hope is that at the end of the day we will have an institutional balance that will be more or less similar to the one we have now with increased power for the states, a few reduced competences and fields of subsidiarity that will be given back to the states, which in fact the Commission should never have gotten in the first place. We will have a strong

Commission with a president who cannot be accused of being a civil servant or a technocrat and who must be a strong character. Jacques Delors, with his strong personality, had a major influence. The Commission can do a lot under such conditions, especially in relation to public opinion.

I will conclude by saying that the central exercise should be in the hands of the executive and that executive cannot be efficient if it does not play a pivotal rule for the Commission. Davignon is right when he speaks about "topical events." They play an important role, even if we tend to forget it afterwards—there is a strategy in the Middle East and if Europe does not have a say there, they will regret it and they will try to play a role in the future.

Frans Andriessen: Let me make some comments about the mandate with regard to Europe, the composition, the direction, and influences from outside.

The mandate is vast. In fact, the Convention itself has even extended the mandate. The members should, in my view, try to limit their scope, not try to create a new concept of how Europe should be integrated. That is not realistic or workable. The people and public opinion need to be convinced that it is important to add new things, and mobilizing public opinion seems to me one of the most important aspects of the operation. They shouldn't make the scope too wide, in my opinion.

I'm not very happy with the composition of the Convention; Where are the representatives from civil society, science, and the public? In my view the Convention is rather elitist: it is all government, Commission, parliamentarians, Europarliamentarians—who are important and, of course, indispensable: but they are not the only influential groups. This is also an operation for the Europeans, as such.

A word about the president and the presidency: I am the first to recognize the qualities of the Convention's president, but I think sometimes that he is perhaps a bit too much "president" to be president of this gathering. Of course, this is balanced by his co-presidents, two very capable men, but the working of this Convention could be damaged if the presidency should weigh too heavily on it. And when I read the newspapers and the declarations, I sometimes think this might be the case. My first observation had to do with influence from the outside, meaning in particular the Council of Ministers. The Convention's procedures include regular reports to the European Council: the president of the Convention goes to the heads of state and government to give a report on the Convention's progress, and they have reserved the right to make comments. That is their right, of course, but it means that the Council of Ministers is permanently involved in the Convention's progress. That can be an advantage, but it can also be a disadvantage if that impact is too great. The time they have given the Convention—about one year and some months—is very brief, given the complexity of the problems they have to deal with. And then the Council has reserved to itself a rather long period to evaluate the Convention's results.

My experience with this kind of evaluation is not always the most positive. Of course, Giscard d'Estaing is not someone who would accept his work being swept under the carpet, but there is a difficult balance to be found, and given the Council's tendencies as far as the division of power is concerned, I have some concerns. I would have liked to have a bigger role for European public opinion inside the Convention, because the big problem we are facing is not the democratic deficit—although I think it exists—but the lack of public interest in what is happening in the European Union. And perhaps the lack of a democratic deficit is one of the consequences of the fact that public opinion is not very interested in what is happening in the European Union, and not the other way around. Mobilizing public opinion, getting people interested in what the European Union is, does and should do is of vital importance for the results of this Convention. Of course, you can discuss subsidiarity; the notion of subsidiarity in treaties is defensive rather than offensive: it is a defense against what they say "leaking competences of the members" back to the European institutions and in particular the Brussels bureaucrats.

I hope there will be a kind of constitutional text, not a constitution in the full sense of the word. The European Union is not an entity in which the normal rules of a constitution are practiced. But the constitutional elements should be in the constitution in such a way that the constitutional and institutional situations should not be frozen. I do agree with François-Poncet that there has to be room for development; integration is a process, and an ongoing movement, which should not be frozen by fixing texts.

Finally, a word on the Commission. I fully agree with what has been said about the Commission's position, there should be a real delegation of executive power from the Council to the Commission. That is not the case at the moment. When one considers the complexities of the "commithology" as we call it in our jargon the way in which the Commission organizes its execution, consults, is dependent on opinions—that will not work in a union of twenty-five (or even more) because it's impossible! I think that the Treaty's Acte Unique of Luxembourg, which states that the Commission is the executive within the rules put forth by the Council, has to be reformulated. Otherwise we will not be able to manage a union of twenty-five, whose complexities, and economic differences will increase exponentially. We will not be able to manage the union if we do not have a strong executive. The question is, will the Convention and its president recognize that we need such a strong Commission? I am not sure about that!

Renato Ruggiero: The discussion has been even more interesting than we might have expected, because we are really speaking openly. Considering the open way in which we work in the European Convention, I would like to say something that might seem unimportant, but in fact it is. European construction has been revolutionary in building Europe, and it is still revolutionary in the history of our countries. Despite the difficulties, we have always moved forward by making progress—sometime quickly, other times less rapidly, but the progress has always been significant.

There is something that we will always remember: the first Council of the enlarged community was held in Paris in October 1969 with the British, the Danes, and the Irish. The hope, which we all held, was that this Council would decide to support elections to the European Parliament on the basis of a popular vote. At that time, French President Georges Pompidou refused to accept the idea because it was premature. When Willy Brandt accepted the French thesis, the dossier was sent back. That was a failure. The first European Council of an enlarged community discarded this important idea and everyone wondered what we were going to tell the public. Now, we're in the European Union. Some heads of government are much more advanced than one might have imagined thirty years ago: no one could have expected that we would arrive where we are now!

As for the Convention, I am looking at it full of hope. Although the present situation is apparently not favorable, we need to go forward, and we need to recognize that we cannot solve all the problems of community development. But at least we're on the right track and making significant progress.

Starting with the constitution, I think that it has a more symbolic value rather than a real one, because we have a constitution in the Treaty of Rome. The problem with a constitution comes from the fact that all the treaties that we have are rather ambiguous and unclear, and in order to express more clearly the so-called European values we will have to be more specific in the treaties. But the main focus that we need in order to go forward is the institutional structure. Thinking that we now have to choose between a community method or an intergovernmental method really oversimplifies things, because no one can destroy the community feelings in areas where they already exist. There we should stick to the intergovernmental method, which differs from a mere agreement because there is always a Commission and a European Parliament. So, there will always be an institutional mix.

So, what do I expect? Well, I think that we will give the European Council's presidency a longer mandate of four years. Another important step, which is basically already completed, is to give the European Council greater and more direct responsibility for defense and foreign relations. In order to maintain an institutional balance, it would be appropriate for Javier Solana or his successor to be nominated by the Council of Ministers, the European Council, but with the possibility of participating in the Commission, which is a dual system. The mere fact that we will improve the workings of the Council will inevitably give the Commission the right to withhold its power of initiative and even to provide the Commission with some other kind of power. I am not certain what we should do with the president of the Commission. I don't think that election by the parliament is the best solution, because the president of the Commission would, in that case, be too much of a politician, rather than politically neutral. Some people have said, "Why not try to do something like what is done in France?" The president of the European Council would have an orientation role, and the president of the Commission would be the head of the executive, but with some links to the European presidency.

As for the European Parliament, we will have to look at its legislative power. While the European Parliament should not be powerless, it would be unthinkable not to give the national parliaments the right to look at what is being done at the European level. The decision would probably be comparable to what we have had previously. We would stick to the institutional balance, with some small changes in the framework of defense and foreign relations, with a European Parliament, national parliaments, European Council and Commission, which would be upheld by adding to this the roles of the national parliaments. If we stick to this model, we would have to extend majority voting, which is definitely necessary, especially in a community of twenty-five.

Let me now take up another difficulty: the problem of the public's disinterest concerning European matters. I see it in my own country, which has always been very progressive in its perception of European construction. I am not talking about the government, but public opinion. In the press, and in the media, we hardly ever speak of Europe, and when we do, it is only in critical terms. There is no longer an active European Party. None of the German, French, or British papers have any summaries of what is done in Europe. Events are totally ignored in Italy: no paper has ever provided a summary of a European meeting or a European Convention. So public opinion is lacking because we don't talk about Europe, and when we do, it is in negative terms. The Stability Pact has become a nightmare for governments, and they need to apply new rules. How can public opinion understand that enlarging Europe would be safer or more positive. When we discuss enlargement, we speak about budgetary constraints, about immigration and the flood of people coming into our countries. How can public opinion be favorable to such construction, considering the information that they receive? I think that we need an active European Party, and we need to be present in the press and in the media. Otherwise, public disinterest will be a real danger for the enlargement of Europe.

Michael Palliser: I'm reminded of the ambiguity and paradoxical nature of the British relationship with our colleagues in the European Union. I personally agree almost entirely with what has been said this morning by François-Poncet and Ruggiero, but many people in my country would not agree with them, and I dare say there are people in their countries, too, that would disagree. I want to come back to this point about the paradox: for many years the Monetary Committee of the European Community and the European Union was chaired by a senior British Treasury official, who was largely responsible for the development of the thinking that led to the euro. This was accomplished without Britain or other European countries knowing about it, but he played a very significant role in developing this extraordinary and powerful implement of the EU.

We've discussed the Convention and its president, whom I first got to know when he was one of the youngest members of the French Assembly and I was one of the younger members of the British Embassy in Paris. I share the feelings of respect and appreciation of his qualities. But we haven't addressed the fact that another important figure in the management of the Convention is the Secretary General John Kerr, who is British and was also my private secretary for about three and a half years. I admire him, and he is undoubtedly going to play an extraordinarily important part in the work of the Convention and the development of its affairs. But once again, I don't think that anybody in my country appreciates this or even knows about it. This brings me to the other point that has already been made but which I would like to emphasize. I very much agree with what Professor Moravcsik says in his paper about the democratic deficit, namely, that there isn't one. There is, however, a deficit of knowledge. Ruggiero made the point that no newspaper in Italy pays any attention to the proceedings of the

Convention, and this is also true for the United Kingdom. And again, in my mind, one of the most interesting features of the past ten days or so has been the revelation that the British government supports the idea of a European constitution. We don't have a constitution in the United Kingdom and for some reason, which has always escaped me, we profess to be very proud of that fact. But this does underline something that is very characteristic of my country: we don't terribly like texts or documents. They're seen as bureaucratic and tiresome, and very often of course they are both. Still, the notion that the British government should say, "Yes, I am in favor of a written constitution," is actually quite revolutionary. It will be interesting to see what content they think should be in that text. And that's why I think it is relevant that there is a senior British figure involved in the Convention. I suspect that one of the reasons why we favor a written constitution relates to the question of subsidiarity. There is something to be said for having a very clear-cut definition of what is a European Union responsibility and what is a national responsibility. The point was made yesterday that in relation to this business of the Commission being sort of everybody's *bouc émissaire*, most of the important domestic political issues are still within the competence of the nation states rather than of the Community or of the Union. On the whole, I think, this is not a bad thing, though of course one needs some means (and this relates to the points made about the Executive) of avoiding situations in which ministers emerge from a meeting where the thesis that they have been developing has not been well received, and they blame Brussels for it. This has been particularly true of British ministers in the past, though it is by no means an exclusively British response. They go back and explain to the House of Commons or explain to the press that of course they'd have liked to do X, Y and Z, but it was those people in Brussels who insisted on doing A, B and C. I think it is desirable that, to the extent possible, the future constitutional arrangements should make clear where responsibility lies. That's difficult to do and there will be tremendous arguments about it, but I think it's important that an effort should be made to do it.

One of the worrisome points is that when ministers don't succeed, they blame Brussels, but also when they do succeed they announce, "We've had a splendid victory and we've beaten all the rest." Both are equally foolish, counterproductive and damaging to the concept of European unity and European Union. To the extent that the Convention can produce rules that make that process more difficult, so much the better.

We haven't talked at all yet about the euro, so I won't talk about it now, but I think that one of the interesting things about the future relationship of my country with the Union is going to be the position that we take on the euro, and the degree of influence that we can exert is going to depend enormously on that.

Laurens Brinkhorst: I am sorry I was not here yesterday, for you had an interesting debate about the transatlantic dimension.

One of the things I remember about the early 1950s was people saying, "Who was the best federator of Europe?" It was Stalin. The curious paradox is that Europe has always responded to external threats, but when there is no threat, we liked to be different among ourselves, because unity is unnatural, and diversity is natural. When there is no threat, it is much nicer to be Dutch or Belgian, or Danish. For the last ten years, we have lived without external threats, and we have been languishing. I have been involved in various capacities in the three Conventions—on Maastricht, on Amsterdam, and on Nice—and my firm conclusion is that we've come to the end of the road with traditional intergovernmental negotiations. Certainly when we move from fifteen to twenty-six, we cannot possibly hope to make any progress at all.

I was in the European Parliament during the Amsterdam and Maastricht Conventions, and it became clear that one cannot expect progress in the traditional way either from the European Parliament or from national structures. So I largely share the view that if there is a hope, it is this Convention. I'm of a slightly different generation than Giscard d'Estaing, but indeed the two original ideas in Europe of the postwar period were largely his. When he was president, he linked the European Council concept with the European elections and it was indeed Giscard d'Estaing, not Pompidou, who accepted that there would be European elections linked with the European Council. And of course, together with Schmidt, he developed the concept of the euro, or the EMU. Lord Jenkins proposed it, but of course it needed political power behind it. I think, indeed, that this Convention is perhaps—as a politician one should certainly never say "never"—one of the very few hopes we have in creating a structure. Certainly the unilateralism of the U.S. may pose a threat, but above all Europeans have to blame themselves. If Tony Blair speaks on behalf of the UK and not of Europe, quite clearly there is no solution for the Convention. And so even in the Convention, we may not find any consensus on how to create a European voice. My one point here is that having a European executive is fine, but having Mr. Solana in both the Council and in the Commission is not going to help because it only enhances ambiguity. On the other hand, I think that there is no chance that the European Commission in its present structure is going to be a real executive on foreign policy.

Secondly, a word about subsidiarity. I believe that it is a *faux problème*. For the past ten years, we have been talking about subsidiarity. If there has been any movement, however, it has been towards more, rather than less, community. When the Third Pillar was created ten years ago, all member countries were concerned about granting asylum and immigration policies to the Community, and it was therefore left as a national responsibility. Ten years later, we realize that national policies on asylum or emigration do not work, and now the community is assuming more responsibility. Frankly speaking, I believe that subsidiarity will not work except perhaps in the financial dimension. Regional policy has largely become a Community matter, and there will be a strong tendency among those who are on the side of the net contributors, like the Germans to reduce public spending.

The third question to consider is national political parties. Having been in both the European Parliament and the National Parliament, I agree that there is no democratic deficit. We should first create power and then the control of power, and as long as there is no power, there cannot be any significant control over it. But to the extent that there is no democratic deficit, we should not have a confusion of roles. On this point I disagree with Ruggiero: I do not believe that national parliaments should have any specific *droit de regard* in the European political framework. I think we should have a division of tasks. But I think granting a separate role to a chamber of national parliaments would add to the confusion and would not help to create a structure of simplicity.

My final point is that I haven't heard anything about how we are going to modify the European Constitution in the future. Yes, we have a constitution, and it might in fact become a simple one, but we must develop a concept in this coming Convention so that the constitution can be modified again. It can be modified by an enhanced majority, a double majority, or whatever, but we must find a solution. If the European Union is going to have any role in the future as a model for a European society, it cannot have a Convention or an intergovernmental conference cropping up every three years.

Herman: I'm very grateful to François-Poncet for having emphasized the necessary role of the Executive. That's the crux of the Convention. Creating a monetary union or a Common Market required tools like regulations and directives. But the creation of a political union requires political power, and that cannot be in the hands of a Council. The Council is composed of people who serve for a short time; their center of attention is their national policy. One suggested formula that I think needs to be emphasized tries to reconcile the role of the Council and the role of the Commission.

With regard to legitimacy, national governments are losing their legitimacy because they cannot solve the problems they are faced with on their own. We've seen that with immigration and the same is true of other problems as well. The problem of legitimacy is different from what it used to be; it now stems from efficiency—the ability to ensure public good.

Everything I've heard so far is extremely useful and constructive, and I would like to add that, having taken part in a number of hearings on the Convention, I think that it is wrong to say that the Convention will not have integrated civil society. My only regret is that the media does not reflect this point.

Mark Eyskens: Since the Convention was summoned, at lot of things have taken place. First of all is the Convention itself, its working method, and a few external threats that might become domestic threats for the Union. The possibility of a world economic recession needs to be mentioned because it could have a serious impact on the enlargement process in Europe, the financing of that enlargement beyond 2006, and the problems that could crop up in the fight against inflation. We have the controversy about the Stability Pact, but recession can still be a major problem when it comes to fighting deflation, or as I call it, re-inflation. With regard to the Convention, I would like to enthusiastically support Palliser's comments about returning to that notion of democratic deficit. We have a European Parliament with 600 members, growing to nearly 700, and elected by universal suffrage. We also have our national parliaments—if I add them up, we have between four and five thousand parliamentarians. What do we complain about? We might have seven thousand in an enlarged Europe. There is a deficit of knowledge, that's obvious. There's also a leadership deficit and an image deficit: Europe has no image, has no face. We have to be careful when referring to democratic deficit because if we had submitted the ECSC creation program to a referendum in Germany and France in 1950, when the Schuman plan was launched, that program would have been rejected soundly.

Coming back to the image of Europe, the idea of appointing a council president keeps being mentioned, and might be combined with a troika. Which would be a combination of a presidential mandate of four and five years, with eighteen-month mandates based on a six-month rotation. It is a complicated system, but Europe is complicated. If we have a president of the Council, he will be a dominating figure and he will not be seen as the president of the Council but as president of the Union, le *Président*. That will of course disturb, if not break, the institutional balance. So for me, the major challenge is to come up with a formula that would simultaneously consolidate the Commission and its rights of initiative and political leadership, as well as provide for a president who would be regarded as the president of Europe. In addition, the president of the Union, of the Council of Ministers, should be called "President of the Union," and he should also be part of the Executive, because we cannot have a Commission below the President of the Union. I fully agree with what Ruggiero said: we cannot simply find ourselves caught between those who are "for" and those who are "against." I remember the story about the Three Pillars, which is a compromise between both trends. The purpose of the exercise is not to fight, but to come to a balanced compromise. How can we achieve that? We also have to think in terms of synergy with new members: new members in the Union should be integrated without giving them a final voice in the decision-making process.

We haven't talked about the Treaty of Nice, which has not been approved yet because of Ireland, so it might appear to be an historical footnote. But I have the feeling that it will need to be altered as soon as it comes off the press. I have said before in the Belgian Parliament that our prime minister defended the small countries in Nice, and he obtained an acceptable weighting for Belgium—making it impossible for the Netherlands to obtain more votes than Belgium—which is very important. But my criticism of the Treaty of Nice is the implicit institutionalization of a *Directoire*, because there are several layers of decision-making: qualified majority, a majority of member countries, and the demographic standard. In other words, decisions must be accepted by 62 percent of the European populations, and Germany, the UK, and France have veto power since they have 41 percent of the votes. That is contrary to the search for balance, and in my opinion that should be changed.

My last point concerns subsidiarity. We would like to have that controlled *ex ante* by entrusting the control to the national parliaments. You can't do that with twenty-five different parliaments. Subsidiarity should be decided *ex ante* by a small assembly. That is logical. But you cannot give each national parliament *ex ante* control on subsidiarity: that would be nonsensical! If we want to reinforce the Union and if we want the Union to face up to challenges, new competences must be transferred to the Union.

Peter Hall: I have been interested to hear how many around this table are in accord with the general defense of European democracy that Moravcsik has mounted. However, I think that the *déficit de visage* is a little more than that, even if is not a democratic deficit. The fact that impresses me is that, on April 27, 2002, more French workers voted for Jean-Marie Le Pen than voted for Lionel Jospin. When I see the effectiveness with which many European political parties that initially reacted against immigration now run against the European Union, I think that the European public needs to hear a more spirited defense of the EU than has hitherto been mounted. The European public does not simply want to know more about what the European Union is doing. Its members want someone to speak on their behalf in Europe. Of course, their governments currently do that, but as some have pointed out, that is not always how each government presents what is happening at the level of the Union. The question is, how might that be possible? One route would be to elect a European president. That would be a risky route, but the Union has taken risks before. A popularly-elected president would have a tendency to strengthen the Executive and would help to resolve this problem. The British tried something like this when they decided to elect a mayor for London. The results have been mixed: the parties have lost control of the process, and I am not sure the transport system has improved. However, for Europe to have the equivalent of Ken Livingstone would not necessarily be a bad thing from the perspective of the democratic deficit.

Andrew Moravcsik: Please let me underscore some points about this public disaffection that are in the paper, but weren't fully developed in my presentation or the discussion yesterday.

My basic point is not just that Europe is democratically legitimate as it stands, that is, as a matter of normative political philosophy. Ultimately what matters most in the real world—and thus my main point—is whether something is pragmatic: efforts to encourage public participation are either futile, or are almost certain to fail. One has to appreciate the paradox of nonparticipation in European affairs: it's not just that citizens cannot participate in Europe, it's that they don't. They have opportunities to vote and they do not exploit these opportunities, even though the polls show that they believe doing so would be efficacious at changing European policy. Europeans believe that if they voted for the European Parliament, it is in fact powerful enough to generate some sort of change in policy. *Nonetheless*, they don't participate. They're not participating in the Convention today, and this is not because Giscard d'Estaing—although I'm sure he might be willing to do this—is putting up barricades against their participation (which would be a wonderful royalist move *à la française*), but because there are no people on the other side of the barricades. It was suggested that they don't participate because the press doesn't inform them. But to a substantial extent, the press writes about things people want to read about, and people don't want to read about the things going on in Europe.

As François-Poncet noted, there is no self-conscious European public opinion, and one of the reasons for that is that nobody has organized them. Why has nobody organized them? The main reason is because fundamentally, structurally, they see no political advantage in organizing around most European issues—with the sole exception of the small and radical Euroskeptical fringe, whose views are both incoherent and ill-informed. Why is this? Because the issues dealt with in Europe are not highly salient or visible issues in the minds of European publics. And that is a structural fact that no amount of institutional reform, no amount of publicity, can change. There are really only two issues in Europe today that people care about in any number, and neither of them are the most salient issues in Europe: one is the environment, and the other is immigration. And there isn't enough political capital to be made in either one to justify an entire infrastructure of European politics. Citizens act instead through their national governments.

This basic structural situation, which we cannot change, has four implications. First, nothing we do institutionally in the Convention or elsewhere can change the level of ignorance or disorganization of public opinion, except perhaps in the purely negative sense of enraging Euroskeptics and creating a cleavage around the issue of Europe itself. Secondly, if we force people to participate when they do not have salient interests that encourage them to organize politically in a structured way, they will behave erratically and will call into question all sorts of aspects of the status quo. That is what we see in the various EU referenda that have been held. The third implication is that a Convention designed to generate more legitimacy is wasting its time because it would require democratic mobilization to be successful. Consider the issue of simplification of the treaties. On balance it is a good thing, but no amount of work can make the treaties simple enough so that European publics are likely to understand them, and if it did, they wouldn't have any particular incentive to pay attention to what's going on. Any understanding of the EU "democratic deficit" must explain why, even when one gives them a chance, European citizens do not participate in European affairs. And the fourth implication is that the functional logic prevails when one wants to do something effective. Thus even those who favor democratic mobilization go back to the old community system when they want to get something done. So Brinkhorst likes constitutional amendment by qualified majority vote of insulated representatives with the participation of the European Parliament. Everybody likes a stronger, more insulated, more autonomous European executive when they are interested in results.

I will close with one paradox that demonstrates this basic point. I'm sure most of you, like most internationalist Americans, subscribe to the orthodoxy that it is a good thing for transatlantic relations, and for sound policymaking, that the United States has "fast track" provisions in place for the Executive to take the lead in trade negotiations, and for Congress to have only limited input. Such an arrangement is, of course, patently undemocratic—it restricts the set of outcomes that the legislator can vote for, largely by eliminating the prospect of amendments. Yet, we internationalists think that "fast track" is a good thing because the outcome of legislative action, absent these provisions, is unrepresentative of the public. Outcomes without "fast track" are more democratic, but less representative. And yet the same Europeans say, "We should increase the democratic participation in Europe to deal very broadly with the same kind of issues." As I have just argued, however, that will likely lead to either the dominance of special interests, or to chaos in a EU that is ruled according to populist plebiscites. This is a more fundamental point, and it explains why the efforts to force the Convention and European immigration in the direction of greater public participation are dangerous and misguided.

Charles Maier: Let me start by admitting that I have a deficit of knowledge on the European Union and Moravcsik knows the subject much better. But despite the virtues of his paper, I have for a long time found myself in close to total disagreement with what he has written. I think certain issues are being confused, necessarily. I am worried about enthusiasm—or lack of enthusiasm. The U.S. created a strong federal government. It required little effort, really, to make much of a democratic government because in fact the effort was in some sense to rein in the London County Council. Rhode Island was the equivalent to the London County Council: it liked to print money easily, and there were trade disputes, and many of the same disputes had to be worked out. The most successful French constitution to date, or the one that's had the longest-lasting regime since the Capetian monarchy, was the Constitution of one line of 1875, the Wallon amendment, which said that the president of the French Republic will be elected by the National Assembly. It served well through 1918 and then it started to fall apart. What has been stated at this conference is that there is no democratic deficit because there is no power. Do you or do you not want power at the European center? I think that power can be created without a deficit. I think subsidiarity has, in many ways, been a sort of "false God". Yes, we can always find issues like *la chasse aux palombes*, or things like the percentage of cocoa that must go into national chocolates in order to be called chocolate. The question is whether subsidiarity is an issue of local control or of having the decisions made by courts and administrators rather than a legislature? Some of the violations of subsidiarity, or federalism, or local control, would not seem problematic if they were made by a legislator. My former colleague, Joseph Weiler, said repeatedly that there is no European *demos*. Peoples are made by elections. You know, when it was said, "*abbiamo fatto l'Italia, facciamo adesso gli Italiani*", the Italians went about making *gli Italiani* because of all the difficulties.They did because they had a liberal government that lasted for fifty-two years and then they resumed, it was a democratic government that lasted another fifty. And having been recently in Sicily, it is Italy, there is a people there. And there are obviously real achievements for Europe: the money, the single currency, basket three, the whole thinking about Schengen and getting Solano in there has had an anti-inflationary bias. It was created under the impetus of the advance of the 1970s and that will have to be re-thought if this recession continues. We know there are real achievements and yet when I read the press, it does not seem to exist, but in 1989 to 1992 there was such excitement among my friends about what was being created at that point in the Delors presidency. It's true: yes, the European public may not be interested in this. Look at the American public: we have a dismal voting percentage and yet, despite that, America is a democracy. Agreeing with Peter Hall, I think there should be some decisive sense of "election in common". I don't know whether bicameralism makes any sense, but a system in which either a president or a head of the Commission or some Executive is elected, whether it is by a public or whether indirectly by the European Parliament, would, I think, make some sense. As Moravcsik stated, when people are given the right to vote, they can vote in unpopular ways. It seems to me there is a possibility for *une grande simplification,* not a *terrible simplificateur*, but a *grande simplification*, and that there exists between Parliament, Head of Commission or other Executive, a notion of a reference to an electoral body without the preexisting national boundaries.

Etienne Davignon: Now I think we should move to another important question that affects transatlantic relations: how do we deal with economics? It is also important to consider whether the Stability Pact is in danger, is the situation dangerous, and what happens with enlargement? I also would like to hear from our American colleagues about what might happen if the euro fails.

Jean Godeaux: If a severe recession were to turn up, the whole system will really be put to the test, and we will see whether we should have made an important step in the financial sector in order to elicit mechanisms for economic and budgetary governance of our affairs. Consequently, our governments should focus on proving that budgetary and monetary policies should be loosened in order not to create a recession. But today, people do not remember the reports from years ago that warned that monetary policy could help. If we overload the boat of monetary policy, we will have serious difficulties.

Renato Ruggiero: I would like to add a few words on this point. I fully agree with what Godeaux said. I'm really worried about the way things stand. Indeed, today there are serious difficulties in some of our member states, even in such an important one as Germany. There is an obvious tendency to link this uncertainty to the Stability Pact. This is an important institutional problem, which is a reflection of our relations with the U.S., because the problem is not one of the relations between the economic and monetary authorities in the U.S. and Europe. There is a void that we need to fill in order to improve the climate that exists on both sides of the Atlantic. But, as we said previously, the main problem is the Executive branch. The governor of the Central Bank needs to be independent, but a central bank alone cannot provide good results.

Frans Andriessen: We don't have one European economy, like the U.S. This means that interest policy—which has to be a Union interest policy—can at a certain time be advantageous for one country and disadvantageous for another. At this very moment, for instance, the Germans need a low interest policy, but fo' other reasons, the Bank has decided that it is not in the interest of all the economies. The Bank's instruments are not adaptive to the diversity of economies that are behind it; that's one of the problems we are facing. A second point is that there is no Union budgetary mass: our budget is perhaps one percent of the GNP of the European Union. So, when

President Bush is confronted with great economic difficulties, he has a budgetary mass that he can access. We don't have that.

The same is true with fiscal policy. The Union has no fiscal policy. Taxation is fully the competence of the member states, with the exception of the Value Added Tax, which means that in budget affairs, fiscal affairs, and even in interest instruments, we are facing great difficulties in managing the economy. And then we have the Bank's mandate—price stability, price stability, and then, finally price stability—whereas the U.S. Federal Reserve has a broader scope of activity.

Jeffry Frieden: I totally agree with what has been said, but I think it may be overdrawing the problems. It is true that there are serious questions about the management of macroeconomic policy, and there have been for ten years, ever since the first discussions. These have not been resolved, although they have moved somewhat closer to a resolution. They have to do with the structure of economic policymaking institutions, the economic government—or absence of economic government—at the European level.

I think there have been three issues. The first is the accountability of the European Central Bank (ECB), which is quite clearly faulty. As an aside, we should recognize analogous regional differences in the U.S. economy, which often lead to the politicization of monetary policy in which oil regions, high tech regions, or manufacturing regions have very different interests. But there is a way for these different interests to be represented in the U.S., and there is much less of a way for them to be represented in Europe. This is a potential problem largely because of the second issue, which is the coordination, or lack of coordination, between the monetary authorities and fiscal policy. It is a little misleading to focus on the Union budget. The principal instruments of fiscal policy in the EU are in national states, which maintain a tremendous amount of fiscal discretion. In fact, I think it would be more consistent to say that it is a good thing for the Growth and Stability Pact to go by the boards, because this will increase the fiscal flexibility of the principal nation states. The problem is that, in the context of a serious recession, it is possible that Europe might experience uncoordinated, even strategically disastrous, conflicts between fiscal and monetary authorities.

The third issue is financial regulation: there has been a gap in Union financial regulations ever since the beginning of the first discussions of Monetary Union. This is a very troubling gap, especially in the context of the financial instability that has hit other areas of the world. Europe has been extraordinarily lucky not to have Asian or Latin American-style financial crises, because the institutions and modalities available to deal with them are absent in Europe and would have to be put together in a very haphazard way. I think that it is a cause of great concern.

So I agree that all these issues are worthy of attention: the disconnect between the needs of economic policymaking and the institutions of economic policymaking. One further point, and then I will move in to the international dimension: many countries have very similar problems. We in the U.S. have a problem of coordination between monetary and fiscal policy. We have had very serious problems with insufficient financial regulation at the federal level, which has cost U.S. taxpayers hundreds of billions of dollars over the last twenty years and has created a great deal of financial instability. These are serious issues in Europe, but I think they can be managed.

There has long been an undertone of exaggerated concern about the connection between monetary union and the position of the EU in international monetary and financial fora. I would divide it again between monetary and financial matters. I don't think many of the things that we've talked about have very significant implications for international monetary relations, because international monetary cooperation is virtually nonexistent, and it almost certainly will remain so. There is very little interest on the part of the U.S. or the European monetary authorities in substantial monetary cooperation, and there is very likely not to be any interest. In fact, I think the creation of the euro has probably reduced European interest in international monetary cooperation. From a number of small open economies, it has become one large closed economy, and that makes monetary cooperation less relevant. So I don't think the international monetary effects are substantial. The effects of the creation of the euro on the structure of international monetary relations were vastly overdrawn, and what's happened has been what most scholars expected: each country, or each zone, pursues its own monetary policies without much regard for its effects on the other, or on the rest of the world economy, except for the normal spillovers.

On the international financial front, many had hoped that the creation of a monetary zone, and almost inevitably a more integrated financial system and financial authority, would increase the possibility of transatlantic cooperation for crisis management. It is certainly true that the lack of coordination and consistency in European macroeconomic and financial policy is a continuing problem. There was a time when the hope was held out that the creation of the ECB would resolve the old problem of who you could call when you wanted to call Europe. But all that it has really done is put one more phone number on people's Rolodexes. So I think that at the level of international financial cooperation, the creation of the euro has not helped, nor has the creation of the ECB, but it hasn't really hurt. I think that the Europeans have found ways through the Bank of International Settlements, the G7, the International Monetary Fund, and through a variety of other modalities to work cooperatively with the Americans in cases that do in fact threaten international financial stability. I am much more worried about the domestic implications of the problems people have identified. I think they are real questions about what might happen were there to be a serious recession, were countries to start engaging in gaming the ECB via fiscal policy, and things of that nature. I think that the international implications of those problems are pretty minimal.

Jean François-Poncet: I would be tempted to endorse quite a lot of what has been said, but I'd like to go back a bit. In my opinion, the main result and purpose of the euro has been reached: to avoid disturbances in the EU countries due to fluctuations in the dollar rate. We've managed to shelter the euro from the ups and downs of the dollar, which can be considerable. In the past, when the dollar was going up or down, there was a merry-go-round in European countries around the deutschmark. That problem has miraculously disappeared. Since the creation of the euro, we have had no exchange rate problem inside the EU. We have witnessed the European crisis with the lira and peseta falling, the German mark going up, the francs clinging desperately to the deutschmark, sometimes paying very high interest rates, etcetera.

Secondly, I have a question: Is deflation realistic and possible? We are obsessed by the case of Japan where we have seen prices drop, and not only in the stock exchange. It is apparently impossible to make a clean start again. Among the industrialized countries Japan has the highest deficits. Is the situation in Europe similar? If we see what is going on in America, it remains a fantastic example for us: America is as flexible as Japan is inflexible. Maybe Europe is somewhere between the U.S. and Japan, and the answer would be to follow the Japanese example rather than get in a rut. Are we really threatened by deflation? If so, is it not the prospect of U.S. intervention in Iraq that is playing a part? Yes, but it's not an explanation that applies to Japan. It's the incapacity of reforming Japanese society that is at stake there. If we are really entering a deflation stage, I think Europe will react.

This brings me back to what Jeffry Frieden just said: I'm not sure Europe is less capable than the United States regarding inflation. I think inflation will remain a permanent threat. I would add that the Stability Pact was imposed upon everybody by Germany. I do not despair about the capacity of Europe and the euro. I think that we will get there easily, perhaps too easily. I worry more about what could happen in terms of the world economy: Are we threatened by deflation?

Charles Maier: As a historian I'm always amazed by how quickly everyone else forgets history and the Stability Pact, which, happily, was diluted to a certain extent by The Economic and Financial Affairs Council. It's like tying Odysseus to the mast so he could hear the sirens of inflation. Well of course the sirens are no longer singing, but since the sailors have plugged their ears no one knows how to get him untied from the mast. The danger of inflation does not exist according to a country's position in the world economy, nor does it exist according to its cyclical or fiscal policies. Japan, despite a zero interest rate, has not succeeded in generating an iota of inflation. The problem in the U.S. is no longer monetary; it is one of asset pricing, especially in equities. We went from having a central bank policy that was designed to sustain full employment for thirty years after the war, to one designed to recover price stability, and then for the 1990s, we went to a central bank policy, that was designed to a certain extent to sustain equity prices. I think the euro, with proper management can be managed. The question is, what about the tremendous waste of human resources that comes with this management?

Jorge Domínguez: I wanted to mention a point that picks up on Ruggiero's original Spaak Lecture. He talked about the relations between the regional international trade agreements and the WTO. An acronym that has not been mentioned in the discussion this morning is Nafta. I'd like to offer an example that I suspect many of you know, but there might be one aspect of it that some of you may know less well. When President Bush established steel penalties, he exempted Canada and Mexico. What may be less well known is the transformation of the political relations of the steel industry in North America. Ten years ago, the U.S. imposed a variety of retaliatory punishments on the Mexican steel industry. Today, the Mexican, Canadian, and U.S. steel industries are one cartel, and they are a powerful lobby behind these U.S. presidential decisions. In this regard, Nafta has succeeded too well: there is not just a U.S. steel cartel, there is now a North American cartel. Unlike in the past, Mexican government officials today describe themselves in public as North Americans, not just the Mexican steel industry. For some years, Mexico has been more important for U.S.

trade than has Germany, the UK, or Japan. Mexico today is much more than an oil well; it is one of the major industrial exporters in the world. This aspect of North American regionalism, I think, is not sufficiently appreciated in Europe.

Renato Ruggiero: Instead of raising the complex problem of regionalism and multilateralism, I would just like to say that even in the WTO, we have nothing against regionalism. We are concerned about some of the effects of regionalism if the multilateral system does not work well, because this is the real issue. The fact that there now exists a steel cartel in the three regional Nafta regions is the natural consequence of regionalism. The problem is whether the multilateral system has a sufficient means to act in ways that this cartel cannot; that is, can it influence the competition in a negative way. This is the real balance.

Unless we have a strong multilateral system, regionalism is a real threat. But if we continue to have a strong multilateral system, regionalism can help the liberalization process at the world level.

A final word about trade. I'm deeply convinced that the fact that we are now beginning a new trade round of liberalization is something of extraordinary importance for the world economy. In a world in which the prospects are so uncertain, where there are ongoing debates about anti-globalization, pro-globalization, anti-liberalization, anti-privatization, anti-market economy, I think that if we fail in this multilateral trade negotiation the consequences could be devastating. In this respect, the relationship between Europe and the U.S. is of fundamental importance. In my experience at the WTO, it was very clear that every time the U.S. and Europe disagreed on an important issue, there was no possibility of making any progress. It is also true that Europe and the U.S. alone cannot impose their will on the rest of the world community, but their agreement is the basis for the success of the round and for every operation. We have to at least pretend that there exists a strong collaboration. I am thankful that Pascal Lamy and Robert Zoellick, two men on different sides of the Atlantic, are trying to create a better political environment for the dispute settlement procedure.

Michael Palliser: On the issue of trade, I very much agree with Ruggiero. But of course, it's not just trade in the Conventional sense, but foreign investment, too, is of tremendous importance. I think, for example, of European investment in the U.S. and, particularly in my case, British investment in the U.S., which is enormous. U.S. investment in Europe is,

I think, also substantially larger than U.S. investment elsewhere in the world. That again is an interesting element, which tends to get forgotten, when we are thinking about the relationship across the Atlantic. There are very powerful economic interests that pull us together, and it's a mistake to forget that.

On the euro, perhaps I can just say a few words from what one might call an unconventional British view. I would have liked us to go into the euro from the beginning, and would still like us to as quickly as we can.

I think Japan is a bit of red herring, except in what you might call the psychological sense. I can't remember now who made the point, but one of the reasons for Japan's current difficulties is in fact the nature of their society. This, of course, is absolutely true of Britain in regard to the euro. Let's remember why the euro was invented. First of all, in order to have a proper common market, it requires a single currency, for a whole range of practical and economical reasons. The second point relates to total confusion created by the American abandonment of the Bretton Woods system. Bretton Woods gave us a degree of comfort and solidarity, but once that disappeared, things became confused and uncertain. Part of the desire to bring it back is that at least a greater degree of certainty would result with the euro.

Why hasn't the euro been as much of an impact on the UK as it has been on the continent? One reason is that whereas from the beginning of twentieth century most continental countries had endured several changes of currency as a result of a whole range of circumstances, in particular World War I, in Britain we had not, until we decimalized our currency at the beginning of the 1960s. In 1959, I had a coin in my pocket that had the head of Queen Victoria on it, and with which I could still buy something. There was this feeling that the currency was immensely solid. Of course, there was also the sterling area, and the whole thing is somehow complex: imperial, domestic, whatever you like, built around the pound sterling. Decimalization was an extremely controversial process, and of course resulted in part very substantial inflation. Inflation was coming anyway, but the decimalization of the currency was poorly executed because we chose the wrong element of currency to decimalize. We should have decimalized on the basis of the ten shillings, which would have made it a logical process. Instead, we decimalized on the pound which, though psychologically the right thing to do, was economically and financially the wrong thing to do. The result was that we had a fairly difficult post-decimalization period, which again made the public skeptical of doing anything with the currency. I think there exists a sort of folk memory of this, which is at the root of the opposition to getting rid of the pound and going for the euro.

The British position is different from the others, and it is perfectly understandable that there is this feeling that currency is something you mess about with at your peril, which was not all that different from the feeling that we have described in Germany about the deutschmark. I think it was, in a sense, more natural for the continental Europeans to accept a change in currency, in addition to all the perfectly valid practical reasons, than it has been for the British.

All that being said, I think that one of the reasons the City of London reckons that whether or not we stay in does not really matter, because the city will always be there. There are two reasons for this: one is the complacency of the city; the other is the fact that our continental partners would like us to be in the euro. The pound would bring with it a country with a strong and effective economy with very substantial trading and investment interests that would actually help to strengthen the euro zone. I hope I am right in thinking that that is the view of a lot of continental colleagues. To my mind, it is one of the reasons for the continuing patience of our continental colleagues with, once again, the intolerable British who could never do anything at the right time.

We've heard of the difficulties of prophesying the future. I'm not sure I ought to even try, but I think there is still a prospect of a decision by the government within the next six to eight months, and a referendum within the next twelve to fourteen months. I'm personally convinced that a referendum in the UK on this subject can be won, but it requires a lot of effort, particularly by the government, and particularly by the prime minister and the chancellor of the exchequer. I think that if they make the decision to do this—which is really taking a risk because it affects their own personal futures—they will fight very hard to achieve it, and I think they will achieve it. But please don't hold me to that in fifteen months time when it hasn't happened!

Etienne Davignon: As any good chairman, before the conference I prepared a long summary of what the conference had said, on the premise that the only good communications are done ahead of time. But I will discard this because of the way the conference went and will instead comment that I believe we've all enjoyed this opportunity, and although we will not necessarily leave more comforted about what the future might hold, certainly the interest was there.

It is significant that we have discussed these issues without the acrimony that is characteristic of the most important aspect of our transatlantic relations. That these discussions are even possible, are best represented by, I think, the end of Monsieur Michel's speech, the quotation by Winston Churchill. For those who have not read it, I think that it is the most optimistic statement that we can make for the future.

But, even more important, all this would not have happened if we did not have the participation of the Fellows at Harvard, professors, and Spaak Lecturers, and so I think the most appropriate thing to do is to thank Frank Boas and to let him have the last word.

Frank Boas: Thank you, Mr. Chairman, you give me much too much credit. The credit belongs to the people here in this room.

Yesterday evening, I mentioned to a representative of the American embassy—a lady who was here at our meeting yesterday—that this is really a gathering of friends. Many of us have known each other for a very long time indeed and have done lots of interesting things together. I told her that we are friends who don't necessarily always agree with each other, but we certainly understand each other. I think that I, for one, will be very anxious to see the *compte-rendu* of these two days reproduced in the book that will be published by Harvard University's Weatherhead Center and by the Spaak Foundation, and we will have a chance to reflect for the third time, since this is the third of a series of conferences, on what has transpired.

Mr. Chairman, I want to congratulate you, personally, on the way that you've conducted these meetings. I think you've done this in the best tradition of what we would call "guided democracy." I think, in conclusion, that Paul-Henri Spaak would have been very happy with what we did here yesterday and today.

Thank you very much.

Louis Michel: Ladies and Gentlemen, dear friends. First let me tell how pleased I am to be with you today. A few days away from the commemoration of the September 11 events, I believe that your reflection is timely and welcome. I wish to express my gratitude to the organizers. It is only natural that I express once again my sympathy and solidarity with the American people, which were struck just a year ago by the deadliest terrorist attack in modern history. "We *were all Americans*" when the hijacked planes were hurled into the Twin Towers and into the Pentagon. We still are today. The September 11 attacks are a denial of freedom and democracy, urging our societies to protect themselves through constant and collective vigilance. Freedom and democracy are at the very heart of the common values shared by Europe and America.

Europe and America have worked together to counter Al Qaeda's plans for attack. Joint initiatives have made it possible to set up an international coalition that has supported unconditionally the efforts to eradicate terrorist bases in Afghanistan, to topple the Taliban regime that protected them, and to establish a responsible and representative government structure. The United Nations have adopted Resolution 1373 that has set new global standards for cooperation in combating terrorism. Police from all over the world, especially in Europe, from where the terrorists came, have contributed all means available to achieve the destruction of a network whose ramifications are still greatly uncharted.

One year later, and this may come as a surprise to many, transatlantic relations seem to have taken a turn for the worse. Misunderstandings and disagreements are piling up. The speech on the "Axis of Evil" delivered early this year has met with criticisms on this side of the Atlantic. The International Criminal Court has stirred controversy. Specifically, the plans to launch an attack aimed at overthrowing the Iraqi regime led by Saddam Hussein causes perplexity and incomprehension over here. It may be useful to remember that many points of disagreement existed way before September 11: antipersonnel mines, multilateral agreements on non-proliferation of weapons, trade in steel and agricultural products, the death penalty, climatic change agreements, only to mention a few. The whole bundle of issues, if you will allow me to put it this way, surfaced again once the shock of Al Qaeda's terrorist attacks had been overcome.

It seems appropriate to reflect on the reasons behind this new development. I actually noted during this summer that there was a lively debate going on, in the media, that is. Work will be done by this Conference that, I hope, will contribute to clarify the ongoing developments. I trust it will, because I see outstanding personalities in this meeting that are eminently familiar with the relations between Europe and the United States.

Let me still submit a few personal thoughts.

The terrorist phenomenon, which has dramatically invaded our daily lives last year, has quite expectably given rise to basic questions on the world geopolitical system. We have to face crime of staggering proportions, bent on hateful and gratuitous destruction, moved by a non-state squad, skilful at escaping, ready to commit suicide, and counting on protection from some governments. The challenge is new by its dimensions and by the feeling of insecurity it causes. Confronted with the unknown, confronted with a new situation, we seem to have developed diverging perceptions in the United States and in Europe. Such is in any case Robert Kagan's assumption, who explains in his paper, "Power and Weakness," that each of the transatlantic partners responds according to his strengths and weaknesses. The United States has considerable military capacity and is therefore prone to favor a military analysis of threats and to develop solutions based accordingly on military options. The European Union, on the contrary, being deprived of the means for military action, is supposedly inclined to favor a "civilian" analysis of events and to seek solutions more in accordance with its capacities: dialogue, diplomacy, coalition, international law, cooperation in police matters and reconstruction efforts.

The picture seems rather simplistic to me. The United States, as I see it, uses more instruments than just a hammer and does not see all the world's problems as mere nails. Conversely, the European Union, or at least some European countries, is not totally absent from the military scene. However, I will readily admit that the task sharing as sketched by Kagan is to some extent accurate.

I believe indeed that Europe has a propensity to seek solutions that favor cooperation between governments, through the establishment of sustainable agreements and structures and through the creation of economic, political and social links that favor trade, interdependence and mutual comprehension. In fact, and Robert Kagan underscores it too, it is a perfectly natural propensity in view of what Europe basically is itself: a gathering of States, totally independent at the outset, currently demonstrating that sustained cooperation, when freely accepted, can engender lasting peace on a whole continent.

We are obviously aware that bona fide international cooperation also has its limits. The Middle-East conflict, the North-South inequalities or the tensions between East and West do not lend themselves to easy solutions or we would surely have already found them. The Monterrey Conference on Financing for Development in which I took part and the World Summit on Sustainable Development from which I came back this very morning have given the measure of the persistent divergences.

Some think that these actually are the underlying causes of terrorism. That link does not seem obvious to me. Indeed, terrorism is also rife in developed and democratic parts of the world like Northern Ireland, the Basque Country or Corsica. And may I recall that Osama bin Laden and his associates are not an impoverished set of actors. While it is true that neglected political situations can foster frustrations and supply terrorism with strong motives, murder candidates, supplies and protections, they do not explain everything.

We should beware from excessive idealism. We know that maintaining stability and peace in the world also requires clear rules, power and compulsory enforcement. This necessity was obvious at the time of the Kuwait invasion and of the crisis in former Yugoslavia. It appeared clearly once more when dealing with the Taliban regime in Afghanistan and therefore seems to be equally applicable when fighting terrorism. "Power," to use the proper term, has a structuring role that remains essential. Referring to the globalization phenomenon, in an interview with *Le Monde* my French colleague Dominique de Villepin talked of a world threatened less by an excess of power than by the "heady lure of a vacuum". He denounces the lack of sense of responsibility on the part of the international community.

"Power," meaning mainly military strength, is effectively needed for governing the world. Today, such power is chiefly concentrated in the hands of one nation, the United States. This situation is exceptional. The simple fact that one possesses the power however does not make the use of it automatically legitimate. To make such use legitimate, the necessity to wield power should be more widely perceived and shared by the international community. The corollary of being a great power is that it has a responsibility, a duty, to listen to the international community. It is a matter of ensuring that the use of force is truly a contribution to international stability and peace and moreover, that it is accepted as such.

This is a hardly veiled allusion to Iraq. A military action against this country, which would not be supported by the international community, would be in dangerous contrast to the situation of 1990 and 1991. The implications for the whole region could be abysmal. In March last, I asked the European Union to take an initiative with a view to exerting pressure on Saddam Hussein and make him comply to the requests of the United Nations. I also decided to meet Minister Naji Sabri and Vice Prime Minister Tareq Aziz and have been entirely outspoken to them. I truly think that all modes of dialogue should previously be exhausted before the international community could possibly consider backing the use of force. As a matter of fact, the discussion at the Gymnich in Elsenör, last week, has revealed that the possibility of an attack against Iraq still raises a great number of questions.

In this connection, there appears to be one obvious and predominant fact: fighting terrorism is the responsibility of the international community as a whole. Despite the enormous means it can throw in, the United States cannot tackle it single-handedly. Indeed there is no sense in talking 'hegemony' when the matter concerns arresting people, sharing police information or detecting dirty money. Holding together a strong international coalition though appears of utmost importance.

As early as September 21, 2001, during the Belgian Presidency, the European Union has taken steps to shoulder its part of the challenge. By setting up instruments set to establish "a common European area of freedom, security and justice" for fighting terrorism. Through police cooperation, through diplomatic mobilization of the countries of Central Asia and through the support given to reconstruction in Afghanistan, Europe has been and still is a strong link of the much-needed coalition.

In spite of all this, there is still much talk of Europe not being forceful enough and less than decisive. This is not an entirely fair assessment of Europe's influence, but all right. It is true that the Union sometimes lacks consistency and the capacity for action, particularly in times of acute crisis. I would even want to go further. These shortcomings could very well explain the difficulties arising on a more general level in transatlantic relations. It actually appears that in the fields in which the European Union has reached a high level of integration of the policies of its member states, those transatlantic relations are easier to manage. This is proved by what happens in fields like competition, trade, currency and soon, justice, only to mention the best known. The strengthening of internal consistency in the European Union generally leads to better management of transatlantic relations. This strikes me as an undisputable fact.

Facing a stronger and more determined Europe, the United States would be engaged in a more significant dialogue, would be offered more tangible cooperation while also meeting with stronger demands for compromise solutions. In my view, there is a fundamental truth: the United States would have less feelings of isolation or of abandonment by its allies if Europe were more powerful and more influential.

I am aware that I only touched lightly upon the subject, but I draw genuine comfort from the fact that you will be pursuing the transatlantic dialogue this very evening over dinner and tomorrow during your next session. My very best wishes are with you. And to give you a clear idea of the size of the challenge before you, I would like to leave you with a quotation from a great European who was also one of America's best friends. At the end of World War II, Winston Churchill liked to quip: "You can always rely on America to do the right thing, once it has exhausted the alternatives." Thank you.

CONFERENCE PARTICIPANTS

This list includes participants who made comments during the conference.

His Excellency Benoît d'Aboville
Permanent Representative of France to North Atlantic Treaty Organisation (NAT0)

Mr. Frans Andriessen
External Affairs Commissioner, European Community

Mr. Frank Boas
Attorney; Administrator, Paul-Henri Spaak Foundation

Mr. Laurens J. Brinkhorst
Minister of Economic Affairs, Netherlands

Dr. James A. Cooney
Executive Director, Weatherhead Center for International Affairs, Harvard University

Viscount Etienne Davignon
President, Paul-Henri Spaak Foundation, Brussels

Professor Jorge I. Domínguez

Director, Weatherhead Center for International Affairs, Chairman, Harvard Academy of International and Area Studies; Clarence Dillon Professor of International Affairs, Harvard University

Mr. Mark Eyskens

former Prime Minister and Foreign Minister, Belgium

Mr. Luc J. B. Frieden

Minister of the Budget and Justice, Grand Duchy of Luxembourg

Professor Jeffry Frieden

Executive Committee, Weatherhead Center for International Affairs; Stanfield Professor of International Peace, Harvard University

Baron Jean Godeaux

Honorary Governor, National Bank of Belgium

Professor Peter A. Hall

Executive Committee, Weatherhead Center for International Affairs; Director, Minda de Gunzburg Center for European Studies; Krupp Foundation Professor of European Studies; and Harvard College Professor, Harvard University

Professor Charles Maier

Executive Committee, Weatherhead Center for International Affairs; Leverett Saltonstall Professor of History, Harvard University

Louis Michel

Minister of Foreign Affairs, Belgium

Professor Andrew Moravcsik

Professor of Politics, Princeton University

Sir Michael Palliser

Chairman of the Board, Montagu and Company

Senator Jean François-Poncet
former Minister of Foreign Affairs, France

Ambassador Renato Ruggiero
former Minister of Foreign Affairs, Italy; former Director General of the World Trade Organization (WTO)

His Excellency Dominique Struye de Swielande
Permanent Representative of Belgium to North Atlantic Treaty Organisation (NATO)

CONFERENCE ATTENDEES

Dennis Abbott
Maïté Abram
Adele Airoldi
Graham Avery
Michael Bartholomew
Luc D. Bernard
Fernand Braun
Jorge Cabezas
Pierre Chevalier
Séverine Cirlande
Gaetano Cortese
François Danis
Jau De Bock
Pierre Defraigne
Fausta Deshormes
Youri Devuyst
André Dumoulin
Jean Durieux
Francisco Fernandez Fabregas
Adrian Fortescue
Christian Franck
Jan Eric Frydman
Joanne Gardner
Renée Haferkamp
Caroline Johnson
James Kanter
Louis Kawan
Kevin Leydon
Jean Victor Louis
Peter Ludlow
Paul Luyten
Ado Malevez
Emile Massa
Benoît Remiche
Michel Richonnier
Jacques Rummelhardt
André Sapir
Peter Martin Smith
Antoinette Spaak
James Spence
Guy Spitaels
Mario Telò
Herbert Ungerer

ABOUT THE AUTHOR

Andrew Moravcsik is Professor of Politics at Princeton University, where he directs European Union Studies activities, and senior fellow at the Brookings Institution. He has authored more than 100 scholarly publications on European integration, human rights, transatlantic relations, international law, and world politics. His commentary appears regularly in *Newsweek* magazine, as well as elsewhere, and has been translated into 17 languages. He served as trade negotiator at the US Commerce Department and editor-in-chief of Washington foreign policy journal. Reprints and additional information are available on the following website: www.princeton.edu/~amoravcs

www.ingramcontent.com/pod-product-compliance
Ingram Content Group UK Ltd.
Pitfield, Milton Keynes, MK11 3LW, UK
UKHW042036051026
476324UK00001BB/61

9 780761 831280